T0271242

Peter Weir: Interviews

Conversations with Filmmakers Series

Gerald Peary, General Editor

Peter Weir
INTERVIEWS

Edited by John C. Tibbetts

University Press of Mississippi / Jackson

www.upress.state.ms.us

The University Press of Mississippi is a member
of the Association of American University Presses.

Copyright © 2014 by University Press of Mississippi

All rights reserved

Manufactured in the United States of America

First printing 2014

∞

Library of Congress Cataloging-in-Publication Data

Weir, Peter, 1944–

Peter Weir : interviews / edited by John C. Tibbetts.

    p. cm. — (Conversations with filmmakers series)

Includes bibliographical references and index.

Includes filmography.

ISBN 978-1-61703-897-6 (cloth : alk. paper) — ISBN 978-1-61703-898-3
(ebook) 1. Weir, Peter, 1944– Interviews. 2. Motion picture producers and
directors—Australia—Interviews. I. Tibbetts, John C. II. Title.

PN1998.3.W44A5 2014

791.4302'33092—dc23   2013039761

British Library Cataloging-in-Publication Data available

"When I waked, I cried to dream again!"
   —Shakespeare, *The Tempest*, III. ii. 152–55

"He who does not imagine in stronger and better lineaments, and in stronger and better light than his perishing mortal eye can see, does not imagine at all. The painter of this work asserts that all his imaginations appear to him infinitely more perfect and more minutely organized than anything seen by his mortal eye."
   —William Blake

Contents

Foreword by David Thomson ix

Introduction: "Unmet Friends": Encounters with Peter Weir xiii

Chronology xxxi

Filmography xxxv

Peter Weir: Reclaiming a Sydney Boyhood 3
    John C. Tibbetts / 2012

Peter Weir: Snapshots in Time 6
    John C. Tibbetts / 2012

Peter Weir: Early Days 40
    Sue Mathews / 1985

Small Screens and Big Screens: Television and Film 47
    Graham Shirley / 1991

The First Features: *The Cars That Ate Paris* 70
    Tom Hogan / 1973

"Weir, Weird, and Weirder Still": The Riddle of Hanging Rock 79
    David Castell / 1976

Years of Living Dangerously: *The Last Wave, The Plumber, Gallipoli, The Year of Living Dangerously* 85
    Sue Mathews / 1985

Interview with Peter Weir 105
    Luisa Ceretto and Andrea Morini / 1999

Peter Weir: Master of Unease 111
    Terry Dowling and George Mannix / 1980

Towards the Center 133
    Tom Ryan and Brian McFarlane / 1981

The Swizzle Stick: Peter Weir and Hollywood Genres 148
    Jonathan Rayner / 1993

The Iceman Cometh: *Mosquito Coast* 161
    Digby Diehl / 1986

Fearless: The Poetry of Apocalypse 167
    John C. Tibbetts / 1993

Poetry Man: *Dead Poets Society* 175
    Nancy Griffin / 1988

Weir's Worlds: *The Truman Show* 183
    Virginia Campbell / 1998

This Is Your Life: *The Truman Show* 191
    Eric Rudolph / 1998

He's Fought His Own Way Back to Work 200
    Terrence Rafferty / 2011

"I Am Your Eyes": Interviews with Russell Boyd, ACS, ASC 204
    John C. Tibbetts / 2012

Appendix: Notes on *Gallipoli* 240
    Interview with Executive Producer Francis O'Brien
    Peter Weir's Anzac Lecture

Additional Sources 253

Index 255

Foreword David Thomson

"I'm master in the darkroom, stirring my prints in the magic developing bath. I shuffle like cards the lives that I deal with. Their faces stare out at me. People who will become other people. People who will become old, betray their dreams, become ghosts."
—Billy Kwan, *The Year of Living Dangerously*

In a few years he will be seventy. He does not seem like a movie director. He is not overloaded with himself. He is not always on interview alert. But since 1974, he has made fourteen feature films. He has been nominated for the Best Director Oscar four times, though he has never won. By and large, he lives in the Australia where he was born, and many of his pictures have involved profound journeys, whether it is a gang of schoolgirls pristine in white going to Hanging Rock in the great heat of Australia or a group of people walking from Russia to India to get out of the way of war. But not every journey is simply physical. In *Fearless*, *The Truman Show*, and *The Mosquito Coast* (at least) the most demanding search is inward, through harrowing ordeal, technological barriers, and alarming violence to the location of the soul. No film by Peter Weir has ever been predictable or expected. The time he takes to deliver a picture seems to demand nothing less than his immersion in a subject. And so, quietly, as it were, or with his characteristic humility, he has stayed away from the busy world of reputations while building the unquestioned status of one of the great directors still at work.

His range is always more than we bargained for. His tone is modest, watchful, ironic, and patient. There is no sense of the bursting egotist in Weir. Yet somehow his body of work seems to rival the largest, most unruly and energized figures in film history—Abel Gance, Fritz Lang, von Stroheim, Welles, or Kurosawa. By the time he does his next film he is likely to be in his seventies, but who can doubt that that picture will be daring, challenging, and unlike anything anyone has done before? Fourteen films in thirty-eight years does not allow for small talk or routine projects.

So what sort of artist or story-teller is he? Well, his manner or style is self-effacing, if epic, and apparently naturalistic. In the great journey of *The Way Back* (2010), wherever it was filmed, every effort was made to make the landscapes credible and geographically truthful. So the snows have authentic depth, and the deserts are as hot and barren as real wastelands. But there are subtle dreams or visions on the journey, as well as intimations of some primal force in nature. When at last we reach the tea-fields of northern India, the bright green foliage is more than tea. It is a spiritual greening and a reward for ordeal. *The Way Back* is a journey based on fact, but it is also a recovery of hope amid the worst assaults humanity has ever known. The film is as convincing a spectacle as, say, *Lawrence of Arabia*, but whereas David Lean could not see beyond the human ego, Peter Weir feels the spirit or the soul. He is too shy or agnostic to be an obvious religious artist, but his films stay with us because of an abiding uncertainty about that dimension.

So Peter Weir seems to be a mainstream director of accessible entertainments like *Master and Commander* (2003), which was a Best Picture nomination, and a movie set in the tradition of *Mutiny on the Bounty*, *Captain Horatio Hornblower*, and even *Titanic*, while being alert to more ideas and schools of thought that those other films appreciated. It was a film about how a sailing ship and a crew worked, with all due honor given to guns, wind, timber, ropes, and canvas. But it was also about how men functioned and saw themselves in a new dawning of science. (The master's ship, remember, is called *Surprise*.)

Master and Commander is an action adventure film in the tradition of *Gallipoli*, Weir's breakthrough as an international director: historically accurate and personally searching. But there was already another Weir in evidence. *The Cars That Ate Paris* (1974) was a surrealist fantasy, *The Last Wave* (1977) was an uninhibited exploration of dream or extra-sensory experience. And *Picnic at Hanging Rock* (1975) was a mystery within a mystery. What seemed like a factual account of a real event was actually the provision of a myth, or a fable. Seen once, it seemed like an intriguing Edwardian who-done-what? Seen again, and it was a reverie on sexuality and the unknowability of heartland wilderness, every bit as suggestive as Nicolas Roeg's *Walkabout*. *Picnic at Hanging Rock* is a calm horror picture without gore, an orgy without orgasm, and an historical recreation based on nothing. It is one of those movies most interested in the mind of the spectator .

In the same way, the plane crash in *Fearless* (1993) is known as one of the most vivid and disturbing disasters on screen. (It may have impeded the film at the box-office, and ruined in-flight showings.) Even more testing is the way *Fearless* rejects the conventional narrative possibilities of mere recovery and sees how the critical experience has had an existential, or philosophical, effect. It is a movie about the proximity of death for an era in which we are still blithely addicted to hair-raisingly narrow escapes in movies.

Gallipoli (1981) is an intense but straightforward account of innocent young Australian courage devastated and betrayed by inept leadership and the new technology of war. But in *The Year of Living Dangerously* (1982) the threat is not just the perils and uncertainties faced by investigative reporters in Indonesia, but the way lives in love are especially vulnerable to accident and misunderstanding. That is probably Weir's most erotic film, thanks to the sensuality of Mel Gibson and Sigourney Weaver, but there is little hint of romance being a safe haven. To be in love in troubled times quickly leads the lover into political puzzles. For Weir, any commitment is hazardous, especially the ones that mean the most.

Witness (1985) could have been just a police thriller (and it was entertaining enough to gross five times what it cost), but it takes Harrison Ford's city detective out of his element and into Amish country. Weir often likes to displace and challenge his heroes. The love affair Ford finds with Kelly McGillis is wrapped in charm but it may have been a little too convenient. These are people from alien cultures, but the film cannot resist their coupling or a certain visual prettiness. It suggests how uneasy Weir is with simple-minded happiness. *Witness* may be his biggest hit, but I suspect it is a film that has not grown much over the years. With a child as the key witness (the adorable, wide-eyed Lukas Haas) it settles for the obvious rewards.

On the other hand, *The Mosquito Coast* (adapted by Paul Schrader from the Paul Theroux novel in 1986) becomes more intriguing. It is a Swiss Family Robinson drifting into dysfunction and the madness of tyranny. The film failed in its day but it can be read now as a lament for vigorous individualism cracking up under the strain of nature and isolation. Civilization is skin-deep, and so *The Mosquito Coast* raised themes that would be returned to in *The Way Back*.

The masterpiece, I think, and the film that gathered together so many of Weir's hopes and fears is *The Truman Show* (1998). Notably, this was an original script, by Andrew Niccol, which Weir took on, removing some of its darker underlinings. He was intent on a mainstream film, a Jim Carrey picture even, but a movie that predicted a world being overtaken by a mosaic of screens and the consequent withering of difficult reality.

We know now that Seahaven, the sunlit but bland prison for Truman Burbank, did not have to be built for the movie. It existed already (Seaside, Florida) as a proud emblem of Americana and its protected communities. But the movie had the prescience to see that a "Truman Show" might be coming—the 24/7 enclosure of real life as an ongoing TV entertainment. Of course, Seahaven is clean, optimistic, and orderly (it's scripted) so that the pilgrim only gradually realizes his shrunken life and resolves to escape. Fifteen years after the film was made, in the new climate of reality television, we inmates may ask "What escape? Where can we go?" The screens have become literal barriers such as Truman bumps into when he tries to sail away.

The Truman Show carried its darker meanings with enough humor to be a critical hit and a commercial success, no matter that it was as much a warning as *Invasion of the Body Snatchers*. In hindsight, the sunniness of Seahaven does not hide a kind of fascism in the TV-dominated community. That's what makes Christof (Ed Harris), the director of the show, as frightening as he is compelling. And surely for Weir Christof is as much an admission on the mixed nature of directing as Scottie (James Stewart) in *Vertigo* was for Hitchcock.

John Tibbetts's searching interview with Weir illuminates not just the quality of his films but the humane, thoughtful man behind them. But as I indicated earlier, it's less an interview than a genuine conversation. For years, Peter Weir has had good reviews, but his work comes at intervals and he sometimes seems far away. You could say the same of Stanley Kubrick working in Britain, and there are instructive parallels. Both directors wonder about man's destiny or significance in an inexplicable world. But whereas Kubrick is sardonic and even nihilistic, Weir is plainly an upholder of humanist filmmaking. He does not much enjoy special effects, but only because of his faith in the power of cinema being so unique.

Introduction: "Unmet Friends": Encounters with Peter Weir

"I'm merely a jester with cap and bells, going from court to court."
—Peter Weir

"I cannot discuss it. I will never discuss it with anyone," declares Lady Joan Lindsay. She has just been asked by filmmaker Peter Weir to reveal the secret of the girls' disappearance in her book, *Picnic on Hanging Rock*. It is 1974 and Weir is preparing his film adaptation of the story. He wants to *know*. . . .

Undaunted, Weir presses on, tongue firmly in cheek: "Would it be going too far, do you think, Lady Lindsay, to say that up on the Rock, a flying saucer might have landed?"

She pauses at length. Finally, she says, "Oh, I think it would have been quite possible!"

Weir recalls this conversation in one of the interviews in this book. "I don't know if she was having me on, or not!" he says.

The lines are drawn. Interviewer and subject are at a standoff.

Now, reverse the angle: In *Peter Weir: Interviews*—the first such volume to be published on the esteemed Australian director—Weir is asked by journalists, scholars, archivists, and colleagues to reveal his own secrets. How does *he* explain the baffling Riddle of Hanging Rock, for example? (You'll have to read further to answer that question.) Indeed, did the story *really* happen at all, as was alleged? Even today, such questions have dogged his most recent film, *The Way Back*: Is it truly *factual*? "Given this controversy," he says, "unless I am satisfied that the walk occurred, I couldn't do the film. So we got that evidence and I was happy and said, 'Okay, I can dedicate it to unknown people who did the walk, and I'll just say it was inspired by the book but I can now change the title, introduce other characters. . . .'"

Weir is all too familiar with the agendas of the interview process, be it a scholarly article, an archival oral history, or, simply, a puff piece and a gossipy "scoop." Despite his gentle and seemingly open manner, he has learned from experiences, like the above encounter with Lady Joan, to be wary—not to suffer fools, to guard against the unwarranted interpretations of his films, and to be watchful of his personal privacy. At close quarters we find him to be a most amiable and gentle opponent. There is something courtly in his manner and disarming in his gentle voice. Yet, he nimbly turns aside our slyest feints with a quiet, yet firm smile that, in the end, brooks no further dispute. Indeed, how can we expect an artist like Peter Weir to open up and define himself in mere words, rather than trusting the ambivalence of the images of his chosen medium to reveal themselves on their own terms? (Besides, is the *whole* of anything ever told?)

And yet, in these pages we encounter revelations at every turn. When he talks about "the precious desperation of the art, the madness, the willingness to experiment" in all his films; when he tells a scriptwriter, "I'm going to *eat your script*; it's going to be part of my blood!"; and when he describes himself as "merely a jester, with cap and bells, going from court to court"—we might paraphrase his own rejoinder to Lady Joan: "Is he having us on, or not?" We encourage, even provoke him to tell his own story, from his childhood in a Sydney suburb, to his apprenticeship in the Australian television industry, his preparations to shoot his first feature, *The Cars That Ate Paris* (1973), his subsequent career in Australia and Hollywood, and his current plans for a new film.[1] Indeed, this book may prove to be the closest thing we will ever get to having his autobiography.

Peter Weir was born in 1944 and grew up in Sydney, Australia, where he spent his restless, formative years pursuing sports, games, movies, and collecting comic books at the expense of a more formalized education at Vaucluse High and Scots College. Similarly, at Sydney University, he was so repelled by the dry, academic approach to literature and poetry (a method satirized later in *Dead Poets Society*) that he dropped out. After a restless two years selling real estate, he pulled up stakes and took a boat to England. On board he and several friends found an unused closed-circuit television camera and created revues and entertainments for the other passengers.

Newly determined on a show business career, he returned to Australia to work as a stagehand at ATN 7 television. Largely self-taught, he attracted attention with a series of prize-winning short films, including a fifteen-minute black-and-white short entitled *Count Vim*, and another short called *The Life and Flight of Reverend Buck Shotte* (which won Weir a Young Filmmakers Award in 1969). The following year he wrote and directed *Michael*, which won the Grand Prix at the Australian Film Awards. A second Grand Prix came the next year with a short feature, *Homesdale*. Then came the three films from the mid-1970s that first brought him international acclaim, *The Cars That Ate Paris*, a holocaust fable about a town whose citizens lured passing motorists to their deaths; *Picnic at Hanging Rock*, purportedly based on an unsolved mystery of the disappearance of four women in Victoria, on St. Valentine's Day, 1900; and *The Last Wave*, a terrifying vision of global apocalypse. After three more Australian films which consolidated his fame—*The Plumber* (1979), an urban fable about cultural dysfunction, *Gallipoli* (1981), which starred a relatively unknown Mel Gibson as one of several young men who participate in a doomed military campaign in World War I; and *The Year of Living Dangerously* (1982), a romance with Gibson and Sigourney Weaver set against the backdrop of the toppling of the Sukarno regime in Indonesia in 1965—Weir left for Hollywood. While his first film, the Oscar-nominated *Witness* (1985), about a Philadelphia cop pursuing in an Amish community a murder mystery, won him critical and box office plaudits; his second, *Mosquito Coast* (1986), about the struggles for the survival of an American family in Belize, was a relative box office failure. He fared better with subsequent Hollywood films, *The Dead Poets Society* (1989), with Robin Williams as a controversial school master; *Green Card* (1991), an urban comedy with Gerard Depardieu; *Fearless* (1993), about the aftermath of a tragic airplane crash; *The Truman Show* (1998), a satire on the consequences of consumer society; and *Master and Commander* (2003), a seafaring yarn based on Patrick O'Brian's classic tales of the Napoleonic era. After a gap of eight years, Weir directed his most recent film, the independently produced *The Way Back*, an epic account of the survival against impossible odds of a group of escaped Soviet Gulag prisoners in 1942. He is currently at work on a new project.

The following interviews flesh out this profile. They confirm not only that the trajectory of Weir's life and work parallels and embodies the growth of Australia's burgeoning television and film industry, but also reflects its national quest to define and express a historical and cultural identity.

To begin with, like his native land, he felt from the start that he lacked historical and cultural roots: "I was astonished," he relates to Sue

Mathews in a detailed account of his boyhood, "that my family hadn't kept any records of where we had come from and who we were. . . . I've asked other Australians what records they have, and have found the same story. A most extraordinary experiment in immigration: Anglo-Saxon people who left the past behind, left their myths behind and began again." As he tells Luisa Ceretto and Andrea Morini, "Growing up I think my great stimulation was nature. I lived by the water, so swimming, rocks and all the elements, the landscape itself, became one's art gallery." He hungrily eyed the ships sailing off to ports unknown; and soon curiosity got the best of him, and he was off to London and Paris, where he spent eight months working at odd jobs, making new friends, and learning something of the wide world out there.

He returned to Sydney in the mid-1960s just in time to participate in the newly developing television industry. It was a time of great ferment and excitement for his generation. The interview with Graham Shirley captures the excitement and promise of those years. "In that first year [in television] as a stagehand," he recalls, "I was so on fire with possibilities; there were sets; there were lights, there were cameras, there was a young, willing crew. Why not make our films? Why not do our own things? But how to do it?" By the late 1960s he moved on to the Commonwealth Film Unit (CFU). "[It was a chance] to work in 35mm film," he tells Shirley. "It's hard to believe that the very sight of a 35mm roll of film with sound was thrilling. To actually touch it was exciting. It was the big time. . . ." He found himself caught up in the youth protests of Australia's allegiance to Britain and British institutions, its alignment with America in Vietnam, and its general subservience to British and American cinema.[2] "The war unleashed energy and conflict, passion," he tells Mathews. "We talked about Vietnam as much as we did about Dylan and marijuana." And in the Castell interview, he says, "We were at war in Vietnam, too. We were involved in our own student demonstrations. It was the long hair, father against son, the music, the dope, the whole upheaval. In some ways, the conflicts were maybe sharper than in some parts of America. Australia was a very sleepy country that was very homogenous in every way, and the war was therefore more shocking."

Along with his contemporaries, Bruce Beresford, Fred Schepisi, Gillian Armstrong, Phil Noyce, among others, Weir made his first feature films with the financial assistance of the newly established Australian Film Development Corporation (AFDC), the Experimental Film and Television Fund, the National Film and Television School, and, after 1972, the South Australian Film Corporation. After a cinematic drought of several decades, a commercially viable product offered local audiences in the 1970s and 1980s their first sustained opportunity to see and hear the recognizably indigenous on their screens. Myth has dubbed this period and that generation the "New Wave" of Australian cinema; although he tells Tibbetts (2012) its reputation has been somewhat exaggerated: "It was a short period, actually, essentially, just a decade and a half. At first, there was really just Sydney and Melbourne. . . . We didn't see much of each other, unless it was at festivals. Then, all barriers were down. We were like frontline troops fraternizing after surviving the battle. But back in Australia there was a big push in the late seventies from critics and academics for us to stop making [historical] period films. We should get relevant and deal with contemporary problems like drug addiction. As if filmmaking was supposed to be some sort of social work!"

Some of the key moments leading to his first features, *The Cars That Ate Paris*, *Picnic at Hanging Rock*, *The Last Wave*, *The Plumber*, and *Gallipoli* are the subjects of many of the interviews. Weir tells Tom Hogan of the chance moment on a French roadside that inspired *Cars*: "There was a barricade across the road and a heavy mist. There were two men, rather frightening looking characters who stopped our car and directed us down a detour. But there was nothing wrong with the road. . . . It was just a funny thing that turned over in my mind and I wondered what lies ahead . . . ?" He reveals to Mathews his first encounters with aborigines in the preparations for *The Last Wave*: "You can't just turn up in tribal areas and hope to sit down and talk about a movie. . . . [I met with] Nandjiwara, who is a highly respected tribal elder and magistrate on Groote Eylandt. . . . He put in all the lines about the law and the Law being more important than Man, and that is really the heart of the film." He relates to Jonathan Rayner his inspiring visits to the historical site of the Gallipoli disaster: "You have one of those odd moments where you know that the history that was in the books actually did happen . . . where suddenly time bends, and you're outside the measured time . . ." And he talks to Ceretto and Morini about the casting of Linda Hunt as Billy Kwan in *The Year of Living Dangerously*, one of the major coups of Weir's career. "I couldn't find the right actor for the [male] part! . . . I had to find the actor or risk delaying, even cancelling the film. . . . It was like Cinderella's slipper—every kind of short actor tried to make it work, without success." The try-out of Hunt clicked, despite the fact she is a woman! "What made it work? Was it the female sensibility inside the body of a man? Was it the deception itself, the mystery of it?" Hunt went on to win the Oscar for Best Supporting Actress.

For his subsequent Hollywood films, he periodically commuted from his home base in Australia to Hollywood, spearheading the diaspora of other Australian filmmakers onto the international scene. Ever restless, he had been ready for a change in scene. "I was stale and thought it was the right time to go and make a picture in America," he tells Ceretto and Morini. "I was looking for fresh landscapes; to be in a way a foreigner, a 'stranger in a strange land.'" He immediately found those "fresh landscapes" in the Pennsylvania countryside in *Witness* and, subsequently, in the jungles of Belize in *Mosquito Coast*: "Here on location [Weir tells Digby Diehl], we have that kind of intimacy that . . . doesn't exist in peacetime, you might say. On location in the jungle you don't have the nine-to-five mentality that you have in city shooting. I like the concentration that results from everybody being at hand and from the ideas that abound in the surroundings. The atmosphere of the film is within the setting all around you. You disappear into the film."

And he found fresh faces. One look at Jim Carrey in *Ace Ventura*, he tells Campbell, was enough to cast him in *The Truman Show*: "From the opening titles of *Ace Ventura*, it was apparent this man was remarkable. . . . Jim has an otherworldliness, and he radiates energy and he wakes you up." A meeting with Gerard Depardieu stimulated the script for *Green Card*: "He came while I was working on the script, because I wanted each scene to be hand-crafted. A lot of the humor, a lot of the feeling in that film—the majority of it I think—came from that period of weeks we spent together" (Tibbetts, 2012).

Weir's American films pursued subjects that had earlier marked his Australian films. For example, in *The Dead Poets Society*, he vented the distaste for institutionalized authority that had fueled *Picnic at Hanging Rock*. He disliked school, he admits to Nancy Griffin. "That's why I could do this film. I would have been a member of the Dead Poets club." He confesses to Tibbetts (2012), that the film was a response to an unhappy experience at Sydney University. The English lecturer had assigned a poem by William Blake, and—Weir takes up the story:

> He told us it was a "lesser poem" by Blake. I came in just a fraction late, and the lecturer was already writing the poem out on the blackboard. (I can still hear the chalk). He wrote it all out, dusted his hands, put down the chalk, and began to talk. He took the poem apart in front of us, like a sort of autopsy. Everyone around me was busily writing. But I got up and left and went to the pub. I had loved that poem! I never went back. I thought, *Am I stupid, am I wrong, do I have to learn this? I can't do this!* This was a beautiful poem.

And this was a wonderful man who had written it. And this cold technician, this mortician, had dismembered this thing of beauty. So I put that into the scene in *Dead Poets*.

The paranoia toward authoritarian surveillance tactics that had surfaced early in the short film, *Count Vim*, reappears in *The Truman Show*. "With the colonization of the airwaves," he says to Eric Rudolph, "with empires being formed by satellites beaming programs down and by the Internet, there are now more people with enormous power and influence in our lives. . . . We know how power corrupts." And, regarding *Master and Commander* and *The Way Back*, he talks to Terrence Rafferty about his love of epic adventures: "I've always been fascinated by survival stories. Even in circumstances that aren't so extreme, the question of what makes anybody keep going is always an intriguing one. *What do you live for?*"

For almost two decades Weir became, in effect, a kind of global commuter. With typical whimsy, he saw himself at the time as a character in a fairy tale: "I think of myself as a character in 'Jack and the Beanstalk,'" he said in the Tibbetts 1993 interview. "I'm Jack and I have my farm in Australia where I have a cow. And there this beanstalk, which is my career, which I've climbed to the land where the Giant lives, which is Hollywood. And I go there every now and then where I'm given the Golden Egg and play the Golden Harp to amuse the Giant at dinner. But then it's time to go home, and the Giant always says, 'Why don't you stay? Why do you want to go home? You've got your own room here!' But no, I keep returning to my farm."

His most recent return to "the farm" these days marks him as a filmmaker combining indigenous and cosmopolitan identities; who can work anywhere, while retaining a home in a country that is his only through what he calls "an accident of circumstances." Weir tells Ceretto and Morini, "I love what Hitchcock said in an interview in response to a question about being English and working in America—'A film is its own country,' and I think that's true." If a film has no nationality, Weir seems to say, neither does he; unless he is his *own* country. As Billy Kwan says in *The Year of Living Dangerously*, "We are divided men. We're not certain we're Australians. We're not quite at home in the world." This points up a profound ambivalence of his sense of personal and public identity as an Australian: He is distrustful of past tradition, convention, and formula. His country, as Allie Fox declares in *Mosquito Coast*, "is always starting from scratch." He even now rejects the personal style so beloved of *auteurist* critics. He tells Griffin, "I've tried, to some extent to disassemble my style, to fight against my own signature." As early as *The Cars That Ate Paris*, we find a reference to a cultural and personal amnesia in the doctor's speech: "Here in the Paris hospital we have people who don't even know their own names. . . . That's the world we live in."

Thus interviewers in this volume who push the *auteurist* label do so at their own peril. They are baffled at Weir's own pursuit of anonymity. Whether he is writing a script, choosing the music selections, or working with actors and crew, he strives to bypass authorial intention and calculation and, instead, trust the instincts of the ancient storyteller.

Weir's working methods are explored throughout these pages. Even in the early days, he tells Hogan, he was indulging in the fertile imagination that would fuel his later films: "I work in a very flamboyant, outrageous way, I suppose. I always think up incredible amounts of incidents, amazing events, strange people." So intense can the project be, as he explains to Ceretto and Morini, "All your senses become so acute when making a film, you hear and see in a different way. It's a kind of trance, I think! You're both focused and open at the same time." That sense of acute awareness of the moment certainly played an important part in the difficult location shot of *The Way Back* where every minute was a budget limitation: "In this case we had to jump out of our vehicles like some sort of SWAT team, ready to go, shoot, because the clock was just ticking away and invariably we had to move from that location to another one some distance the next day; you couldn't come back." And all the while, he tells Dowling and Mannix, he's plumbing the Jungian "basement": "[Jung's] famous archetypal images, and the studies he conducted of primitive tribal groups and how these people possessed a different perception of the world—all of this came together for me around the time I was finishing the script of *The Last Wave*. I was just looking through a doorway that he entered. I'm still peering after him."

Further, he explains to Ryan and McFarlane: "I direct with my body: I use my sexuality to direct. I have explored the masculine and feminine in my own personality to direct actors and actresses, and that's meant they must explore their duality too. In this way I think I've gained from Jung."

Weir refers frequently to his passion for music. On the set he carries a boom box and plays a diverse menu of classical, African, and ethnic music to suit the moods of scenes. "Music is the fountainhead of all the arts for me," he tells Ceretto and Morini. "If you'd asked me one of those trick questions like 'What would you be if you weren't a film director,' I'd have answered 'composer.'" He declares to Dowling and Mannix, "I think music is undoubtedly the greatest key to those hidden passageways in your mind." He describes to Rayner his approach to selecting and planning his music: "I've tried not to analyze it too much, because that's something that's coming intuitively, and you can inhibit the process by analyzing it too much."

Although he is relatively unversed in the history and mechanics of music, he demonstrates again and again an uncanny knack for discovering music—sometimes quite by accident—that best expresses and amplifies the visual text. Examples are numerous in these pages. Perhaps the most celebrated use of music in his films occurs in *Picnic at Hanging Rock* with Gheorge Zamfir's pan-pipes. It seems entirely appropriate, as those pipes surely evoke the myth of the seductive god Pan. However, as Weir explains to Tibbetts (2012): "It happened by a sort of accident. While I was looking for the right 'sound' of the film, I told my composer, Bruce Smeaton, that I just didn't think we had found it yet. . . . Then the co-producer, Jim McElroy, came in one day and told me there had been a program on the suffering in Biafra the night before; and that they had played this haunting music on some sort of flute. . . . I played it and realized we had found the perfect 'sound.'"

No one is closer to Weir's daily working methods—and has contributed more to his films—than his Director of Photography, Russell Boyd. It's a particular pleasure to bring interviews with him into these pages. It's admittedly stretching the comparison, but his role with Weir could be likened to photographer Billy Kwan's collaboration with journalist Guy Hamilton in *The Year of Living Dangerously* (which Boyd also photographed). As Billy says, "I am your eyes." Their association—Weir describes them as "gentlemen's agreements"—span Weir's entire career, from *Picnic at Hanging Rock* to his two most recent films, *Master and Commander* and *The Way Back*. In the concluding interview in this book, Boyd provides a "ground-level" perspective on Weir at work. For example, Boyd explains the challenges he confronted handling the peculiar quality of Australian light on *Picnic at Hanging Rock*: The miraculous impressionistic scenes of the picnic with the girls were achieved by patiently waiting for the overhead light that lasted each day for but one hour: "When we chose the location, I said to Peter, 'I think we can only shoot for an hour a day here, when the light's just perfect.' You see, in the morning, the area was too shadowy from the trees. By late morning, it was perfect. After an hour it was completely in shadow again. I'm afraid they thought I was mad, and that I was going to get fired off the movie then and there! But eventually the producers agreed. It took us five or six days for just that one scene."

Boyd also confides "inside" tips about the shooting. He confirms, for example, that a different ending was shot for *Picnic* than the one we know. For *that*, you'll have to read on in these pages. And so it goes, film after film, details of more alternate endings (*The Last Wave*), the challenges of shooting in the Galapagos Islands (*Master and Commander*, for which he won an Oscar), and the rigors of the extremes of hot and cold climates encountered in *The Way Back*. His collaborations with Weir benefited them both greatly: "Peter elevated my career," Boyd concludes with characteristic humility. "It gave me the reputation of being able to put something on the screen."

In a strange symbiosis, Peter Weir deftly melds the material reality of the *craftsman* with the visionary dreams of the *artist*. On the one hand, while filming *Heart, Head and Hand*, a 1979 documentary about pottery making, he had an opportunity to meet the Japanese master, Shiga. It was a moment Weir has never forgotten. "I knew nothing about pottery," he confides to Tibbetts (2012). "We just chatted into the night, waiting to open the kiln. We talked about art, what art is, the difference between the West and the East, certainly between Japan and Europe. And suddenly, I knew this was somehow meaningful to me in my own life as a film director. Just to be content with the *craft* and let the art take care of itself. Every now and then the gods will touch the potter's hands, and that object will be a work of art. Self-consciousness can impair that."

In the interview with Dowling and Mannix, he says, "To some extent I still think of myself as an apprentice learning the craft of filmmaking or of storytelling." Thus, for example, in *The Truman Show* and *Master and Commander*, we have two films that underpin the story with the canny accumulation of physical details. His dreams are erected on solid foundations rather than a ropes of sand. "I tend to believe that myriads of small details," he tells Rafferty, "from wardrobe and costume to dirt under the fingernails will all somehow play their part. . . . Attention to detail affects everybody on a film." The results, whether it's the Napoleonic period recreation of *Master and Commander*, or the construction of an artificial world of consumerism in *The Truman Show*—"that vast enterprise of cosmetic surgery"[3]—are utterly convincing: "We took a lot [of the look of

Truman] from the current vogue for extreme wide-angle lenses in commercials" he tells Rudolph, "and we borrowed our high-key, somewhat glossy lighting approach from commercials and situation comedies. We often used a lot more light in interiors than one would normally use, to keep it all sparkly and clean. We were always reminding ourselves that in this world, everything was for sale."

On the other hand, the visionary aspect appears as early as his little-known short student film, *The Life and Flight of Buck Shotte* (1969), which is discussed in the Tibbetts interview (2012). Weir himself appears on screen in the persona of the spiritual guru, "Buck Shotte," who proclaims, "Free yourselves from your own feet!" It's a bizarre sight: Weir wears a feathered cloak and carries an imperial scepter as he urges his "flock" to abandon all worldly claims: "Free yourselves from your own feet!" Buck's clarion call could also be Weir's personal motto. The superbly self-possessed Buck is the ancestor of the many other "angel figures" that appear in Weir's later films. They strive to loosen the "surly" bonds of system and authority—Miranda in *Picnic*, Billy Kwan in *The Year of Living Dangerously*, Allie Fox in *Mosquito Coast*, Max Klein in *Fearless*, and Mr. Keating in *Dead Poets*, to name just a few—while portending imminent apocalypse. They don't just wish to *escape* from the bad old world, but, rather, they yearn to *complete* it. "God has left the world incomplete," declares Allie Fox in *Mosquito Coast*. And, unfettered, we might share in the Dream-Time of the aborigine, which "is more real than reality itself" in *The Last Wave*. Facing the apocalypse that awaits him at Gallipoli, Archie declares, "There's a feeling that we're all involved in an adventure that's somehow larger than life." Peter Pan–like, Weir would seduce his characters (and viewers) into a Neverland not on any map. He makes "Lost Boys" of us all. Perhaps some of us are likewise bewitched, never to return, like Miranda's companions on Hanging Rock.

It's no surprise that Weir at times has been labeled a mystic, an eccentric. By 1976 articles were appearing in the foreign press with titles like "Weir, Weird, and Weirder Still."⁴ Tongue firmly in cheek, Weir *flaunted the absence* of the girls in the Castel interview about *Picnic at Hanging Rock*: "I think that Rock literally opened and swallowed them. The girl who survived saw something that was so beyond description—to see into the earth any distance and to see her friends falling—that the mind could not possibly accept what it saw and retain sanity." Spending any amount of time with him, however, confirms that he is as normal, solid, and sane as the next man. That is, if you accept G. K. Chesterton's paradoxical dictum that only the "sane" man can "feel the full insanity of all extreme tendencies. . . . He feels eccentricities, because he is in the center."[5] In a letter to this writer, Weir himself commented, "Well, we are banal, ordinary; but we can't afford to be so when making a film!"[6] He finds his "center" in his home life. "I do a film every couple of years," he tells Campbell, "and then I drop out and go to a house that's well outside of Sydney and live a very simple life . . . just allowing your imagination to revitalize itself and to engage with life rather than be dictated to by images." When an inspiration does come, it is likely to occur during nothing so banal as a trip to the supermarket or during a morning drive: "Driving to work you see street scenes—a face, a hat, a detail—that you often end up putting into the film that very day. I saw a man with a plastic bag on his head with just the face part cut out and a straw hat on top of that and said, 'Let's do that'" (Castell). Wisely, he leaves the interpretative apparatus to critics and academics. "The words and analytical thinking, which come from your side of the table," he tells Ryan and McFarlane, "represent something I have unlearned. It is a tool I was brought up with through my education . . . [but now] something I have found I didn't want to use or live with."

In sum, these interviews reveal Weir both as the potter shaping humble clay, and the other-worldly angel who flies free of gravity. He is both—and he is neither. Rather, he is positioned somewhere *midway*, on a *threshold*, suspended in a restless equilibrium.[7] Again, we can find hints of this kind of uncertain equipoise, even in his earliest films. Midway through *Michael* (1969), we meet the title character, a very buttoned-down young business man, who has taken up with a number of youths living on the fringe of the anti-Vietnam counter-culture. Michael faces a choice between joining the security of the robot-like workers of one world and the instability of the restless free spirits of the other. In a key moment midway through the film, he stands, hopelessly conflicted, before the revolving door to his office. Does he enter or does he leave? Seconds pass. The indecision leaves him paralyzed.

All of Weir's films likewise are revolving doors positioned between modern-day Sydney and the aboriginal underground in *The Last Wave*; the city of Philadelphia and the Amish community in *Witness*; Mrs. Appleyard's school and Hanging Rock in *Picnic*; East and West in *The Year of Living Dangerously*; Welton Academy and the Indian Cave in *Dead Poets*; the New York apartment garden and the African jungle in *Green Card*;

the civilized order of shipboard and the raw nature of the Galapagos Islands in *Master and Commander* ("No naval discipline *here*"); etc.

In this wise, perhaps it is not a stretch to claim his elective affinities with the ranks of the great Gothic and Romantic visionaries of the generation 150 years before him, including poets Novalis, William Blake, Percy Shelley, Edgar Allan Poe, John Keats; composer Robert Schumann; and painter Caspar David Friedrich.

Weir would doubtless be astonished, certainly bemused, to find himself placed in this "community of like-minded spirits," as Shelley put it.[8] Yet, allusions, direct or indirect, to Romantic imagery and texts, abound in his films. We know that he paid tribute to Poe in *Picnic at Hanging Rock* and to Shelley and Keats in *Dead Poet's Society*; and that he referenced Coleridge's *Rime of the Ancient Mariner* in *Master and Commander*, etc. (Perhaps an extended study is long overdue about Weir as their cinematic heir.)

For example, Weir's angel figures and portents of apocalypse remind us of Blake's "bright visions of eternity" where "the heavens are shaken & the Earth removed from its place."[9] The luminosity of light and richness of surface recall Novalis's dictum: "[A sense of wonder lies in] giving the commonplace a heightened meaning, the ordinary a mysterious appearance, the known the dignity of the unknown, the finite an infinite aura—I thus romanticize them."[10] Weir's explorations of the tenuous borders between reality and dream find expression in his quoting in *Picnic at Hanging Rock* of lines from Poe: "Is all that we see or seem/ But a dream within a dream?" and Keats's famous lines: "Was it a vision, or a waking dream?/ Fled is that music—Do I wake or sleep?"[11] He understands Shelley's love of Gothic terrors and twilight enchantment: "Have I mixed awful talk and asking looks/ made such magic as compels the charmed night to render up thy charge . . . ?"[12] He positions music and image in a kind of counterpoint that is analogous to the "enharmonic" modulations of Schubert and Schumann: "I dream, a silent chord," wrote Schumann, "but under the hands of those who comprehend me, I become an eloquent friend."[13]

Moreover, the baffling conclusions of many of his stories—Miranda's unknown fate high on the Rock; the freeze-frame of Archie's last moments at Gallipoli, David Burton's view of the mysterious "last wave," Truman's pause on the precipice between Seahaven and the outside world—all remind us of those solitary figures in Friedrich's landscapes who stand, frozen in space and time, their backs to us, gazing out into the formless void.[14] And we can't ignore that supreme Romantic figure, the poet-musician Orpheus. Like him, who could charm Death itself but, standing on the threshold of his escape, would fall victim to his human failings, Weir "looks back" to our mortality, and, like the survivor Janusz in *The Way Back*, is unable and unwilling ultimately to forsake it.

Parenthetically, we might imagine Weir's demeanor during the above recitation. He's probably turning to us now, eyebrows arched, perhaps looking for the exits, replying, simply, "Is that what you think . . . ?" He's probably remembering those awful academic dissections and hearing again the *scraping* sounds of the chalkboard during his university days. "Sometimes I've wanted to tell the audience more, to share more with them," he admits in the interview with Dowling and Mannix, "but I've not really known how."

Finally, as we venture into these pages, we would recall the question that Billy Kwan in *The Year of Living Dangerously* addresses to the journalist, Guy Hamilton: "Could you be the unmet friend?" A curious question— an inquiry, an invitation, a hopeful but cautious expectation . . . perhaps how Weir confronts the interrogators in these pages? Indeed, it is the same question that this book, *Peter Weir: Interviews*, directs to *us*: If we would be those "unmet friends," then we wonder, like Billy, "What then, should we do?" Follow Billy's advice. Recognize "a potential, something immediate, a possibility" in Weir and his work. Take him at his word. Remove the calipers and measuring sticks of critics and stuffy academics. *Believe* in what is, after all, the enduring, yet elusive *strangeness* of his films. Avoid the trap of the man in the Henry James story who sacrifices his life and sanity in a fruitless quest for an author's secret meaning, the "figure in the carpet."[15] Instead, as Weir puts it, accept our own role not just as his inquisitors but as the "final participants" in his films.

Stand before the "threshold" of this book. Teeter on the brink, embracing, exulting, sharing the exhilaration of the riddles therein. Know that he, like us, is also searching for his own meanings—an endless inquiry. . . . And savor the wry humor when in one of the interviews he returns to the Riddle of Hanging Rock:

> Question: Do you take a secret delight in the sometimes baffling ambiguities of your pictures, particularly the endings to *Hanging Rock* and *The Last Wave*? Peter, do you sit back, snickering through your fingers at our confusion?
>
> Weir [After a pause and a mock desperate gesture]: No, I've probably got my fingers firmly on my brow, thinking, Is *this* the right ending?

Editor's Note and Acknowledgments

The interviews included in this book are arranged chronologically in three sections. The first section comprises three interviews (Tibbetts and Mathews) that cover Weir's boyhood in Sydney and his first travels abroad; the next seven interviews (Shirley, Hogan, Castell, Mathews, Ceretto/Morini, Dowling/Mannix, and Ryan/McFarlane) span his television years, the award-winning short films *Michael* and *Homesdale*, and the Australian feature films that first vaulted him to international notice (*The Cars That Ate Paris, Picnic at Hanging Rock, The Last Wave, The Plumber, Gallipoli, The Year of Living Dangerously*); and the last eight interviews (Rayner, Diehl, Tibbetts, Griffin, Campbell, Rudolph, Rafferty, and Boyd) encompass Weir's films in Hollywood and as an independent producer, from *Witness* to *The Way Back*. The Appendix features Peter Weir's 2001 Anzac Lecture.

Appropriately, many of these interviews were conducted by Australian journalists, filmmakers, and archivists, who best know the historical and cultural contexts of Weir's life and work. They include hitherto unpublished conversations with Graham Shirley, of the National Film and Sound Archives in Sydney, Australia; and with Tom Hogan, former colleague during Weir's formative years in television, who has been tireless in his patient answers to my many inquiries about the history of Australian film. Other interviews appearing here for the first time were conducted especially for this volume during this editor's sabbatical trip to Sydney and Melbourne in July 2012—including long overdue conversations with Russell Boyd, the celebrated cinematographer and longtime colleague of Weir, who photographed six of his most famous films; and with Peter Weir himself, who seizes the occasion to reflect on his career, past and present. Grateful acknowledgment and thanks are due to them all.

I cannot express sufficiently my debt to the friendly collegiality of the officers of the NFSA—Simon Drake, Collections Access; Graham Shirley, Manager, Access Projects; Anna Nolan, the Library Manager of the National Film and Sound Archives; and to Zsuzsi Szücs, the Collections Access Officer of the Melbourne branch of the NFSA.

Thanks also to the hospitality of the personnel at International Studies at the University of New South Wales, Drs. Anna Martin, Associate Director of Global Education and Student Exchange, and Elena Sinitsyna, Coordinator and Student Advisor of Global Education and Student Exchange. And my gratitude to Rocky Wood for the invitation to come to Melbourne and scramble about Hanging Rock.

Special recognition goes to my colleagues at the University of Kansas in the Department of Film and Media Studies, who both facilitated my sabbatical and have read portions of the manuscript: Chair, Tamara Falicov; the School of the Arts, Associate Dean, Liz Kowalchuk; and International Programs, Rene Frias; to other "Jayhawks," Baerbel Goebel, T. L. Reid, and Pam LeRow and Paula Courtney of KU Digital Media Services. And thanks go to my colleague Zach Ingle for his work indexing the manuscript; and to other colleagues who took time to read and comment on the manuscript and who assisted in the interview contacts and transcriptions, Kevin Brownlow of Photoplay Productions in London; Cynthia Miller of Emerson College in Boston; James M. Welsh, Emeritus Professor of Salisbury University, Maryland; and Erik Battaglia of the Verdi Conservatory in Turin, Italy,

To David and Louisa McCrae, thanks for your hospitality and lodgings at Manly during my Australian trip.

And finally, to Peter Weir: It was my turn to meet you on *your* end of the Beanstalk. Thanks for your time and consideration.

JCT

Notes

1. For insightful analytical studies of Peter Weir's films, see Michael Bliss, *Dreams Within a Dream* (Carbondale and Edwardsville: Southern Illinois University Press, 2000); Brian McFarlane, and Geoff Mayer, *New Australian Cinema*. London: Cambridge University Press, 1992); Brian McFarlane, *Australian Cinema 1970–1985* (Melbourne: Heinemann, 1983); Jonathan Rayner, *The Films of Peter Weir* (London: Continuum, 2003); Don Shiach, *The Films of Peter Weir* (London: Charles Letts, 1993). An extended study that takes an auteurist position is Serena Formica, *Peter Weir: A Creative Journey from Australia to Hollywood* (Chicago: Intellect, 2012). See this volume's Bibliography for other pertinent texts.

2. The Vietnam protests led to the subsequent withdrawal of Australian troops from the conflict. The interrogation of allegiance to Britain led to supplanting "God Save the Queen" with "Advance Australia Fair" as the national anthem.

3. With apologies to Baudrillard, the words seem singularly apt to *The Truman Show*. J. Baudrillard, *The Transparency of Evil*, trans. James Benedict (London: Verso, 1993), 45.

4. Editor's Note: As a practicing television journalist for CBS Television in the 1980s, this writer frequently heard such remarks about Weir in the course of attending film promotions hosted by the Hollywood studios.

5. G. K. Chesterton, *Charles Dickens, the Last of the Great Men* (New York: The Reader's Club Press, 1942), 158–59.

6. Peter Weir e-mail to John Tibbetts, September 6, 2012.

7. For a discussion of the "threshold effect" in Romantic literature, see John Fetzer, *Romantic Orpheus: Profiles of Clemens Brentano* (University of California Press, 1974).

8. In his essay on Percy Bysshe Shelley, biographer Richard Holmes notes that the spirit of Romanticism "tells those who come after what remains to be tried. . . . More a haunting than a history, [it is] peculiarly alive and potent." See Holmes, "Exiles," in *Footsteps: Adventures of a Romantic Biographer* (New York: Vintage Books, 1985), 135.

9. William Blake, *Vala*, II, 5–16.

10. Novalis, *Henry von Ofterdingen* (New York: Frederick Ungar, 1982), 26. Baudelaire frequently expressed similar ideas, defining Romanticism as "the driving force of the imagination . . . an aspiration to the infinite, expressed through all the means that the arts contain . . . the infinite in the finite." See Rosemary Lloyd, *Charles Baudelaire* (London: Reaktion Books, 2008), 68.

11. Edgar Allan Poe, *A Dream within a Dream*, lines 10–11; and John Keats, *Ode to a Nightingale*, VIII, 9–10.

12. Percy Shelley, the opening invocation to *Alastor*.

13. Robert Schumann, "The Old Captain," in Fanny Raymond Ritter, ed., *Robert Schumann: Music and Musicians: Essays and Criticisms*, First Series (London: William Reeves, n.d.), 101.

14. Friedrich's *Wanderer above a Sea of Fog* (1818) is the iconic image in this context. One might see it as a visualization of the famous words of Novalis, written eighteen years earlier in the unfinished novel *Henry von Ofterdingen*: "He saw himself on the threshold. . . . He was on the verge of immersing himself in the blue waters of the distance" (77).

15. The unnamed narrator in James's short story, "The Figure in the Carpet," is "shut up in his obsession" for the elusive meanings behind the works of a famous novelist. In the end, succumbing to frustration and madness, the hapless inquisitor finds his quest is "only rounded off with a mystery finer and subtler" (310). See Henry James, "The Figure in the Carpet," in Henry James, *Selected Tales* (New York: Penguin Books, 2001), 284–313.

Chronology

1901	The Commonwealth of Australia is established on January 1 (population: 1,795,873).
1915	Australian troops land at Gallipoli, Turkey.
1919	Australia's first film classic, Raymond Longford's *The Sentimental Bloke*, is filmed.
1944–56	Peter Weir born August 21, 1944, in Sydney, New South Wales, Australia. His family moves several times in twelve years, including residences in Watson's Bay and Vaucluse. Attends a private school but drops out.
1956–60	Attends Vaucluse High School. Television comes to Australia.
1963–64	Drops out of Sydney University after one year. Writes the University Architecture Revues. Works with co-writer/performer Grahame Bond. Sells real estate for two years. The Sydney Film Festival holds its 1964 forum around the theme "The Australian Film Industry: What of Its Future?" in which Senator Vincent spoke of the need for lobbying to implement his report deploring the dominance of Australian film and television by foreign countries and encouraging more local government and state support. Out of this forum came another public forum the following year: The National TV Congress. Aboriginals given full rights as citizens.
1965	Quits real estate and takes passage to Europe aboard a Greek ship to Piraeus and Europe. Spends nearly a year in London. Meets and marries Wendy Stites.
1966	Back in Sydney, independently produces a Christmas entertainment review for the Social Club.
1967	Joins ATN 7 Television to work as a stage hand, later production assistant. Works on several television series, including the *Mavis Bramston Show* and *Beauty and the Beast*. On his own time directs the fifteen-minute *Count Vim's Last Exercise*.

1968   Directs *The Life and Flight of the Rev. Buck Shotte* for ATN 7
            Television.
1969–70   Leaves Channel 7 and takes a job at the Commonwealth
            Film Unit (now Film Australia) as assistant cameraman and
            production assistant. Works on training films, such as *Stir-
            ring the Pool*. *Buck Shotte* accepted at the 1969 Sydney Film
            Festival. The Film and Television School established in north
            Sydney. Jerzy Toeplitz became its first head.
1971   Directs *Michael* for the Commonwealth Film Unit; and
            Homesdale, an independent production for the Experimen-
            tal Film Fund. Both win the Grand Prix from the Australian
            Film Institute. Travels to Europe and the Middle East with a
            study grant from the Interim Council. Visits the Pinewood
            and Elstree facilities and meets Alfred Hitchcock during the
            shooting of *Frenzy*. Visits Tunisia, where he gets the first
            inspiration for *The Last Wave*. The Australian Film Develop-
            ment Corporation is established.
1972   Directs *Boat Building*; *The Computer Centre*; *The Field Day*;
            Three Directions in Australian Pop Music; *Incredible Floridas* for
            Film Australia.
1973   Works with film critic, John Flaus, in Hobart, Tasmania, in-
            volving the introduction of more than fifty Tasmanian high
            school teachers to the new subject of screen studies. Directs
            Whatever Happened to Green Valley? and *The Fifth Facade* for
            Film Australia. Daughter, Ingrid Weir, born. Sydney Opera
            House opens. The South Australian Film Corporation is
            established.
1974   Directs *Fugue* for Film Australia.
1974–75   Directs *The Cars That Ate Paris* for Salt Pan Productions and
            Royce Smeal Productions, his first film for producers Hal and
            Jim McElroy. First meets Director of Photography, Russell
            Boyd, with whom he will make six films. The Australian Film
            Commission is established.
1975   Directs *Picnic at Hanging Rock* from Cliff Green's adaptation
            of Joan Lindsay's novel. It is the first film financed by the
            South Australian Film Corporation and the Australian Film
            Commission. First collaboration with Russell Boyd. It is not
            widely released in America until 1979.
1976   Roger Corman and New Line Cinema releases in America
            an unauthorized, re-edited version of *The Cars That Ate
            Paris* under an altered title, *The Cars That Eat People*. Stanley

Kubrick recommends him to Warner Bros. to direct an adaptation of Stephen King's *Salem's Lot*. Weir declines the invitation.

1977   Directs *The Last Wave* for Ayer Productions. Son, Julien, born. Directs two episodes of *Luke's Kingdom*. Signs contract with the South Australian Film Corporation.

1979   Directs *The Plumber* for TCN-9 Australian television (funded by the South Australian Film Corporation). Turns down an offer to direct the ABC TV mini-series *The Thorn Birds*. Directs *Heart, Head and Hand* for the Crafts Council of Australia.

1980   Signs a two-picture deal with Warner Bros., but turns down the first project, *The Thorn Birds*. Remains in Australia.

1981   Directs *Gallipoli* for Paramount to a screenplay by playwright David Williamson.

1982   Directs *The Year of Living Dangerously* for Wayang Productions/MGM from a novel by C. J. Koch. It is the first Australian feature film to be financed entirely by a major Hollywood studio, MGM.

1985   Travels to America to direct *Witness*, his first fully produced "American" film, for Paramount. Earns first Oscar nomination as Best Director. For the next decade, he keeps his home base in Sydney between projects for American studios.

1986   Directs *The Mosquito Coast* for the Saul Zaentz Company, from Paul Schrader's adaptation of Paul Theroux' novel.

1989   Directs *The Dead Poets Society* for Touchstone Pictures.

1990   Receives the AFI Raymond Longford Award.

1991   Directs *Green Card* from his original screenplay for an Australia-France co-production for Touchstone Pictures.

1994   Directs *Fearless* for Warner Bros.

1998   Directs *The Truman Show* for Paramount from a script by Andrew Niccol. It is his highest-grossing film to date, and it earns Best Director Oscar nomination.

2001   Delivers the 2001 Anzac Lecture in Washington, D.C.

2003   Directs *Master and Commander* for Twentieth Century-Fox and reunites with Director of Photography, Russell Boyd. Earns Best Director Oscar nomination. Boyd wins an Oscar.

2010   Directs *The Way Back* for Newmarket and Image Entertainment. Delivers the 2010 David Lean Lecture in London on December 6. Recipient of a Career Tribute at the Telluride Film Festival, Colorado.

Filmography

Short Films

Count Vim's Last Exercise (1967, ATN7 Television). 16 minutes
The Life and Flight of the Rev. Buck Shotte (1968, ATN7 Television). 20 minutes
Stirring the Pool (1970). 6 minutes
Tempo: Australia in the 70's (1971, Film Australia) (as co-writer). 25 minutes
Boat Building (1972, Film Australia). 5 minutes
The Computer Centre (1972, Film Australia). 5 minutes
The Field Day (1972, Film Australia). 5 minutes
Three Directions in Australian Pop Music (1972, Film Australia). 11 minutes
Incredible Floridas (1972, Film Australia). 10 minutes
Whatever Happened to Green Valley? (1973, Film Australia). 25 minutes
The Fifth Façade (1973, Film Australia). 30 minutes
Fugue (1974, Film Australia). 5 minutes
Heart, Head and Hand (1979, Film Australia). 20 minutes

Short Features

THREE TO GO—MICHAEL (1969)
Commonwealth Film Unit
Producer: Gil Brealey
Director and Screenplay: **Peter Weir**
Photography: Kerry Brown
Editing: Wayne Le Clos
Musical Score: The Clevves
Cast: Matthew Burton (Michael), Grahame Bond (Grahame), Peter Colville (Neville Trantor), Georgina West (Georgina)
28 minutes

HOMESDALE (1971)
Independent Production and Experimental Film Fund
Producers: Richard Brennan and Grahame Bond
Director: **Peter Weir**
Script: **Peter Weir** and Piers Davies
Photography: Anthony Wallis
Editing: Wayne Le Clos
Musical Score: Grahame Bond and Rory O'Donahue
Cast: Grahame Bond (Mr. Kevin), Kate Fitzpatrick (Miss Greenoak),
Geoff Malone (Mr. Malfry), James Lear (Mr. Levy)
50 minutes

Features

THE CARS THAT ATE PARIS (1974)
Salt Pan Productions/ Royce Smeal Productions
Producers: Hal McElroy and Jim McElroy
Director: **Peter Weir**
Screenplay: **Peter Weir**, Keith Gow, Piers Davies
Photography: John McLean
Editing: Wayne Le Clos
Musical Score: Bruce Smeaton
Cast: Terry Camilleri (Arthur Waldo), John Meillon (the mayor),
Melissa Jaffer (Beth), Kevin Miles (Dr. Midland), Max Gillies (Metcalf),
Peter Armstrong (Gorman), Edward Howell (Tringham), Bruce Spence
(Charlie), Derek Barnes (Al Smedley)
91 minutes

PICNIC AT HANGING ROCK (1975)
South Australian Film Corporation, Australian Film Commission
Producers: Hal McElroy, Jim McElroy, Patricia Lovell
Director: **Peter Weir**
Screenplay: Cliff Green, adapted from Joan Lindsay's novel
Photography: Russell Boyd
Camera Operator: John Seale
Editing: Max Lemon
Musical Score: Bruce Smeaton
Gheorgyhe Zamphir (pan-pipe), Beethoven, Fifth Piano Concerto
Cast: Rachel Roberts (Mrs. Appleyard), Dominic Guard (Michael

Fitzhubert), Helen Morse (Dianne de Portiers), Jacki Weaver (Minnie), Vivean Gray (Miss McCraw), Kirsty Child (Dora Lumley), Anne Lambert (Miranda), Karen Robson (Irma), June Vallis (Marion), Christine Schuler (Edith), Margaret Nelson (Sara), Peter Collingwood (Col. Fitzhubert), John Jarrett (Albert Crundall), Ingrid Mason (Rosamunde)
116 minutes

THE LAST WAVE (1977)
Ayer Productions, South Australian Film Corporation, Australian Film Commission
Producers: Hal McElroy and Jim McElroy
Director: **Peter Weir**
Screenplay: Tony Morphett, Petru Popescu, and **Peter Weir**
Photography: Russell Boyd
Camera Operator: John Seale
Editing: Max Lemon
Musical Score: Charles Wain
Cast: Richard Chamberlain (David Burton), Olivia Hamnett (Annie Burton), Gulpilil (Chris Lee), Frederick Parslow (Rev. Burton), Vivean Gray (Dr. Whitburn), Nandjiwarra Amagula (Charlie), Walter Amagula (Gerry Lee), Roy Bar (Larry), Cedric Lalara (Lindsey), Morris Lalara (Jacko), Peter Carroll (Michael Zeadler), Athol Compton (Billy Corman), Hedley Cullen (judge), Michael Duffield (Andrew Potter)
United Artists
104 minutes

THE PLUMBER (1979)
South Australian Film Corporation for the 9 network, Australian Film Commission
Producer: Matt Carroll
Director and Screenplay: **Peter Weir**
Photography: David Sanderson
Editing: Gerald Turney-Smity
Production Design: Wendy Weir
Cast: Judy Morris (Jill Cowper), Ivar Kants (Max), Robert Coleby (Brian Cowper), Henri Szeps (David Medavoy), Candy Raymond (Meg), Yomi Abioudun (Dr. Matu), Beverly Roberts (Dr. Japari), Meme Thorne (Anna), David Burchell (Professor Cato), Bruce Rosen (Dr. Don Felder)
76 minutes

GALLIPOLI (1981)
Producers: Robert Stigwood, Patricia Lovell
Director: **Peter Weir**
Screenplay: David Williamson and **Peter Weir**
Photography: Russell Boyd
Camera Operator: John Seale
Editing: William Anderson
Music: Albinoni, "Adagio in G Minor"; Jean Michel Jarre, "Oxygene";
Bizet, "The Pearl Fishers"; Johann Strauss, "Roses from the South";
Paganini, "Centone di Sonata No. 3"
Production Design: Wendy Weir
Cast: Mark Lee (Archie Hamilton), Mel Gibson (Frank Dunne), Bill
Hunter (Major Barton), Robert Grubb (Billy Lewis), Tim McKenzie
(Barney Wilson), David Argue ("Snowy"), Bill Kerr (Uncle Jack), Ron
Graham (Wallace Hamilton), Charles Yunupingu (Zak), John Morris
(Colonel Robinson), with the men of Port Lincoln and Adelaide; the
16th Air Defense Regiment; cadets of the No. 1 Recruit Training Unit,
Edinburgh, South Australia
Paramount
110 minutes

THE YEAR OF LIVING DANGEROUSLY (1982)
Wayang Productions
Producers: Hal McElroy and Jim McElroy
Director: **Peter Weir**
Screenplay: David Williamson, **Peter Weir**, and C. J. Hoch (from
Koch's novel)
Photography: Russell Boyd
Camera Operator: John Seale
Editing: William Anderson
Musical Score: Maurice Jarre (uncredited, Stathis Vangelis)
Richard Strauss, "Four Last Songs" ("September")
Cast: Mel Gibson (Guy Hamilton), Sigourney Weaver (Jill Bryant),
Linda Hunt (Billy Kwan), Bembel Roco (Kumar), Domingo Landi-
cho (Hortono), Michael Murphy (Pete Curtis), Noel Ferrier (Wally
O'Sullivan), Mike Emperio (President Sukarno), Bernardo Nacilla
(dwarf), Kuh Ledesman (Tiger Lily), Norma Uatuhan (Ibu)
MGM
115 minutes

WITNESS (1985)
Producer: Edward Feldman
Director: **Peter Weir**
Screenplay: Earl Wallace and William Kelley
Photography and Camera Operator: John Seale
Editing: Thom Noble
Musical Score: Maurice Jarre
Beethoven, Fifth Piano Concerto
Cast: Harrison Ford (John Book), Kelley McGillis (Rachel Lapp), Josef
Sommer (Deputy Commissioner Schaeffer), Lukas Haas (Samuel Lapp),
Jan Rubes (Eli Lapp), Alexander Godunov (Daniel Hochleitner), Danny
Glover (McFee), Brent Jennings (Carter), Patti Lupone (Elaine), Angus
MacInnes (Fergie)
Paramount
112 minutes

THE MOSQUITO COAST (1986)
Producer: Jerome Hellman
Director: **Peter Weir**
Screenplay: Paul Schrader, based on novel by Paul Theroux
Photography and Camera Operator: John Seale
Editing: Thom Noble
Musical Score: Maurice Jarre
Cast: Harrison Ford (Allie Fox), Helen Mirren (Mother), River Phoenix
(Charlie Fox), Jadrien Steele (Jerry Fox), Hilary Gordon (April Fox),
Rebecca Gordon (Clover Fox), Jason Alexander (clerk), Dick O'Neill (Mr.
Polski), Andre Gregory (Reverend Spellgood), Martha Plimpton (Emily
Spellgood), Conrad Roberts (Mr. Haddy)
Saul Zaentz Company
117 minutes

DEAD POETS SOCIETY (1989)
Producers: Steven Haft, Paul Junger Witt, and Tony Thomas
Director: **Peter Weir**
Screenplay: Tom Schulman
Photography: John Seale
Editing: William Anderson
Musical Score: Maurice Jarre
Beethoven, Ninth Symphony ("An die Freude")
Production Design: Wendy Stites

Cast: Robin Williams (John Keating), Robert Sean Leonard (Neil Perry),
Ethan Hawke (Todd Anderson), Josh Charles (Knox Overstreet), Gale
Hansen (Charlie Dalton), Dylan Kossman (Richard Cameron), Allelon
Ruggiero (Steven Meeks), James Waterson (Gerard Pitts), Norman Lloyd
(Mr. Nolan), Kurtwood Smith (Mr. Perry), Carla Belver (Mrs. Perry),
Leon Pownall (McAllister)
Touchstone Pictures
128 minutes

GREEN CARD (1990)
Producers: **Peter Weir** and Edward Feldman
Director and Screenplay: **Peter Weir**
Photography: Geoffrey Simpson
Editing: William Anderson
Musical Score: Hans Zimmer
Production Design: Wendy Stites
Cast: Gérard Depardieu (Georges Faure), Andie MacDowell (Bronte
Parrish), Bebe Neuwirth (Lauren Adler), Gregg Edelman (Phil), Rob-
ert Prosky (Bronte's lawyer), Jessie Keosian (Mrs. Bird), Ethan Philips
(Gorsky), Mary Louise Wilson (Mrs. Sheehan), Lois Smith and Conrad
McLaren (Bronte's parents)
Touchstone Pictures
103 minutes

FEARLESS (1993)
Producers: Paula Weinstein and Mark Rosenberg
Director: **Peter Weir**
Screenplay: Rafael Yglesias from his novel
Photography: Allen Daviau
Production Design: John Stoddart
Art Direction: Chris Burian-Mohr
Editing: William Anderson
Musical Score: Maurice Jarre
Design Consultant: Wendy Stites
Cast: Jeff Bridges (Max Klein), Isabella Rossellini (Laura Klein), Rosie
Perez (Carla Rodrigo), Tom Hulce (Brillstein), John Turturro (Dr. Bill
Perlman), Benicio del Toro (Manny Rodrigo), John de Lancie (Jeff Gor-
don), Spencer Vrooman (Jonah Klein)
Warner Bros.
122 minutes

THE TRUMAN SHOW (1998)
Producers: Scott Rudin, Andrew Niccol, Edward S. Feldman, and Adam
Schroeder
Director: **Peter Weir**
Screenplay: Andrew Niccol
Photography: Peter Biziou
Editing: William Anderson
Musical Score: Burkhard Dallwitz and Philip Glass
Production Design: Dennis Gassner
Design Consultant: Wendy Stites
Cast: Jim Carrey (Truman Burbank), Ed Harris (Christof), Laura Linney
(Meryl Burbank/Hannah Gill), Noah Emmerich (Marlon/Louis Col-
trane), Natascha McElhone (Lauren Garland/Sylvia), Holland Taylor
(Truman's mother), Brian Delate (Kirk Burbank), Blair Slater (Young
Truman), Ron Taylor (Ron), Don Taylor (Don), Judy Clayton (Travel
Agent)
Paramount
103 minutes

MASTER AND COMMANDER (2003)
Producers: Todd Arnow, Duncan Henderson, and **Peter Weir**
Director: **Peter Weir**
Screenplay: John Collee and **Peter Weir**, from the novels of Patrick
O'Brian
Photography: Russell Boyd
Editing: Lee Smith
Production Design: William Sandell
Art Direction: Bruce Crone and Mark Mansbridge
Music: Mozart, "Third Violin Concerto"; Boccherini, "La Musica Not-
turna delle Strade di Madrid"; Vivaldi, "Concerto for Four Violins and
Orchestra in B Minor"
Costume Design: Wendy Stites
Cast: Russell Crowe (Jack Aubrey), Paul Bettany (Stephen Maturin),
James D'Arcy (1st Lt. Tom Pullings), Edward Woodall (2nd Lt. William
Mowett), Chris Larkin (Capt. Howard), Max Pirkis (Midshipman Blake-
ney), Jack Randall (Midshipman Boyle), Robert Pugh (Mr. Allen)
Twentieth Century-Fox
138 minutes

THE WAY BACK (2010)
Producers: Joni Levin, **Peter Weir**, and Duncan Henderson
Director: **Peter Weir**
Screenplay: **Peter Weir** and Keith Clarke, from "The Long Walk" by
Slavomir Rawicz
Photography: Russell Boyd
Editing: Lee Smith
Music Score: Burkhard Dallwicz
Costume Design: Wendy Stites
Cast: Jim Sturgess (Janusz), Colin Farrel (Valka), Ed Harris (Mr. Smith),
Mark Strong (Khabarov), Saoirose (Elena), Gustaf Skarsgård (Voss), Alex-
andru Potocean (Tomasz), Sally Edwards (Janusz's wife)
Newmarket, Image Entertainment
133 minutes

Peter Weir: Interviews

Peter Weir: Reclaiming
a Sydney Boyhood

John C. Tibbetts / 2012

Interview conducted July 9, 2012. Previously unpublished. Printed by permission of the author.

"It's been a long time since I've explored these areas," murmurs Peter Weir from behind the wheel of his car. We are on a tour of his childhood haunts in and around Sydney. It's a sparkling Sunday afternoon, July 9, 2012, with mild breezes and flying blue skies. It's been many years since we first met, back in America, on the premiere of *Fearless*. With only sporadic correspondence in the intervening years, we're getting to know each again. The trip proves to be not just an affectionate visit to his past, but it affords me a fleeting glimpse of the rich history of Sydney and environs. Moreover, says Weir, "It gets us to talking again."

Our adventure begins when Peter picks me up at my lodgings in Manly, a coastal suburb which is one of the oldest settlements and beach areas in Sydney. It spreads across from the coast to the northeastern edge of Sydney Harbor; and a twenty-five-minute ferry ride delivers you to the heart of the city. Melbourne is an hour-and-a-half further south by plane (for the curious, Hanging Rock is located near Melbourne). From Manly, Peter's trajectory includes Vaucluse, an eastern suburb of Sydney, located on the South Head Peninsula; the adjacent eastern suburbs of Watsons Bay and Rose Bay; and the historic area around Camp Cove.

Camp Cove is close by Sydney Harbor, part of the coastline first chartered by Captain James Cook on his First Voyage in May 1770.[1] Originally dubbed New Holland, it was here that the first colonial settlement and penal colony were established. "This is a famous spot," Weir explains as we enjoy the spectacular views of cliffs and breakers. He smiles mischievously as we walk. "This is an old convict area—let's walk here and break the law! There you see South Head, the entrance to the harbor. After mapping the coast, Captain Cook sailed out of Botany Bay and sailed northward. He'd come here from Tahiti, where he'd been covering the Transit of Venus." Walking further along the rocky edge of an area called The Gap, he pointed out the area far below us where in 1857 the *Dunbar*, a square-rigger carrying free immigrants, foundered on the rocks, leaving only a handful of survivors. "A relative of ours, a woman, just missed that ship," he explains, as we peer at the furious spray of the whitecaps below us. "The jumpers like it—a quick death." He has to raise his voice above the roar of the breakers. "Kids thrilled to the sense of danger here. I was just ten or eleven when I came down here one day and saw a corpse with its feet sticking out from under a blanket. I've never forgotten it. And there—" he guides me toward a cliff wall, where a gigantic stone anchor, fully ten feet in height, was mounted—"is the anchor from the *Dunbar*. Sydney is built on these massive rocks." Further along, Peter pauses again. "Here's something from my childhood." He gestures toward a fence along the cliff edge. "These were gun emplacements, with tunnels underneath for storage, built after the outbreak of war with Japan. We thought 'they' were coming." He smiles: "Now they come as tourists! My father had been an air-raid warden, and he was on duty the night two Japanese subs got into Sydney Harbour. He remembered the sounds of shells bursting, and I got him to tell me the story over and over."

It is a short distance to Watsons Bay, near Camp Cove, where Peter lived from age eight to twelve; and another hop to the eastern suburb of Vaucluse, where he spent his high school years. He remembers the Weir family real estate shop, St. Michael's Church, and the family home on Parsley Road, which is still standing. He notes that the famous Australian film star, Chips Rafferty ("a kind of Bryan Brown of his day"), had also lived in Vaucluse. "My family is fourth generation immigrants mostly from Scotland," he muses. "We had a scrapbook, but there was no writing on the photos to identify them. But people didn't care. They came to Australia as immigrants and never looked back."

At each stop, we leave the car and walk around, enjoying the breezy weather and bright sunlight. At one point we pause for a seaside late lunch of fish-and-chips. Shielding our eyes from the sun, listening to the merry beach sounds on all sides, our conversation skips from topic to topic—from his work with cinematographer Russell Boyd ("he deeply understands Australian light"); a film retrospective in Bologna; a visit to the famed Turin Film Museum ("the past is not patronized there"); handcrafted "Miranda Bears" (in honor of Anne Lambert, the "Miranda" of *Picnic at Hanging Rock*); Harrison Ford's carpentry on the set of *Witness* ("he loved building that barn"); his love of the works of Robert Louis Stevenson ("I'd like to have travelled with him, made up stories with him"); the etiquette of journalists ("don't quote me!"); and Australian pronunciations ("we tend to lose the 'l' in 'Australia'"). And, of course, there were occasional musings about what might be dubbed "The Australian mindset": "We're deracinated mongrels; we don't have a lineage to be snobbish about."

We are back on the road. "I remember the local movie house," he says, as we alight in an area he calls The Glen. "It's now an antique shop. It and another cinema, at Rose Bay, is where we saw the serials and westerns and lots of American films. My favorites were the Hammer horror films. And I distinctly remember seeing *The Wages of Fear*." We walk along an inviting expanse of open grass, nestled within surrounding trees. "This was the place to go—the Glen. Some of the more daring kids would chase trams and unhook the power cables. You could sense danger here, so essential to childhood. Can you imagine children now? I was lucky to grow up in an era when kids played *outside*. Would parents now let them loose at twilight, like we were?" I notice a clump of spectacular, twisting trees. "Those are the Morton Bay Figs." He pauses, the sounds of birds racketing all around us. "I spent so much time here . . . eight years here. Long, slow, idyllic years. I sailed for one or two seasons in the bay, but I was always falling in. But it was a fun thing and a good way to meet girls! You could drink in the pubs at age seventeen. The P&O liners would anchor in the bay. I began to realize I wanted to go where the ships went. This was the crucible of my imagination."

Having driven past Bondi Road, we cut across to the Kensington suburb, where we drive past the University of New South Wales ("not as attractive as Sydney University") and Centennial Park, Sydney's central park and an oasis of calm. ("Forty years ago, there was virtually nothing here"). But in the here and now the traffic is increasing. . . .

Time to turn back. . . .

Note

1. In January 1787 British Captain Arthur Phillip, in command of eleven ships full of convicts, arrived at Botany Bay on January 18. Finding the poor soil and the region's lack of strategic cover, he settled instead at Port Jackson, farther north. The settlement became Sydney. Lord Sydney's decision to colonize Australia grew out of Britain's need to relieve its overcrowded prisons; moreover, Australia was of strategic importance to Britain and provided a base for the Royal Navy in the eastern sea. European settlement of Australia began in 1788 when a British penal colony was established on the east coast. Australia Day is now celebrated on January 26 each year to commemorate the first fleet landing.

Peter Weir: Snapshots in Time

John C. Tibbetts / 2012

Interview conducted in Sydney, Australia, July 9–20, 2012. Previously unpublished. Used by permission of the author.

[Note: Imagine a sunny afternoon in Manley. Peter Weir and I are outside, in a little corner of a back garden. He sits across from me at a table, entirely at his ease. His trademark hat shadows his forehead from the intense sun. Despite the afternoon cool, he wears a black tee-shirt. He frequently accompanies his remarks by shifting in his seat and gesturing with his hands.]

John C. Tibbetts: Catch us up on what you are doing now.
Peter Weir: Well, I'm working on a screenplay, an adaptation of a novel. It's a work of fiction. When I'm offered a new project today, usually when my agent sends me something, it's a true story. Fiction is seen as a sort of poor cousin, from the other side of the tracks, in terms of movie subject matter. I've given up making jokes, like, "have you got any fiction left???" And they've given up trying to understand why I resist true stories. I don't mean historical settings, you know, I've obviously dealt with those with *Gallipoli* and *Master and Commander*. But I always say "no" to biographies. They would make me feel constricted. I would be obsessive about not changing anything, of being certain that what I was doing was respectful. I did once consider doing two weeks in the life of the British sea captain, Captain Cook. I thought he was long enough dead, so there's no books to cover the conversations I would have to imagine. But even then, I was wary. So now I'm very pleased to be working on a fictional piece. If it's a script that's in very good shape—which is rare for me—you've got a shot in starting preproduction within three to six months.

Tibbetts: You have patience, don't you? You don't rush these things. Years go by between projects. All of us hate you for that. [both laugh]
Weir: Well, I would love to work at a greater rate. But it's just the nature of my approach.

Tibbetts: Was it quite a process to lock on to this project, I mean, were there other projects that fell by the wayside, like *Shadow Divers*?
Weir: No, that, period you're referring to with *Shadow Divers* was between *Master and Commander* and *The Way Back*. It was just a run of bad luck (I either abandoned projects or others withdrew).

Tibbetts: But you say you have closed the door on a biographical dramatization of some kind, of a real person, that is.
Weir: I think, maybe, there could be an exception to that. One has to be careful. I think you never say "never." I did consider a subject I came close to, and had meetings with the subject, and that was Oliver Sacks. It was *Awakenings*. I went to Fire Island, where he lived, and we sat and talked; and I said to him, "You know, this is your life's work I'm considering putting into a film; and, it's a good screenplay by Steve Zallian. Are you happy with this?" And he said, "Well yes, and no. The 'yes' part is the lovely Mercedes you saw in my driveway, which the option money bought. [laughter] The 'no' part is that it is not a fairy tale, the sort of thing where someone with this particular disease is awakened from a long, long sleep by dopamine." Anyway, that's as close as I ever came to that.

Tibbetts: There is no real set format for writing a screenplay. Do you prefer to work in prose first, breaking it down into shots and dialogue?
Weir: Yes, it's a very odd document you're reaching for. Scripts are never reread, they're never sold, other than to film schools. It's an uncomfortable form to read, you know—"Interior: Day: A New York Street." Then, "Walking towards us is Harold with a brown satchel in his hand; blah, blah, blah."

Tibbetts: "—Cut to Close-Up."
Weir: It's just very awkward. Sometimes I will just go to the short story form. Of course, you don't write anything for some time. You *research*.

Tibbetts: Do you allow yourself already to think about things like music?

Weir: I think less so in the last few years than I did earlier. In the past I used to use the music more to get myself into some kind of a "fit." To work myself up, to get into a passion. And now I prefer almost the opposite. I would almost rather write "cold," or cooler, at least, and let any heat come through of its own inherent power rather than kicking up a musical storm.

Then and Now

Tibbetts: Well, you've kind of gone through a career arc; I mean, the European style film, then gradually you came into the Hollywood fold; now it seems as if there's a return to a European sensibility, or at least market, with the independently produced *The Way Back*.
Weir: Yeah. I think that's true; although, when you think about it, *Fearless* and *The Truman Show* are not conventional Hollywood fare.

Tibbetts: Well, none of your films are, when you get right down to it.
Weir: People sometimes say to me they prefer my Australian films to the American ones. To me, they're all stories and you tell them. You know, they're set here or they're set there. But, yes, I think it's more the case I no longer work with the studios. And I started working with *Witness*, 1984, through *Master and Commander*, let's say, 2004. So, that was my studio period, and they no longer make those kinds of films. As somebody from a studio said to me recently, "We're not in that kind of business anymore."

Tibbetts: Let's consider the Peter Weir that was and the Peter Weir that is now. What were you like in your earlier days; and have you changed in any way?
Weir: Difficult to answer that. I'd say I strive for simplicity now in my work, not something I'd have been capable of as a young filmmaker.

Tibbetts: Thanks to the National Film Archives, I've recently had a chance to go back and look at some of your earliest films from the late 1960s, *Count Vim's Last Exercise* and *Buck Shotte*, for example. There's scarcely any references to them in the books written about you. But I think they're fascinating. And we see you as an actor, too. There you are, in *Buck Shotte*, on camera, dressed in priestly robes, a sort of hippie guru—
Weir: —Those are from the Christmas Revues I did.

Tibbetts: And there's a line where you say to your congregations and acolytes, "Free yourselves from your own feet!"
Weir: Right. He's airborne! [chuckles]

Tibbetts: Peter Pan would say something like that. So many of your characters seem to invite us to do just that.
Weir: Well, that's for you to say.

Tibbetts: Am I making too much of some of this?
Weir: Absolutely. [laughs]

Tibbetts: And Buck has what he calls this "Cage Corps," where he and his, er, flock, go out on a mission, free the birds of the world, free the imagination.
Weir: I haven't discussed this since 1968! Now, you know, those early films of mine did not have any slot you could post them in. They didn't fit anywhere. I remember David Stratton, the film critic here said, "Our Peter Weir's a maverick."

Tibbetts: And Buck wants to "have a perch," in every state, bird seed in every home, as he puts it. Isn't that what a filmmaker does; get your film out there, in the theaters, in everyone's imagination? Here I go again! [laughs]. . . . You're not buying any of this, are you?
Weir: No, no, not at all.

Tibbetts: Let's see. And then there's *Count Vim's Last Exercise.*
Weir: My first film. 1967. I was working as a stage hand at a local television station, and in my spare time had gotten involved in various amateur revues as a writer/performer, with a friend, Grahame Bond.[1] I suggested to the head of the station Social Club that we put on a staff revue at the end of the year. I said we could include a short film in the program if he could get me permission to borrow a camera from the news department and processing from the company lab. This was agreed to and I made the film on weekends, while writing and rehearsing the revue. And the big night came. We rented a hall in the city, a 350-seater. And it was all friends and families of the actors. We had a 16mm projector. We would open the second act with it. So I went that day, very excited, to pick up the print. And the guy at the lab said, "Sorry, we didn't get a chance to marry your sound with the image." I said, "I've only got the

image?" So, I wondered, What am I going to do? The show's on tonight. So I took the work print, got to the theatre early, and asked for a "live" mic, so I can narrate the film myself. I'll sit in the front row and keep the mic under the seat at the interval. So I sat where a seat had been kept for me, with the puzzled looks of people on each side of me. But I forgot about the auditorium lights going out! I couldn't read my script. So, I had to do it from memory; and I did all the sound effects, the wind howling [imitates wind sound], feet crunching on gravel [sounds]. So, I did all of this with a very good mic and very good sound system!

Tibbetts: Just call you "Mr. Foley," yes?
Weir: [laughs] Anyway, most of the people there didn't know what was happening, other than those sitting beside me. Later, I got a live mic, watched the film, and recorded the same kind of soundtrack. And that's what's on it. Me doing all the effects. Anyway, it got me a promotion. I got a job directing film sequences for a variety show.

Tibbetts: Now, about these two shorts, *Buck Shotte* and *Count Vim*— they show a side of Peter Weir, if I may say so, that we don't know enough about. More of a clown?
Weir: Yeah, yeah.

Tibbetts: Cap and bells?
Weir: Absolutely.

Tibbetts: It hasn't really disappeared from your work, has it?
Weir: Well, it was a way of starting. I was born to be a member of the show business fraternity. Humor's probably the quickest way to know how you're dealing with an audience. I wasn't interested in classical acting. I didn't know if I'd be a writer, actor, or producer. I didn't even think about directing. But I wanted to be a performer, really, a writer-performer. And that was my plan, with Grahame and a couple of other guys. We were auditioning for television stations while I was making these short films. Then I went to London, as I mentioned, on this study trip, funded by the newly established Australian Experimental Film Fund, the plan being they would then set a second fund up to make feature films. You could apply with a plan. Mine was to go and get experience in the British studios for six months. And my wife and I went and lived in London, and I worked in the special effects department. While I was there, for the first time I saw Monty Python. We had heard all about them, Grahame and

I, but in those days programs didn't come over to us as quickly. So, they hadn't been shown in Australia. *Monty Python* was doing the sort of stuff we were doing, but much better. And I thought, that's a door closed. We couldn't compete with them.

Tibbetts: Can we think of these early shorts as "chips from the master's workbench"? Would you like to have them better known to the viewers now?
Weir: No, no. I consider them only of academic interest.

Tibbetts: But when you have a sword duel with your mirror image in *Count Vim*, isn't that what a director does in making a movie? [Weir laughs] Isn't that what you do; continually contesting with yourself?
Weir: Of course, you are constantly playing chess with yourself. . . .

Tibbetts: And right away, so early in your career, *Count Vim* forecasts the kind of surveillance state you depict later in *The Truman Show*. Somebody says, "The state is watching you."
Weir: Well, yeah. I grew up with the history of the Second War and the rise of fascist states, and the Nazis and the Soviets. It was in the air. You know, Big Brother will come again.

Tibbetts: And Vim's execution is terrifying—he's sort of "escorted out of life," as is said. The line is "Well fallen, Vim. Well fallen."
Weir: No, John, I never thought of it in that way. Everything was done so fast and—

Tibbetts: And while I'm at it, what about your documentary spoof, *Green Valley*? That's hardly mentioned anywhere in studies of your work. It's hilarious. And in a short film-within-the-film you made this wild satire where you are onscreen as a news reporter. I'd love to see that plucked right out of the rest of it and stand alone.
Weir: Well, you know what happened, I was about to say farewell to my day job with Commonwealth Film Unit, as it was then called. I was a round peg in a square hole. I was not good at documentaries. I wasn't interested, I liked fiction. So I was about to start my first feature film, *The Cars That Ate Paris*. I was given this one last assignment to make a film about this area where people were living in an experimental community, Green Valley.

Tibbetts: A real place?

Weir: Yes, an experiment where working-class people were moved out of the city into state-provided housing. So I went out to see it. It was way out of Sydney, you know. The people were very sick of the press. So when I arrived, it was like, "Oh, not another person with a camera!" I would ask them about their problems, and they would sum things up in a few, slick lines and complain it was not the way the press portrays it. So I decided to pick a few people and give them cameras to tell their story. And then I would make a film satirizing what I was doing as a newsman intruding in their lives.

Tibbetts: You were the on-camera voice of a news show called *Spotlight*!

Weir: [laughs] That's right.

Tibbetts: Was there actually a television news program called *Spotlight*?

Weir: No, no. I made it up as a sort of pre-*60 Minutes*. [laughs] I had a ball with it.

Tibbetts: This reporter is so pedantic. And intrusive. Paddling about in a rubber boat. And there you are, measuring a withered tree with your tape measure. You could be like, like Mr. Keating in *Dead Poets*—

Weir: —measuring poetry!

Tibbetts: I mean, the ever-ready tape measure. "The leaf is two inches long . . ."

Weir: [laughs] I haven't thought about it in ages. You bring it back. Reporters are constantly like that. And it probably was a reaction to school in some ways which hadn't been that long before.

Tibbetts: And then, at the end—"The *Spotlight* might be on your suburb next week!" That's pretty scary. Here's another *Truman Show* thing.

Weir: And in *Michael* I put in also another television program, called *Youth Quake*. In which again, television reporters are trying to package up opinions and ideas and news as entertainment.

Tibbetts: Are you dismissive of these early projects of yours?

Weir: Yes and no. Let me put it this way, John: I think most films are made for the time, to be consumed at the time. Of course, they live on, but most of them don't deserve to. I think very few things have another life other than the time in which they were released. Unless they can be, as I say, of academic interest.

Tibbetts: But did you ever have in your television days an ambition to actually be a news reporter or an on-camera commentator?
Weir: No, no.

Tibbetts: Even though you have great fun sending it up in *Green Valley*?
Weir: Well then, therefore, I couldn't really do it, could I? You know, I've made my statement.

Tibbetts: Now, what a contrast we have in your documentary, *Fifth Façade!*
Weir: I don't even remember that. Was that the Sydney Opera House? I just co-wrote that with Keith Gow.[1] He directed it.

Tibbetts: But you know what?—there we have at the end of the film, images of people attending a performance; we see them, rising up in ranks, rising up the staircase to the fantasy world above. You say, "Leaving the world behind to the Fantasies above." Isn't it like the girls ascending Hanging Rock?
Weir: Is that what they do?

Tibbetts: You know I'm out of my mind, don't you?
Weir: [laughs]

Tibbetts: Is it entirely obnoxious that viewers like me might come to you with things like this?
Weir: I don't think I'll see these films again. They're safely inside the vault. You were rummaging around.

Tibbetts: It's a pretty memorable image, those ranks of people rising up into the "empyrean," I would call it, rising towards the light.
Weir: I was just a writer. I took a check. I think many of us, it's like we're soldiers back from the trenches: We don't talk much. We're asked, "What's it like out there?" We get through things, day by day. The more you've seen and experienced of the cut and thrust of this kind of work, trying to get things right, not to mention the long days and problems with actors—the more you do it, the less you talk about it, like those frontline soldiers.

Tibbetts: But you do make statements about your work—at least in your films. The Archive showed me your documentary about the potter, Peter Rushworth, *Heart, Head and Hand.*
Weir: Oh, did you see that?

Tibbetts: Remember how you opened it up?
Weir: On the beach. Yes, with the children making sandcastles. It struck me when I went and watched Peter throwing some pots, that that's what we do as kids. We are so creative on the beach. Peter had set up his kiln in nearby St. Ives. We had this problem at the beginning of the shoot, because I was looking for an angle, a way to make it. I told him I'm not great on documentary. So we talked about his life, about his teaching, and the Japanese potter Shiga, who had inspired him. Peter said something or other about his imprisonment in Changi in the Second War. And yet, even though he had suffered under the Japanese, now his greatest inspiration is a Japanese potter! Wow, there's the angle. I told him we could rebuild a part of the prison camp. We'll have actors playing you and the Japanese guard. And he said, "Oh my, god, no. I couldn't do that, that would be offensive!" I assured him we would do it tastefully, with him reading by lamplight under the watch of the Japanese guard—and then cut to Shiga, as he throws a pot all those years later. Peter still refused. He was right. He was a very gentle man, a very kind and honest man, and he'd come to peace with his wartime experiences. He didn't want to reopen them and didn't want anyone fiddling with that memory. And so I respected that; I thought, fair enough. That was the night that was so influential for me. I've talked about that a lot. While we waited for the pots to cook, I took the opportunity to talk with Shiga. He had come to live here for a period, as a kind of expatriate. I knew nothing, nothing about pottery. It was only subsequently that I found out he was a very big name. (He died only recently, and there was quite a big obituary in the paper here.) We just chatted into the night, a couple of hours or so, waiting to open the kiln. We talked about art, what art is, the difference between the West and the East, certainly between Japan and Europe. And suddenly, I knew this was somehow meaningful to me in my own life as a film director. Just to be content with the *craft* and let the art take care of itself. Don't try to be an artist. That's what I got from what he said. Not in so many words, you know; but that's what the Japanese artist or craftsman is all about—making utilitarian objects without singing about them. Self-consciousness can impair that.[3]

Tibbetts: Have politics ever played much of a role in these films? Were you more politically overt then than now?

Weir: I think politics and the interest I've had in them has been fairly slight and not very interesting. I think when I enter the "door" of a film, you know, which is at the script stage, I have no interest in politics, *other than the politics of the story itself*. I think it's wise to leave your politics at the door, when you go in. Avoid the possibility of contaminating the material. You know, I'd hate it to be contaminated by my prejudices, which would lead to the danger of making a propaganda film.

Tibbetts: Do you think very much about those past days? There's a quote by G. K. Chesterton that I'd like to read to you.

Weir: Yes, go ahead, sure.

Tibbetts: [reads] "I'm concerned of what's become of a little boy whose father showed him a toy theatre, and the schoolboy who nobody ever heard of, with his brooding on doubts and dirt and daydreams, of crude conscientiousness so inconsistent as to be near hypocrisy. And all of the morbid life of the lonely mind of the living person with whom I have lived. It is that story that came so near to ending badly that I want to end well."

Weir: I think it's a lovely quote.

Tibbetts: Does it mean anything to you though, or am I pushing something that's . . .

Weir: That could be said by somebody maybe close to the end of his life, and therefore in a situation where he could reflect. But right now, I think I'm too preoccupied with my new project. So I tend to not spend a great deal of time on reflection.

Tibbetts: But we want it to "*end well*," as he says.

Weir: Oh, I love that line! It's in my head.

Tibbetts: Do you still have the love and enthusiasm for cranking the camera and working on a script that I assume you once had?

Weir: Yes, I protected that very carefully over the years. I always wanted to protect the pleasure that I've found in making films.

Tibbetts: But about the politics . . . there's something timeless about the political situation you describe in of *The Cars That Ate Paris*. Many people have commented on that.

Weir: Yes, I think so, although no one ever mentioned that in any of the first reviews of the time. I like to leave sleeping metaphors lie. I don't like to put them in, but if I find one or two *already* in a story, then I prefer to leave them alone.

Tibbetts: Were you amused to find years later George Miller populating the screen with automobiles in the "Mad Max" movies that looked a lot like the ones we see in *Cars*?

Weir: [laughs]

Tibbetts: Did he thank you for that?

Weir: I guess you could just say it was in the air. Around the same time was Sandy Harbutt's *Stone* [1974], with the "Grave Diggers Motorcycle Club."

Tibbetts: But where did you get that idea of "dressing up" the cars to look like wild animals? You hear them "growling" on the soundtrack.

Weir: They reflect the state of the young people, who are without any moral values of any kind. They've grown up in such a hypocritical society. You know, there was a hint at the beginning of the film that I wish I'd explored more, the title sequence—

Tibbetts: Oh, the commercial.

Weir: Yes, and following the commercial, the central characters are driving through the countryside on their way to Paris. And they pull up in the little town, and there's a couple of soldiers around an army truck. You can see newspaper headlines on the front of the store. And the headlines are all about some sort of economic crisis, here troops are called out and the country is becoming a banana republic. So I'd hoped in that subtle way to convey that this country is in turmoil. But, it wasn't obvious enough.

The Notebook

Tibbetts: While we're looking back, I would like to talk about the notebook you loaned me a few days ago. You copied out in longhand a bunch of quotes from Matisse and Van Gogh.

Weir: I think that was in 1987, after *Mosquito Coast* had flopped. I was thinking at the time, What am I doing; how to go forward? So these painters gave me some directions. I think I just wanted to touch something they touched. That was why I wanted to write out their words by hand, I wanted to feel what it felt like to actually write those words.

Tibbetts: I'm going to read some of them back to you. Let's see. Matisse: "Individuality exists within tradition."
Weir: Remember, I started in Australia in a very organic way, shooting short films in '67. I knew nothing. But in a reasonably short time I was in the Hollywood studio system, shooting with major stars. So I think having one big success with *Witness*, my first film, and then a complete reverse of that with *Mosquito Coast*—well, it stopped me in my tracks. So then I'm thinking, Should I keep in this hit-making system, or should I go work only in Australia?

Tibbetts: And so in your notebook you turned to these fierce individualists, Matisse and Van Gogh. . . . .
Weir: I also wanted Cézanne to join in, but as far as I can see, he only said things like, "humpf" and "Go away!" [laughs]

Tibbetts: Or, "All I want to do is paint the damn mountain!" Here's another related quote from Matisse: "I have accepted influences but I have always known how to dominate them."
Weir: An influence is different from copying. I suppose I was saying, "relax with those influences, don't be so self-conscious." I tried to reassure myself with that quote.

Tibbetts: Matisse says: "Do I believe in god? Yes, when I work."
Weir: It opens up a whole realm, a creative cave, a *keep*, if you will—when you know you're in the deepest part of the creative keep. That's why I say leave politics at the door. I don't read newspapers, I sort of drop out of the world when I'm working on a film.

Tibbetts: And then we have Van Gogh. He says, "Before I close my eyes forever, I shall see the *rayon blanc*." Circles of light? Everywhere you look in your films there are circles of light.
Weir: Oh, really. I must look at them again. [laughs heartily]

Tibbetts: Circles of light are everywhere in *Fearless*. How did you come across the Bosch painting we see Jeff Bridges looking at?

Weir: *The Ascent into the Empyrean.* What a piece of work! I finally saw it, too. I saw it in Venice, in the Palazzo Ducale. It was as big as this wall. I was researching in books for anything with mandala shapes.[4]

Tibbetts: And Jeff is obsessed with those circles.
Weir: Jeff drew a lot of them himself. You know, he is an artist. He drew quite a number. In San Francisco we went into a great cathedral which reproduced the maze in Chartres cathedral outside Paris. You know, it's like another circle, the shape of the interior of the aircraft in that film, a tunnel, as if Jeff's character had been between heaven and hell.

Tibbetts: Seems like there are "musical" circles, too, like those intertwined lines of music by Górecki. When did you decide on that music?
Weir: You mean the Third Symphony [1976].[5] My wife told me she had heard this beautiful piece of music in the store where she had been buying props. She found out what it was and bought it and gave it to me. So I put it into the film. I found out it was inspired by the Holocaust.

"Only Connect—"

Tibbetts: I think of the grandfather in *Witness*, when he says, "What you take into your hands, you take into your heart." It seems that you can't stand it, unless you can literally get your hands on the props and materials related to a film. And I'm thinking now of that moment we see in some of the special features attached to the *Master and Commander* DVD, when you're surrounded by props and models from the film. You touch them, you love them; and you say how important it is to actually touch these things. Is that how you are on a shoot? You have to get out there and connect with everything?
Weir: I think to touch something is to know that it's true. I think the touching is more important with a historical film in some ways than with a contemporary film. But I also collected props for *The Truman Show*, even though it's completely fiction. I found a tin suitcase one day with a plaid pattern in a junk shop in Los Angeles, and I thought, This is Truman's little case. So I bought it and gave it to Props. I told them to give it to Jim for the scene when he thinks he's leaving town. So that's one kind of touching. I've long been fascinated with the fact that you can *think* you know something is true intellectually, but it's a very different thing to be actually on the site, to touch the object, to meet the person. So, in *Gallipoli*, for example, you find yourself at the pyramids. To really go there, to see them and touch them, well, you *know* them now.

Tibbetts: And stage a football match at the base of them! "At play in the fields of the Lord."
Weir: Today, you would shoot that with CGI, isn't that funny? It would just be cheaper.

Tibbetts: Yet, temperamentally, it doesn't seem like you. You would rather get your hands on the situation.
Weir: Well, depending on the circumstance. If it was too costly, I'd say it's not worth it. If you want the Eiffel Tower in the background, you don't need to go to Paris for a one-day shoot. As the years have passed, I have begun to see some of the great things about shooting in the studio. *Master and Commander* was an example. That was essentially shot on a stage, and in a tank, with only a week at sea. We got more work done. We could concentrate on the performance, so it could be about the actors. We could create the mood through artifice. So, I no longer need to go there, as you say, unless it serves the work. . . .

Tibbetts: Certainly there's no artifice about the details, like the attention to getting those ropes properly braided and tarred.
Weir: We had the experts help us with that much detail. Still, there should have been more rigging on the ships, you know, and so on.

Tibbetts: What happened to the ship?
Weir: I think it's in the Naval Ship and Maritime Museum in San Diego. In fact, I just had an e-mail from my sound designer, Richard King, who won the Academy Award for his work on that film. And he told me he's doing a soundscape for the museum installation. It plays when you go on board.

The "New Wave" Generation

Tibbetts: While we're talking about what's old and new, then and now, what about that wonderful generation of your contemporaries coming out of Australia in the late sixties and seventies? Did you all feel part of what we now call a "New Wave"?[6]
Weir: It was a short period, actually, essentially, just a decade and a half. At first, there was really just Sydney and Melbourne, two cities that were like two football teams. The competition between the two didn't always come in a pleasant way.[7] We didn't see much of each other, unless it was at festivals. Particularly Cannes or London was where you would bump into people in those days. Then, all barriers were down. We were like

frontline troops fraternizing after surviving the battle. But back in Australia, there were always people critical of what we were doing, saying we should be doing this or that. For example, there was a big push in the late seventies from critics and academics for us to stop making period films. We should get relevant and deal with contemporary problems like drug addiction. As if filmmaking was supposed to be some sort of social work. We had some young people who went in that direction and their work wasn't really noticed.

Tibbetts: Do we romanticize too much, then, about a real community, an "Australian New Wave"?

Weir: The "wave" is already passed by the time it's being written about! You have to remember, John, there was nothing here. There was no film industry as such.[8] Quality dramas done on television—I'm talking about, the late sixties—were poor and the imports were fantastic. American movies were great at the cinema, European movies were wonderful at the festivals, and so was British BBC and Canadian broadcasting. We didn't do anything of any significance, except the odd thing. So, we were very, very new to it, and everything was a milestone—the first feature film made by an Australian in so many years; the first to go to Cannes; the first to be accepted in competition; the first sale to America; the first good review in a major English newspaper; the first person to work in Hollywood. We were so busy building that we had no time to stand back and have a look at things.

Tibbetts: I'll tell you what, though, in the States we knew little of Australian history; and we looked forward to the release of those films. Who among us knew about Gallipoli and the tragedy that befell Australian and New Zealand troops in 1915?[9]

Weir: Great to know. I think that we—I say we, though I can't speak for everybody—knew that a film had more reach in the pre-Internet days than any other form of communication. People began to know about our country as a result of those films.

Tibbetts: So, to bring it up to the present, then, is there still any kind of continued contact among all of you?

Weir: I think it's gotten less as the years have gone by. I keep in touch somewhat with Bruce Beresford. We exchange e-mails, every now and again. And I see more of Jane Campion. She and I have stayed the most in touch, I think. Fred [Schepisi] is down in Melbourne, and we occasionally chat on the phone, asking about an actor or producer or something. Fred lived for a period in New York, and he may still have an apartment there. Bruce has, I think, got a flat in London. It's a new generation, now. It's an international business, but you're still just as liable to have down time elsewhere as in Australia.

View from the Apocalypse

Tibbetts: Ever since I interviewed you years ago on the release of *Fearless*, I've been struck by the presence in your films of characters that I guess could be called "angels," portending some sort of apocalypse. My god, surely people have talked to you about this before. [See the Tibbetts 1993 interview in this volume.][10]

Weir: You know, there was a period when I was younger where they also said, "You always have 'water' in your films, like *The Last Wave!*" So I made sure that in the next film there were no rain scenes. [laughter]

Tibbetts: Sorry to push it, but I don't necessarily mean this in a religious sense, but mysterious characters that lead us to a revelation of some kind, benign or otherwise—Miranda, Billy Kwan, Allie Fox, Truman—even the character of Elena in *The Way Back*, whose death scene is described by Mr. Smith as "an angel going to heaven, her home."

Weir: Sometimes when we're talking about my films, I feel like the person I'm talking to knows more about them than I do! And that's not just because they've studied them, but simply because I don't quite know what happened. . . . Well, I did think literally of angels when I was shooting the scene in Penn Station in *Witness* when the little boy looked up at the angel sculpture.

Tibbetts: And you dwell on that shot two times.

Weir: It was just what I thought the child would see; but I wasn't using the child as a host for any of my own ideas. So, again I come back to serving the story; what does it need, how to express these ideas. However, it's not that surprising that I will bring my own preoccupations, or even unconscious impulses to a film. But no, I'm not conscious of it. And I don't care to pursue it. You just get into a kind of a trance, I think, when you make a film. Or write a poem. Once I saw a book from Les Murray, the great Australian poet. He says he thinks he gets into a bit of a trance when he writes. And to some degree it's gone the minute you've finished it. And you wonder what happened. It's sort of like getting struck by lightning or something. It doesn't make the film good, necessarily;

the film can fail. But you still have been in this state. You know, I'm not saying that I'm Edgar Cayce. I don't lie on a couch and give instructions to the crew through some sort of trance. An actor once said to me after I had been talking to him, "You're trying to hypnotize me!" We were disagreeing about something, in a minor way, but I realized that I had crossed into some area. Other directors have hinted at it but no one talks about it. Nor is it something everybody shares; but I've seen a reference to it from Eisenstein. Others refer to a hypnotic power that can come to you, like the ability to read minds and influence people. . . .

Tibbetts: These "angel" figures sort of illuminate the stories from within. Okay, so maybe you do this intuitively. But there is something beyond those images.

Weir: Oh, there has to be. I love it, I search for it, I've had some extraordinary moments. Probably the greatest moment was with Jeff Bridges in *Fearless*. He had to do this scene where he ate the strawberry (it sounds so lame to talk about it out of the context of the film). He gets an attack, an allergic reaction. He is close to death. And in a sort of trance he thinks he is back on the aircraft before the crash. So he's lying there on the floor, his wife's trying to revive him. Now we shot that in a day. It was fairly early in the morning, and he had this quality about him . . . something different about him. I mean, there was nothing between him and the lens. There was no artifice. Think of early photographs, before people knew what cameras were, or children, when they didn't know they were looking into a camera. They didn't know what a camera was. They didn't project anything. You saw it in the faces of young people when the Berlin Wall came down in '89. People who had not grown up with Kodak cameras. They had grown up unselfconsciously. And I thought, if ever I do a period film, I'm going to get people from a country like Poland and use them as extras because they've got the "look" of the period *before the camera*. Which is what I did for *Master and Commander*. We had a casting session in Warsaw. Eight hundred people we saw, and we took a dozen to Mexico, where they became the key background. Those faces were faces that had not lived in our century, in our time.

But, back to Jeff. He had this—well, it's nothing like an angelic look or anything—but a look of some utter purity. There was nothing physically or emotionally demanding. What I was photographing was a *soul*. I kept it to myself at the time. Anyway, I had a job to do, and every shot was perfect. Every take was brilliant. We finished the day. So, I went home that night, thinking that was one of the greatest experiences of my life as a filmmaker, to have watched, to take that close-up. So, I went in the next morning, to carry on with our work. And I was told Jeff was ill. What happened? He's developed some kind of influenza, and he's going to be out for a week to ten days. "My god," I said. "I've never heard of anything like this!" So, we worked around him. He later came back and said, "I've never had that in my life; I'm a very healthy person." He said it was like getting shot with a bullet. My own theory was that he'd lowered his immune system during those scenes. *He went to death's door*, in my opinion.

I was then reminded of a conversation I once had with Oliver Sacks. Remember, I had turned down *Awakenings*. I was talking to him about that moment with Jeff, and he told me about working with De Niro on *Awakenings*, about how he would get so close to this sleeping sickness, that he worried about him. He thought De Niro was actually on the edge. We all know that some people will decide to die, and they simply do. It's not just a case of stopping eating but they give up life. I knew this from the aborigine I worked with in *The Last Wave*. The night we shot that scene in *The Last Wave* where Nandjiwarra, the tribal elder, points the bone. He asked for everybody to be cleared from the set in front of that bone. We laughed, but he insisted he didn't want to point it at the actor. So, we had to cut it into two shots. So, if you believe that you will die from the bone, you will die. So I'm trying to get as close to what Jeff got close to that day.

Tibbetts: You seem to really love characters like this. Not just Jeff Bridges in *Fearless*, but even somebody like Allie Fox in *Mosquito Coast* and Mr. Keating in *Dead Poet's Society*. They're so locked in to themselves. And they're not necessarily likeable or benign, either.
Weir: Why would you say that of Keating?

Tibbetts: You and I may lock horns on this one. I mean the moment when Keating has his students tear up their textbooks. I thought, maybe some of those kids might have liked some of that poetry, given a chance. But he's denying them that.
Weir: [after a pause] You know, Andrew Sarris (may he rest in peace), wrote an open letter in the *New York Times* to Robin Williams about that scene.

Tibbetts: To Robin Williams?

Weir: Yeah, he didn't send it to me, but he should have. He was very upset about it. As was Roger Ebert when I talked with him one day.

Tibbetts: What did you say to them?
Weir: Once when I was at the beginning of my second year at Sydney University, I was doing an arts course and went to the poetry lecture. It was on William Blake. I was one of two or three hundred sitting there. We had been asked to look at a poem and talk about it. So I came in just a fraction late, and the lecturer was already writing the poem out on the blackboard. (I can still hear the chalk.) He wrote it all out, dusted his hands, put down the chalk, and began to talk. He took the poem apart in front of us, like a sort of autopsy—called it a "lesser" Blake poem.

Tibbetts: —like Miss McCraw, analyzing the geological structures at Hanging Rock.
Weir: Everyone around me was busily writing. But I got up and left and went to the pub. I had loved that poem! I never went back. I thought, Am I stupid, am I wrong, do I have to learn this? I can't do this! This was a beautiful poem. And this was a wonderful man who had written it. And this cold technician, this mortician, had dismembered this thing of beauty. So I put that into the scene in *Dead Poets*.

Tibbetts: Yes, in my mind Keating is a tyrant, a monster. We've all had teachers like that. They're so inspired, everything ends up being all about themselves.
Weir: John, you felt this scene personally, because you're a teacher! You know, that scene replaced the original idea we had. The original scene was not a Blake poem, but a Victorian sort of sentimental ditty. It was all about the heart and love and tripping flowers and tweeting birds and whatever. And Keating mocked the poem and took it apart on the blackboard. It was quite an amusing scene. But one of my very good men, a set dresser, said to me, "Do you mind if I say something about the script?"; and I said, "No, what is it, John?" And he asked me why Keating criticizes such a lovely poem to the class? He said, "I think it's lovely!" So I went home and ripped the scene out of there. Don't forget that "introduction" to the textbook Keating talks about clearly states that a poem *must be analyzed* in a particular way. If it had been a Soviet or Nazi textbook, and the introduction said that you *must* evaluate it only on racial lines . . . or that the poem is no good because it's *bourgeois, then* you would accept the teacher telling you to rip it out.

Tibbetts: Would you say that is one of the more-talked about scenes in any of your films?

Weir: Not with the public, but I have struck it with teachers and academics. I think teachers have been critical of the film. Some of them have written me, and I've accepted that. I'm sorry Sarris took it so hard, because if he'd really looked at it and thought about it, there are such things as bad books and bad instruction. And these people were being taught each year, this is how you evaluate poetry, with a graph and calculations and so forth. Perhaps it was a bit excessive, with all the "Rip, rip, rip, rip it out—let me hear the sound of ripping. . . ." but it's not a license to then go ripping out all introductions or dismissing old books.

Tibbetts: And what about Truman? He's a messenger of an apocalypse, when his little boat rams into the edge of the cyclorama—

Weir: End of the world!

Tibbetts: Yes! I suppose a scene like that was there from the very beginning? You can almost wrap a whole film around a scene like that.

Weir: Yes. The producer Scott Rudin said it was the reason he bought Andrew Niccol's script. Scott was running the project as the producer for Paramount. Andrew and I had a wonderful collaboration, one of the best I've ever had, I think. He was so relaxed, so open to my changes. When I joined the project, he had done a draft. And I said, "I love this script, what's the background?" I found Andrew was from New Zealand. The script had been shown around, and a lot of people were interested. Spielberg nearly bought it; and Brian De Palma was very interested in it. But Andrew had a condition in the contract that he wanted to direct it. Scott would only agree if Andrew did a test scene first. He shot a test scene, but Scott did not like it, and exorcized that clause. So, I met with Andrew in L.A. and I asked him if he would go with me, even if I made changes. And I warned him as I would with any writer that I'm working with, that this could be a painful process for him; and I said what I've always said—"I prefer to work with dead writers!" But if they happen to be alive, and can accept the changes I make, we can become a team. In fact I changed the whole feel of the story, beginning with changing the New York setting to a tropical paradise. Jim [Carrey] was not available for a year, which was a big disappointment. But I couldn't see anybody else doing it, so I waited for him. So, Andrew and I shuttled the script backwards and forwards via fax. And did nine drafts on it, until it became the film that you see. But it's, it was, you know, if you look at an earlier version of it, it's really quite different.

Tibbetts: Now, do you sometimes enjoy destroying the world in scenes like this? I'm not being entirely facetious. I've talked to many science fiction writers, like Greg Bear and Gregory Benford, who have written novels where people leave the world as it's blowing itself up. And he told me he actually enjoys that, to imagine that, to see what it would be like. It's not a destructive impulse, it's creative, in a way.¹¹ Now, you don't literally destroy the world, unless it's in *The Last Wave*—
Weir: That would have been a tsunami!

Tibbetts: But is there something in you . . . ? Like an apocalypse would usually signal some kind of a cyclical rebirth, or transformation?
Weir: Death is the apocalypse. I think apocalypses are an easy way to end a film.

Tibbetts: Or forgetting who you are. That's a kind of death, isn't it? There's always somebody forgetting their name in your films.
Weir: Is that right? Don't look too closely!

Tibbetts: As you go from film to film, is each film kind of an apocalyptic experience that leads to a "rebirth" to the next one?
Weir: In the sense that I always hope not to die before I finished it! Because you're creating a little world and I'm trying to get all of the logic right in that little world, at every level, emotional, intellectual. In a way it *is* over when the world has been built. It's been like a life. Like a life to you. It used to take me a couple of weeks to get back to civilian life afterward. Now, I don't really want to cheapen this, but I think probably the closest thing it would be to somebody who had been in combat, where life and death were bound together. You come back to the world of the supermarket and the bus, of chatting to neighbors. They'll say to me, "How was the shoot?" "Oh, it went well." "Um, when will the film be out?" Sometimes I'll take, as I did after *The Way Back*, a week off on the way home, in a hotel room, in the tropics, as in Bali, to simply get rid of the dreams. You know, those dreams?—the ones that haunt you, wake you up, of scenes you missed, scenes you hadn't shot. So that period passes and you can be "normal" again.

Music

Tibbetts: Let's talk about music. There's that lovely, lovely sequence in *Gallipoli* with the music from a Bizet opera. What possessed you on the eve of the fatal charge to have the officer listening to the aria from *The Pearl Fishers*? It's so unexpected, yet so haunting, so right.

Weir: I heard the opera for the first time in Melbourne, before the shoot, just by chance. It's rarely staged. That duet came on. I was so alive to anything that might be useful in my film, anything could be relevant; and I heard these two male voices entwined. And I thought, This is Frank and Archy! And wondered if I could put it in the soundtrack. What if the officer had a wind-up record player? Soldiers took all kinds of stuff with them. So I put it into the story, and it had all sorts of resonance.

Tibbetts: And tells us a lot about the officer, too.
Weir: The music was something of such beauty in amongst the loss of these young lives. It was irresistible and painful. Here was a case where I could say a lot about destruction and death through that man listening to that music, with the distant thump of shells and the knowledge in the morning they would have to go over the top.

Tibbetts: And another example, the way you use the music of Boccherini at the very end of *Master and Commander*. It was like Captain Aubrey says to Maturin, "Oh, yes, the enemy is getting away . . . but let's play some Boccherini first!"
Weir: [laughs] You know, in Keith Richards's recently published biography, he says that he and Mick Jagger are like Aubrey and Maturin—playing different music together, of course! That would be interesting casting. [laughs]

Tibbetts: Somebody must have raised their eyebrows and said, "You're going to end the movie like that?"
Weir: Yes, another studio hierarchy might have said, "You've got to go on to the Battle of Trafalgar!" or something. "You cannot simply build up all of this emotion, get to know these guys, without having them at least trying to save England!" But, remarkably, it was approved. It's because of Tom Rothman, the co-chairman of the studio. That's because Tom loved those books. We're talking about making one of those books, or an amalgam of those books, into a major feature film with a great whopping budget. It was a risk, a real risk. When you started the question, I thought you were going to refer to a scene with Linda Hunt in *The Year of Living Dangerously*—

Tibbetts: You mean, musically speaking?
Weir: Yes. She had told me she would take on a man's part if I would never lose faith in her. So, I was looking for anything to help her. I'd been playing this very powerful piece from Richard Strauss' *Four Last Songs*.[12]

It had been inspiring. There was something in Kiri Te Kanawa's voice that was transcendent. I felt it had something to do with this film, but I didn't know what it was. I gave her a copy and I forgot about it. I don't use music to brainwash actors. Musical taste is very personal. She came back to me and said, "I'm playing it and it's helping me; it's getting me through this." So we put it into the movie.

Tibbetts: But then, these are classical examples. You certainly feel free to use jazz, pop, and tribal rhythms and things like that, too.
Weir: There's all of that in *The Plumber*. The character of Max really was a tribal man, yet he played, or composed, a kind of Dylanesque music challenging modern arrogance.[13] And she, who was very educated, would play her recordings of Burundi tribesmen thumping their drums. It was an interesting switch, in a way, each was playing the other's music. A telling contrast.

Tibbetts: A kind of tribal drumming is all through *Green Card*. When Andie MacDowell responds to the drumming in the streets, right away we know what will happen with her and Depardieu. When he sits down at the keyboard, in that highfalutin society party, he just bangs away! It's the musical equivalent to Walt Whitman's "barbaric yawp" in *Dead Poets*, I guess.
Weir: [laughs] We had that piano scene put in, because in the script he was named "Fauré," like the French composer. So, I then listened to some music by the real Fauré and I realized that Depardieu's character might not really be a composer; or maybe we just don't know. If he's asked to play, what would he do? So we had a piano put in Gerard's hotel room and I asked him to practice something. Well, he couldn't play, so he just went into the scene just like that—

Tibbetts: How many takes? Does he just bash away?
Weir: It's different each take. [laughs] It didn't matter what; it worked.

Tibbetts: It's the "Depardieu Songbook!"
Weir: He has this great line in the letter he writes to Andi: "The elephants are restless tonight!"

Tibbetts: That could almost be an epigraph to all of your films. "The elephants are restless tonight!"
Weir: I thought *Green Card* was a film that should be seen at five o'clock

in the afternoon. It was just a perfect sort of late matinee. I never thought it was a "night-out" kind of film. Depardieu and I had a great collaboration. He came here and stayed while I was working on the script. Because I wanted each scene to be hand-crafted. My French was better than his English at first; then it ended up well the other way. But at that stage, we mostly talked in the present tense in an abbreviated vocabulary: "I go, you stay. You come, me go?" So we were very much like children. You couldn't express any complicated thoughts. You could only be expressive through mime or movement. So no complications came into the friendship, there were no disagreements about anything, because we couldn't get into those conversations. A lot of the humor, a lot of the feeling in that film—the majority of it I think—came from that period of weeks we spent together. And in New York, we would do things like going down to city hall to watch some weddings. Gérard ended up giving a bride away! And we went to the café across the road, and we realized, this could be his "Africa" café! It was a film that was lived in, in a very real sense. It was a wonderful experience.

Tibbetts: What about that ending: They're in love now, but they're going to have to be separated.
Weir: The last time I had this conversation was with Jeff Katzenberg on the pavement at Sherman Oaks, outside the preview theatre. He said, "Peter, how much money would you like to make with this film?" He said, "Let me put it another way; how big do you want it to be? It could be much bigger." I asked him what he was talking about. And he said, "Reshoot the ending! If they don't separate, and if they somehow humiliate that wretched immigration officer, you will have a very big result." And I went away to think about it. It *is* an entertainment piece. But I somehow just couldn't think to end it that way.

Tibbetts: Thank you! There is a place in Paradise reserved for you! 'Cause that's the only way it could be.
Weir: I think so. And when you think it through, she would eventually follow him to Paris.

Tibbetts: We can't end this musical discussion without the music of Zamfir's pan-pipes in *Picnic at Hanging Rock*. Of course, Pan and his pipes are part of pre-Christian myth, a seductive lure to some sort of pagan wild. Is that the sound you were after?
Weir: It happened by a sort of accident. If I had thought of it myself,

I probably would have done it; I probably would have. But while I was looking for the right "sound" of the film, I told my composer, Bruce Smeaton, that I just didn't think we had found it yet. He said, "Give me another go; I'll come up with something else." Then the co-producer, Jim McElroy, told me there had been a program on the suffering in Biafra the night before; and that they had played this haunting music on some sort of flute. He offered to ring the producer and get it. I played it and realized he had found the perfect "sound."

Tibbetts: The fact that it's a pan-pipe is just a happy accident?
Weir: Yes and no. We had been listening to all kinds of things, and that pre-Christian quality seemed to me just right.

Tibbetts: So was there ever a recording session with Zamfir playing the pan-pipes?
Weir: He turned out to be a man with an enormous ego, and when I spoke to him in Paris, he said, "I recorded that some years ago. No, you don't want that. What you want is my new stuff!" He sent some things to me, and it was not what we wanted at all. And then we began to talk to him about rerecording what we had originally heard. He got nervous about it. The signals were clear: just walk away. Just buy it, which is what we did. It's just came right off the vinyl. It was so successful that he did a tour!

Tibbetts: There's also a piano concerto that you quote, not just in *Picnic* but in *Fearless*. A favorite of yours?
Weir: The Beethoven "Emperor" Concerto was one of the first classical pieces I'd heard. I always use the Wilhelm Kempff version. That playing, it's like breathing, when I hear it. And so when I've been in a tight corner sometimes, you know, like a soldier with only emergency rations, I reach for my Wilhelm Kempff and put it on. As kids we were in our early teens and starting to listen to rock and roll, and my mother felt we should also have some classical music in our lives.

Tibbetts: Of course, although I'm disappointed that you haven't used any Schumann yet.
Weir: [laughs] Well, you're going to get me into Schumann.

Tibbetts: So we're going to have to work on that!

Adaptations and Screenplays

Tibbetts: When we started our conversations you mentioned a book by Jean-Claude Carrière, *The Secret Language of Film* [1995]. He worked on scripts with Pierre Etaix, didn't he?
Weir: Yes. And the great Jacques Tati, at least as an assistant.

Tibbetts: Oh my, I'm not worthy.
Weir: Tati's comedy was incredibly exciting for me as a young man. *Hulot's Holiday* and *Mon Oncle*. You know, he was a big influence on me and on my interest in performing. My mother would get me to tell stories, at the drop of a hat. I had a knack for it as a young boy. I could come home and there'd be an incident on the tram, on the trolley or on the bus, some minor incident, you know; maybe a lady's shopping bag burst and fruit and vegetables were rolling around the bottom of the bus. But I would take something like that and go home, and my mother would have a cup of tea for me and say, "Anything happen?" And I'd start talking about the lady and the bag of oranges. "Really?" she'd say. "And *then* what happened?" So I would put a kind of twist on things, maybe about a boy who trod on a tomato and how angry the lady was, because she was very poor. That sort of thing. The problem was, that a day or two later if my aunt dropped in, my mother would say, "Peter, Pete, come and tell Aunty about the bus and the bag of vegetables!" And I'd think, Oh my, god, I'd forgotten what I'd said. She'd tell everybody to sit down; and then I'd have to crank it out, get myself back into the spirit of the thing.

Tibbetts: Some kids have to play the piano for the relatives.
Weir: Did you do that? [laughs]

Tibbetts: And they never listened! I'd be so mad. I'd have to play, and then I discovered in the next room everybody was laughing and talking about something else.
Weir: And then you'd hear a "Very nice, dear!" from the other room.

Tibbetts: But how wonderful of your mother to say, "And then what happened?!"
Weir: She didn't know she was training me for my profession! At the time, all I was thinking about was just getting down that hill and into the park and muck around.

Tibbetts: About Carrière's book—I looked it over and you could have written it yourself!

Weir: If I had met Carrière, I feel I would have had a rapport with him. It's also crossed my mind that I'd love to work with him.

Tibbetts: I was struck by Carrière's comment that a proper screenplay ultimately vanishes. What did he mean by that?

Weir: He says that literally, doesn't he? How confident of him to say that. It shows real confidence that comes from great talent. He knows what he does. That's why he doesn't need to bang the writer's drum, as a lesser talent would. . . .

Tibbetts: I mean, is there a "Hanging Rock" out there for screenplays? Where they vanish and undergo a metamorphosis, melt into another form?

Weir: Isn't that interesting! Like a mold which you pour for the shooting. And then the mold is broken off. And you have the facsimile. Why do you think so many young writers want to direct? They say it's because their work's interfered with, otherwise. But I think it's because for some writers it's too painful to watch your script disappear. But that's the point. It's the art. Carrière says, "Screenplays are always the *dream* of a film." Isn't that wonderful? When I sit down sometimes to work, and I'm a bit stuck on a script—and I'm working on one, right now—I'll think of a great cutting room. I'm in a cutting room, sitting at this desk. And in that cutting room, hanging in the trim bins or stored in the data and memory of the computer, are any scenes you want. You want President Kennedy to appear in the film, to walk in the door, ah, as a young man? Okay, you can do that. Anything you want. Just put it down on the paper. And it gives me a wonderful freedom, that I can reawaken the dead or bring people to life who didn't exist—anything can serve the story. It's a very liberating mental exercise.

Tibbetts: But are you overwhelmed by the endless options you have?

Weir: No, no. It frees me. It frees me up. Carrière talks about his writing rituals with Luis Buñuel. They'd go out to the country for a few weeks; work in the morning, take a bit of the afternoon off. Next morning, they'd have to recount any dreams they'd had. Then they'd meet in the bar before dinner for a couple of drinks and tell stories—make them up or draw them from life. . . . These were *exercises*. Exercising the storytelling muscles. The more you do it, the better you get at it. I don't want to make too much of it, but here in the 1960s, when I was lucky enough to be around and doing short films, we were really starting at the beginning, almost like those people in the silent film days. Like those early filmmakers, we had no one's feet to sit at.

Tibbetts: How did you guys regard movies made in Australia in the late sixties and early seventies by "outsiders," like Fred Zinnemann's *The Sundowners* and Nicholas Roeg's *Walkabout*.
Weir: It was like a shout saying, "Come on, you could do this, too!" I loved Roeg's picture. Others loved Ted Kotcheff's adaptation of Kenneth Cook's novel, *Wake in Fright*, which is from around the same time. But there were no Australian filmmakers to go to. Yes, there was Ken G. Hall, but he was a more commercial director and not interested in the poetry or the artistic side of things.[13] He was a television executive then; but no one else. So you had to really kind of invent the wheel. You see all the foreign films at the festivals and the new American pictures. But nothing was really stirring until the early seventies. Our actors weren't used to saying lines, our writers hadn't written anything for the screen. Directors hadn't done anything, either. Documentary was the quick way into the business, but really not interesting. Not anybody could make a fiction film with screen actors.

Tibbetts: So, there was a kind of innocent vision coming to bear upon this new experience with film? Do you sometimes wish that you could return to that kind of innocence?
Weir: No I don't. It's not my way of thinking, to look back, to wonder if I had this or if I didn't have that. I'm happy with what I see before me and not look back.

Tibbetts: Somewhere, you talked about adapting a book by turning it upside down and letting the words fall out.
Weir: I mean, the first thing you lose is the prose. If you're dealing with a classic, the work of a giant—I'm thinking of Baz Luhrmann taking on Scott Fitzgerald's *The Great Gatsby*—you have to lose those chiseled, diamond-like sentences. Well, shake up the book, and they all fall out! What you're left with is the plot.

Tibbetts: But that's a gutsy thing to do, instead of kneeling before the altar of the book.
Weir: I do understand that old saying, that it's easier to make a good

film of a bad book, than the other way around. That's because you don't expect anything from the bad book, so you're not inhibited. Maybe you only like the title or one of the characters. But with a book you love, the danger is you're too much in love with it. You have to understand what it was that initially drew you to it. It's as if there's a shadowy image in you that matches something in the book. But it's rare to be able to put it in words. In fact, it's unsayable. You may not even know what it is until you've done the film! It's always the most awkward question I get in press interviews afterward: "Why did I pick the book; what made me choose it, etc.?" And the right answer is, "I don't know!" But that just comes across like you're trying to be difficult. It's like why you feel love for somebody. Well, I don't know what that is, but it just happens. The danger in trying to answer questions like that is that you can find yourself in a room full of mirrors, just reflecting yourself. You have to be tough. And I have these images, I kick the book in the backside. I mean, when no one's looking, I give it a kick, like that. And that's one of the things I'll do to disrespect the book. Another thing I'll do is turn my back on it and go in another direction and just write something to do with the story that's not in the book to see if the book comes and taps me on the shoulder. I'll ignore it, I'll try to ignore it, try to dislike it, anything to get myself free of its tyranny so the film can breathe. It might as well be making music from a book. It's that different to make a bunch of images and sounds that correspond to something you read.

Tibbetts: You describe the book as if it's a living presence you have to contend with.
Weir: That's true. With all the books I've worked from, I've had great respect for the writers, and met many of them. But when I've met them, I tell them: "This is difficult for me and will be difficult for you. You probably won't like the film, unless it's a big hit, or your friends like it; and you may come to terms with it."

Conclusion

Tibbetts: Now, let's place this in time. It's been almost two weeks ago since you told me about your new screenplay. Now, in these two weeks have you thought more about it, and have you been putting more words to paper?
Weir: At that point, I was a month away from delivery of this fifth draft, after six months work, enough time to live with it and rewrite it.

Tibbetts: Is anyone else working with you on it?

Weir: No. Although I love co-writing. It's lonely on your own, it's tough. But some scripts require that privacy while I search out the reason I chose it. It's been a comfortable daily routine the past few weeks, altering sentences here, shifting things slightly around. But I had a shape and I was happy with it. But then, two or three days ago, I had a completely new idea. And that idea is now causing me to have to work very hard and fast. It's changing things structurally.

Tibbetts: It doesn't let you get complacent, does it?

Weir: No. I've gone back into major surgery. I think of myself as a surgeon, you know, where this patient was in recovery, and now I'm saying, "We're going to go back in, because we've made a mistake. We've got to open it up again!"

Tibbetts: Now, I've talked to a number of people, the wonderful playwright August Wilson and the novelist Peter Straub, for example. They cannot write unless they're in a hotel lobby, or a café, where there's people milling back and forth, all those myriads of stories floating around.

Weir: Interesting. Yes, it's what's good for them. You know, I don't think it matters, people have all kinds of different routines, I'm sure, but I think mostly, it would be a solitary occupation, in a kind of room somewhere. There's just no way that you can organize the muse. No way. The point Carrière's making is that the actual physical writing of the thing is the lesser side of it. It's the thinking and the *not* thinking, as a Buddhist would say. Not thinking. That's when things happen. Probably the more important point of a writing time is what you do in between writing. Is it physical? Is having a few drinks a way of getting the cattle prod working, getting you available for the muse, for the lightning bolt, the flash, the light bulb? That's what you're hunting for. Or leaving yourself open so the muse comes to you. Music will do it for me. Music can jam the radar, as I call it. I play it, during a film, very much in the evening, after a day's work. And you've got the day, tomorrow to think about. You know, I'll usually have a couple of glasses of wine, very much part of the process. I'll put something on, and it does jam the radar, it stops conscious thought and allows the unconscious free play. Because you can't think while you're listening to music. Music strikes a very strong chord with you. You have to *listen*, and then, somewhere within that, I'll have a pen and paper there. A telegram will come through the brain.

Tibbetts: Now, as we begin to wind down, I'm going to quote back to you a cartoon that you mentioned while we were driving around Sydney last week. There's a woman standing before a movie theater marquee—
Weir: Yes, she looks a bit dragged down, a bit beyond middle age, holding a shopping bag. She's got her money in her hand, and she's saying to the clerk in the box office: "But will it give me back my sense of wonder?"

Tibbetts: Why did that stick with you?
Weir: Because most films won't do that! [both laugh] That sense of wonder she's talking about is the child in her, maybe her first experience of wonder in the cinema. Many people never get past it; they love only the films of their childhood. How many adults have you met, of a certain age, who get a smile on their face at the mention of *Indiana Jones*? I didn't, because I didn't see it as a kid (although I certainly appreciate the film!). Sometimes those people's taste remain infantilized. They can really only go to films that are part of their childhood. But, you know, a sense of wonder is not something exclusively in the province of the child. It's just very hard to re-awaken it for adults. They've seen all kinds of films and images. And in a way they're going to have to cut through all of that knowledge and prejudice in order to reawaken that feeling again. And when they do, they are very grateful because it's pretty rare in adult life to be touched that way by a film.

Tibbetts: Is there a better testament to any artist, in this case a filmmaker, than to achieve that?
Weir: Absolutely. But you mostly fail; or you only achieve it for a small number of viewers. It's a deep thrill when, after time has passed, somebody says, "Oh, you made that?" Especially someone who's not a film buff. "You made that? You directed that? I saw that!" And then they'll tell you the details of virtually everything, what they were wearing, the evening, what it was in their life, and what they felt coming out. That's a wonderful tribute, and that keeps you going.

Tibbetts: And so, when the time comes, as it must to all of us—sounds like Charles Foster Kane— [laughs]
Weir: —To say farewell?

Tibbetts: —to say, as you wrote at the death of Count Vlm—
Weir: Ha! "Well fallen!"

Tibbetts: Did you write your own epitaph?

Weir: I see what you mean. But don't forget the word "fall" is a very potent word in Australia. Because it's generally used in reference to the war dead.

Tibbetts: Oh.

Weir: Those who fell in battle. It's almost a Victorian usage of the word, a way of avoiding nasty works like "killed" or "blown up"; so they "fell." We honor the fallen, that they fell in defense of our values and way of life. So we'll hear the word, once a year around Anzac Day, the memorial of the Gallipoli landing. [See the Appendix, Weir's 2001 Anzac Lecture.]

Tibbetts: Well, maybe you'll forgive me if I change "well fallen" to "well done!"

[Both laugh]

Weir: That I love! Don't write my epitaph just yet.

Notes

1. Longtime associate of Peter Weir and a popular Australian television performer, Grahame Bond received the Member of the Order of Australia in the most recent (June 2012) Queen's Birthday honors.

2. Keith Gow (1921–1987) made eighteen films at Film Australia (formerly the Commonwealth Film Unit) as senior cameraman, director and producer. He co-wrote *The Cars That Ate Paris* (1974) with Peter Weir and Piers Davies.

3. It has been argued that Weir's emphasis upon the self-effacement of individual intention in favor of the absolute selflessness of the Japanese potter, Shiga, is misplaced. "What is interesting about Weir's adoption of this attitude, however," writes Gary Hentzi, "is his belief that it can be transferred intact into the realm of mass culture, even though it is essentially a pre-individualistic philosophy which assumes a social world organized around the institutions of the village or tribe" (10). See Hentzi, "Peter Weir and the Cinema of New Age Humanism," *Film Quarterly* 44, no. 2 (Winter 1990–91), 2–12.

4. *Ascent into the Empyrean* is one of four vertically elongated panels that are part of an altarpiece by Hieronymus Bosch (the central panel is lost). It depicts six souls, accompanied by an angel, flying toward the heavenly light. The altarpiece is generally known as *The Blessed and the Damned*. It dates from approximately 1520. "When the altarpiece was opened, the panel showing the tunnel of light would be to the far left. It expresses the metaphor of a unification with God: "The sun will draw us with blinded eyes into its light where we will be united with God" (304). See Roger H. Marijnissen, *Hieronymus Bosch: The Complete Works* (Antwerp: Mercatorfonds, 1987).

5. Henryk Górecki (1933–2010) was the third member of Poland's impressive avant-

garde *troika* with Penderecki and Lutoslawski. His Third Symphony of 1976 was scored for solo soprano and strings, woodwinds, horns, harp, and piano. The work consists of three movements, each a lament or "sorrowful song" to Polish texts with deep spiritual or humane connotations. See Wilfrid Mellers, "Round and about Górecki's Symphony No. 3," *Tempo*, no. 168 (March 1988), 22–24. For Górecki's own account of the work, see the account of Tony Palmer's documentary film, *Górecki: The Symphony of Sorrowful* Songs (1993), in John C. Tibbetts, *All My Loving: The Films of Tony Palmer* (London: Chrome Dreams/Voiceprint, 2009), 146–50.

6. By the 1980s a new generation of Australian filmmakers began to mount a counter-reaction to the seventies' "New Wave." Most of the original sevenites bunch had moved on to Hollywood, where they either flourished (Weir, Schepisi, George Miller) or struggled to survive (Gillian Armstrong, Bruce Beresford). Jane Campion, John Hillcoat, Ann Turner emerged to deploy a new Australian modernism with more dissident themes and experimental styles. See especially *Don't Shoot Darling*, by Annette Bionski (1988) for an examination of the role women played in this new phase of Australian cinema. See also, David Stratton, *The Last New Wave: The Australian Film Revival* (Sydney: Angus & Robertson, 1980). For an especially thoughtful and probing examination of Australian culture's ongoing engagement with "Americanism," see Philip Bell and Roger Bell, "'Americanization': Political and Cultural Examples from the Perspective of 'Americanized' Australia," *American Studies* 37, no. 1 (Spring 1996), 5–21.

7. Sydney and Melbourne were indeed rival cities. Sydney was seen as the center of film production in the country, the home of the Commonwealth Film Unit, Cinesound, and the Australian Broadcast Commission. Melbourne, on the other hand, was regarded as oriented more toward a "serious" cinema, with its Melbourne Film Society. "Tensions have always been very real between the cities," reports David Stratton in *The Last New Wave*, "and in the late sixties, when the time came to lobby for government support for a film industry. . . ." (10).

8. Once boasting a thriving national film industry at the turn of century, Australian cinema was indeed at a low ebb by the 1960s. This can be attributed mostly to years of government indifference, a diaspora of Australian filmmakers overseas, and the predominance of American and British film and television on local screens and channels.

9. The Gallipoli campaign has played a vital part in the formation of an Australian self-image, particularly in affirming the concept of "mateship" (comradeship among males). Australian and New Zealand troops, the "Anzacs," landed on the Aegean side of the Gallipoli peninsula in April 1915 and fought through December of that year. The climax of Weir's film dramatizes the suicidal, senseless attack on Turkish trenches by the Eighth and Tenth Light Horse Regiments of Anzacs. See Bill Gammage, *The Broken Years: Australian Soldiers in the Great War* (Penguin Australia, 1974), which was a major resource for Weir's film.

10. A thorough study has yet to be written about Weir's use of "angel" and "apocalyptic" iconography and thematic material in his films, from the figures of Miranda in *Picnic* to Elena

in *The Way Back*. Haunting these films is a sense of the impermanence of the world and the imperfections of man. A final destruction of the cosmos necessarily leads to a re-creation/rebirth. How such topics have informed art and culture is examined in Francis Haskell, "Art & Apocalypse," *New York Review*, July 15, 1993, 25–29. An overview of the presence of angels in western culture, from the Bible to Milton's *Paradise Lost* to New Age culture is in Nancy Gibbs, "Angels Among Us," *Time*, December 27, 1993, 56–65.

11. Science fiction writer Greg Bear destroys the Earth in *The Forge of God*. "Writers are bloody-minded individuals," he says in an interview, "and we have the most fun doing the most horrible things. . . . So, as a hard science fiction writer I say, 'What's it *like*?'" See his interview in the chapter, "The Heresy of Humanism," in John C. Tibbetts, ed., *The Gothic Imagination* (New York: Palgrave Macmillan, 2011), 359–381.

12. The music is "September," from the *Four Last Songs* of Richard Strauss. One of the eighty-four-year old composer's last works, it is his farewell to art and to life. The text is by Hermann Hesse:

> Golden leaf after leaf
> Falls from the tall acacia.
> Summer smiles, astonished, feeble,
> In this dying dream of a garden.

13. Crouching in the doorway of the demolished bathroom, he declaims:

> Why don't you look in the mirror
> And tell me what you see;
> You be standin' in my shoes.
> 'Cause I'm me, babe. Etc.

14. Ken G. Hall (1901–1994) was an important Australian filmmaker who began making fiction and actuality films in 1928. On January 1, 1972, Hall was awarded the Order of the British Empire for his services to the Australian motion picture industry.

Peter Weir: Early Days

Sue Mathews / 1985

Excerpted from *35mm Dreams* (Australia: Penguin Books, 1985). Reprinted by permission of the author.

[Editor's note: In this first of two excerpts from the interview by Sue Mathews, Peter Weir speaks of his early days growing up in Sydney, Australia.]

In conversation Peter Weir has a youthful intensity, choosing allusive, literary phrases to capture nuances of feeling as he recalls the past. He is more comfortable talking publicly about events and stages in his life than in reflecting on more general issues and approaches, either to his own work or to the Australian cinema in general. This interview reflects that: in checking the transcript Weir excised many of the analytical and interpretive comments. His lucid, evocative grasp of language makes him "excellent copy," but Weir clearly finds public discussion of his work an ordeal. Though relaxed, direct, and professional in the recording of this interview, agreement on the final transcript was difficult to reach and the published version is the last of several proposed revisions.

Weir lives just north of Sydney in an old house overlooking a remarkable tree-framed view of sand and water. "I don't really feel as if we own this," he says, and you know what he means: it is a view almost too beautiful to be private property. The house has a comfortable yet slightly exotic air. Furnished with timber, bamboo, and Asian fabrics, its large windows make the interior seem continuous with the surrounding garden. Weir's study, apart from the house and past a small rock garden and waterfall he built himself, has a similar atmosphere. Volumes of war history and a collection of World War I helmets and weaponry are ranged a little incongruously alongside the novels on which his films have been based, and diverse works of fact, place, and theory from Montezuma to the Australian Stony Desert.

Weir is one of the most successful of Australia's directors, both at home and overseas. He is polite and quietly spoken with a boyish look. A man of strong attractions and dislikes, he vehemently defends his films against criticism from those writers he labels "academic" who expect a different sort of clarity from him, demanding that conclusions be drawn and answers be given. Such critics have, he says, a view of art and life so remote from his own that he doubts he will ever satisfy them: "I can only wave across a distance," he says, "as the person heads in another direction."

Sue Mathews: Where did you grow up?

Peter Weir: Sydney. We moved quite a bit until I was about twelve; my father was a real-estate agent and he would buy a house and move us into it for three or four years and then move us to another one. At one time we settled in Watson's Bay which was the beginning of a wonderful period. The settings are very exotic around there and I was fortunate enough to be brought up in the pre-television generation, so after school I'd be out in the streets. They'd be full of kids right through to dark; there would be balls bouncing and bits of things rolling down the street and neighbors chatting to each other and sitting outside; it was almost a village feeling. There was always a gang of kids: we would go over to the Glen and jump on trams as they went through, or explore caves that were supposedly Aboriginal or go to the Gap which was nearby. There seemed to be a lot of danger, which I think adds so much to a child's life, the forbidden things that one shouldn't do or go near. When I was twelve we moved to Vaucluse. We were at the top of a little hill that led down to the park at Parsley Bay where there is a big suspension bridge. I was never out of the water, snorkling or spear fishing. Those years were linked with the water and the sea. I used to watch the ships going out, those huge liners going to Europe and from as early as I can remember I used to think that I'd like to be on one.

Mathews: This was before television was introduced in Australia—did you have much contact with other areas of popular culture?

Weir: Comics! They were a big part of a kid's life; I used to collect them, swap them, sell them. I liked the Phantom and Scrooge McDuck—I always preferred him to Donald Duck—especially the ones that were about adventures in South America and Lost Cities. Then there were the pictures, the Saturday afternoon flicks. My father used to take me to the Wintergarden in Rose Bay. I loved Westerns, and the serials . . . it's interesting to see Spielberg and Lucas reproduce those for other generations.

Mathews: Did your parents mind you collecting comics—did they feel you should be interested in other sorts of pursuits?

Weir: No, not really. From my earliest years I played very elaborate games. They took various forms, though they were generally war games, beginning with lead soldiers. There were very strict rules: if you got shot you really had to lie down, and you couldn't go "pow," you had to make it sound like a gun. When I was twelve or thirteen, my parents became very concerned about these games, and had a talk with me, more or less saying that these sorts of games have gone on too long. I remember that conversation at the breakfast table really having some impact on me, and I moved onto other things after that.

Mathews: Do you think that constructing those games was a precursor to an interest in making films?

Weir: Well, I think there is certainly a link between games and creativity. For example, many Japanese are very concerned because their children don't play anymore, it's all scholastic achievement from a very early age. My problem at school, however, was the study side. Actually I don't think I ever stopped playing games. In my teen years they took on a certain bizarre aspect. I would go to parties disguised as various characters—a visiting American student, a trainee priest, or a German merchant seaman. I very carefully rehearsed the friends who collaborated in these elaborate jokes. Most of them worked far too well and caused all sorts of problems, but they certainly livened things up.

Mathews: Did you read novels?

Weir: I don't remember much reading. My father was a good storyteller, so when I was a young child, rather than reading a book before bed, my father would tell me stories. He had one enormously successful serial which ran for about two years. It was called *Black Bart Lamey's Treasure*, an exotic tale of the South Seas in the pirate days. I did read adventure stories—the *Famous Five*, *Biggles*, things that were popular in those times. Then when I hit secondary school, books were introduced as part of the examination process. I was one of those students who reacted extremely badly to that and saw reading books as a chore. It took me many years after I dropped out of university to get back to reading novels, and I've only just begun to get back to Shakespeare. Poetry I still can't touch.

Mathews: *Biggles* and the *Famous Five* are English books—did you have a sense of England as home or where we really belonged?

Weir: Not really. I do remember an intense period of interest in who we were and getting out the family Bible and looking at some old photos. I was astonished that our family hadn't kept any records of where we had come from and who we were on either side of the family. I've asked other Australians what records they have, and have found the same story. A most extraordinary experiment in immigration: Anglo-Saxon people who left the past behind, left their myths behind and began again. It's helped me to understand why many of our films have been period films, and why Australian audiences have been so drawn to them—because of this need for myth.

Mathews: How long ago did your family come to Australia?

Weir: I'm fourth generation—my great-grandfather and mother on both sides were immigrants from England, Ireland, and Scotland. I think it's the Celt side that has come out most strongly.

Mathews: Were you aware of things from America and things from England as two separate sets of influences on Australia?

Weir: I was less aware of the English than of the Americans. In the fifties American culture had a kind of exotic quality about it. I remember once a friend of the family bringing us back long strips of chewing gum before we had that shape here. After 1956 I'd see odd American television programs and I was fascinated with those.

Mathews: Were you aware of a tradition of Australian filmmaking?

Weir: Not really. I saw *Bush Christmas* and liked it, and I certainly loved Charles Chauvel's *Jedda*, seeing it as a kid.[1] I can still recall the powerful highly colored images from that film, but it was like looking at a film from another culture. Everyone knew of the actor Chips Rafferty. He *was* the industry in a way. A sort of one-man band.

Mathews: What about Australian literature?

Weir: I had very little interest in our literature and history—I always felt that the grand events and the great adventures lay outside this country. The image of that ship sailing out summed it up: the world lay elsewhere.

Mathews: You've described your experience of literature at school as a fairly unhappy one—what was school like overall?

Weir: Well, the word "unhappy" is something I've come to apply since. I was happy enough—but it was after school that things really began. I remember running down the hill, ripping my tie off and jumping on a tram and getting down to "real life." I went to a private school where the emphasis was on sport and academic achievement and I was not particularly good at either. I failed the Leaving Certificate and went to Vaucluse High where the atmosphere was very different. We had a history teacher called Bill Kneene who in the first class asked us to come up with our own ideas about the causes of the First World War. I recall that day very clearly: he was asking us to do our own research, telling us it mightn't be all known! History came alive for me that day. Of course, we didn't find any illuminating facts, but from then on that year just took off and I passed and went on to Sydney University.

Mathews: It sounds like that was a more or less automatic transition?
Weir: It was what I wanted to do. I'd built up a picture of what university was going to be like. It was really a picture that might have been true in about the fifteenth century, you know, "the student life," where we would all be singing and arguing into the night. But the first lecture I remember was on the novel *Portrait of the Artist as a Young Man*. I looked around and I couldn't believe it—there were 599 other people in this vast lecture theatre and an ant down the front with a microphone squeaking away for an hour about the meaning of the novel. I just looked at a couple of friends next to me and we all raised eyebrows and it wasn't too long before I was cutting those lectures and going to the pub.

I went to a poetry lecture where we'd been asked to read a Blake poem. I loved the poem and though we had to write something on it, I couldn't, I was so moved by the poem, so excited by it. I thought, well, it'll come out when we talk. Then in the classroom the lecturer put the poem on the board—it was very short—cut it up with his chalk into various sections and proceeded to introduce the seminar by saying, "This is really a poor example of Blake's work and a very bad poem for the following reasons. . . ." I looked around and everyone was writing it down and I felt a flush come to the cheeks—I felt embarrassed that I had been moved by it. I didn't say a word during the whole thing and crept out—and began to cut those lectures too.

So I failed the first year, and pulled out and went into real estate. My father was glad I was out of University; he liked me getting down to business and earning some money. He had a one-man business and the plan was pretty clear that I would join him, and in the meantime get a couple of years' experience with other real-estate agents.

Mathews: Working with other agents, not your father?

Weir: Yes, from about eighteen to twenty. I sold land. I went and visited all my blocks and made notes on them and then went back to the office. I remember the boss coming out and saying "what are you doing?" I was ripping all those ones I didn't like out of the listing book. I said "well, you can't sell something you don't think is any good." Anyway I sold the lot and I'll never forget when I came in one morning and there was one of the other agents, ripping out all the houses in his book he didn't like. With the money I made I bought a one-way ticket to Europe with the intention of working in London, and set off on what was supposed to be a three or four months' visit.

Mathews: How did it feel to be on a boat sailing out?

Weir: It felt like a beginning; I knew that whatever it was, it was going to happen.

Mathews: You've said that the trip itself was quite a formative experience?

Weir: It was a Greek boat heading for Piraeus where it was due for a refit and as I came to know, when a ship is due for a refit, there is a kind of malaise amongst the crew. This affected the entertainment side of things and the Entertainments Officer had organized something like a fancy dress night, but not much else. So a few of us suggested a ship's revue and he said "if you want to organize it, go ahead." We also found a closed circuit TV on board—God knows what it was used for, but there was a little studio and TV sets in all the bars and some very bored passengers, so we asked if we could do a show.

Mathews: On the TV?

Weir: Yes. We'd left Australia in the heyday of *The Mavis Bramston Show*, *The Phillip Street Revue*, and *Barry Humphries*, so we did a kind of revue format of satire and interviews with passengers.[2] We got off the ship pale— we used to live in that little studio.

Mathews: Did being in Europe alter your perspective on Australia significantly?

Weir: It was such an innocent time to travel—a time that was about to come to an end, as the ship voyages were about to end. It's one of those things that I responded to in Christopher Koch's book about events in 1965 [*The Year of Living Dangerously*]. You could draw a line through that year: it was a beginning and an end; it was the end of the fifties. It was just prior to the hippie wave and every young person hitching was a student. One evening in Spain I was dropped off towards sunset and climbed a hill with some bread and wine. And during that evening it struck me very strongly that I was a European, that this was where we had come from and where I belonged. That was probably the beginning of an interest in thinking about immigration to our country and where we were in the world. Those of us who went to Europe for the first time by ship were very lucky—that understanding of the distance, of just how far away we were from our culture.

Mathews: Were you working in England?

Weir: I was there for ten or eleven months. I had various jobs—grocery driver, lifeguard. They were great days—a feeling of optimism, of change, a wonderful period to be in London. In fact, it's always been difficult to go back. It was like a membership in a giant club, just to be young. 1965— it was "Flower Power," anti-Vietnam marches, rock and roll, and "swinging London," as it came to be known. It was a feeling that I carried back with me and no doubt it contributed to my decision not to go back into real estate but to do any sort of work until I could get a job in television.

Notes

1. Charles Chauvel directed *Jedda* in 1955. His last film, it featured a love story between two aboriginal characters, Robert Tudawai as "Marbuck" and Ngarla Kunoth in the title role. It was the first Australian film to be shot in color and won more international attention than any previous Australian film.

2. During the 1960s Barry Humphries was a top Australian entertainer specializing in one-man shows. He was responsible for the original *Barry McKenzie* comic strips, entitled *Aussie in Pommieland*. Humphries's most popular character is "Edna Everage." Edna was incorporated into Bruce Beresford's *The Adventures of Barry McKenzie* (1972).

Small Screens and Big Screens: Television and Film

Graham Shirley / 1991

Conducted February 26, 1991. Never before published. Permission granted by Australian Film and Sound Archives, Graham Shirley, and Peter Weir.

[Editor's Note: Graham Shirley worked for four decades as a director, writer, and researcher on Australian historical documentaries. He is author (with Brian Adams) of *Australian Cinema: The First 80 Years* (published 1983 and1989). From 2006 to 2010 he was a senior curator with the National Film and Sound Archives (NFSA). He is now the NFSA's Manager, Access Projects. He recorded this conversation with Peter Weir February 26, 1991, for the National Film and Sound Archives in Sydney, Australia. It has never been published. In a letter to this editor, he wrote the following biographical and introductory note.]

On NFSA's behalf, I have also recorded video oral histories with Fred Schepisi (focusing on his Australian works) and Gillian Armstrong (covering her entire career) last year and at the start of this year. I've been recording oral histories with film industry people since my first one in 1971. In 1972 I visited California, where I interviewed special effects pioneer and director Norman O. Dawn, who directed *For the Term of His Natural Life* (1927) and two other features in Australia, besides travelling around Australia to film actualities made prior to World War I. At that time, I also interviewed a number of other Hollywood special effects pioneers and present-day practitioners, including Linwood Dunn, Jim Danforth, Byron Haskin (who also covered his career as director) and A. Arnold Gillespie. Some of those interviews were published in Australian film magazines while others have never been published. Oral histories are something I've had a passion for over the years, and not long before I joined NFSA I was moving out into broader areas of interviews, covering the lives and careers of war veterans for Australia's *Australians at War Film Archive* project (which has its own website, complete with transcripts), and people relating their experiences of World War II in two of my documentaries, *Behind the Lines: The Secret War of Z Special Unit* (2001) and *Road to Tokyo* (2005).

On the 26th of February, 1991, Peter and I sat down in a restaurant at Ocean Road, not far from Palm Beach, to talk about his early work up to the time of his first feature films. He took great pleasure in talking about this formative phase, for, as he put it, earlier interviews had paid little attention to it.

[What follows are excerpts from that interview.]

University Years

Graham Shirley: Let's talk about your early work. . . . *Count Vim*. It's been given the title *Count Vim's Last Exercise* and *Count Vim's Last Experience*. Which is correct?
Peter Weir: It's the first, *Count Vim's Last Exercise*.

Shirley: Does a copy still exist?
Weir: Yes I've got it, the one and only copy. I must give it to the Library or something. I did have it put on tape at one time.

Shirley: Does it stand up well, do you think?
Weir: No!

Shirley: This is why you have it?
Weir: That's right! I mean I look at it, and I'm kind of appalled to think that I had enough confidence to keep going after having done it.

Shirley: But obviously someone at Channel 7 was impressed enough by it?
Weir: Oh yes.

Shirley: To give you that opportunity.
Weir: I had done one independent revue, and had written material for the University Architecture Revue and had got to meet Grahame Bond and Geoff Malone and Geoff Atherden and that sort of fantastically creative Architecture group. So that was enormously stimulating for them and for me. You know, the feeling that we could go on beyond

university, because I wasn't from that background. In that first year there as a stagehand, when I was so on fire with possibilities, there were sets, there were lights, there were cameras, there was a young, willing crew. Why not make our own films? Why not do our own things? But how to do it? The most expensive area was stock and processing, the only area you couldn't get for free, through you know, the black market you might say. So that's when I heard about the Social Club. And I went to them and I said, "What is the social club?" He said, "Oh well, we have a raffle once a year at Christmas, and a Christmas party." And I said, "Why not do something theatrical? We should do something like a revue!" And he said, "Oh yes, but who would organize it?" And I said, "The only thing we need is stock and processing." And they agreed to get that. I asked Bruce McDonald, who was an assistant cameraman in the news department, "Can you get a camera?" And he said, "Sure, on the weekend, no one will notice!" So he slipped a Bolex in his bag for the weekend!

Shirley: You had continued those revues a couple of years after you left university, didn't you—or were they spin-offs?
Weir: Spins-offs, yes.

Shirley: There was *Candy-Striped Balloon*, wasn't there?
Weir: That was its commercial or its festival name. It was called *Balloon to Bloom*, which was the show we did at the Cell Block Theater [part of the National Film School], which was backed by Pact Theatre [a small theater in suburban Sydney]. And we used to rehearse at Pact and they gave us $500 to stage the show. And I think we did a one-week run at the Cell Block, and that gave us confidence to keep going, to attempt really to get onto television by doing a series of pilots. I think we did one for Channel Ten. And we were constantly talking to people. That was going to be my career.

Shirley: And you were working on a revue-type format where you were sending up Ampol [Australian Motorists Petrol Company] and various other companies. And you were a performer as well?
Weir: That's right, yes. Writer/performer.

Shirley: So is that where you saw your career going at the time in terms of writing/performing?
Weir: Yes, although the word "career"—I didn't ever really think of it in those terms, because there was nowhere to go beyond getting a show on,

getting a show up. No grand plan, no long term. Certainly not in film because there was no industry. The only films were those that came from overseas to shoot here. So it was just the mixed event, "What's happening next? What are we doing?" Planning things, but never thinking in terms of a career. In fact I think I rejected the very idea of that because it was part of the times. Everything I was doing was to do with the Vietnam War period and all of the change that occurred during the war and after the war.

The Television Years

Shirley: After you returned from your first visit to Europe, did you immediately seek employment at the TV stations?
Weir: Yes I did. I wrote letters to all of them and my biggest hope was the ABC [Australian Broadcasting Commission (now the Australian Broadcasting Corporation)].

Shirley: Why was that?
Weir: Their programs were more interesting, I don't know, it just seemed to be the most sympathetic interview. It had a kind of image as a place where you could get training. And I must have talked to a couple of people who had gotten jobs as stagehands. That's what I was applying for, stagehand. In fact I came across this morning just by chance a draft of a letter, well, two letters, one to Mr. Eisdel at ABC Radio who was, I think, a producer and an occasional on-air announcer who was a family acquaintance. And what was curious about Mr. Eisdel was there was this draft letter saying—just like letters like I get today—"You know, I've applied for a job there; can you tell me is there any other way that I could get a start?" Obviously was hoping that he could have influence with Mr. Wolveridge, who was the second letter.

Shirley: Stan Wolveridge
Weir: Yes, at the ABC. Is he still around?

Shirley: I've seen him around; I think he's there as a sort of staging consultant; but he no longer runs the department.
Weir: And I'd mentioned in the letter to Mr. Eisdel that I'd written to Mr. Wolveridge and had had an interview, and I was on some sort of waiting list. Many years later, when I was shooting *The Last Wave*, and I was doing a sequence in Sydney here, I recognized one of the extras. And I went over and said, "Mr. Eisdel?" And he said "Yes." And I said,

"Good heavens, what are you doing?" And he said that he'd retired from the ABC and did a bit of extra work now and then. I said, "Remember me?" and he said, "Yes I remember you coming to see me." It was a curious moment, but there was Mr. Eisdel, looking much the same as he had when I'd sat opposite him at his desk, kind of giving me the usual sort of advice—you know, "Really there's nothing I can tell you that will help, nothing I can do."

Shirley: So Channel 7 was part of your circuit of applications?
Weir: You know something, several months after I'd been out for an interview, they wrote saying there was a position. I grabbed it. Before that, I could last just about six weeks in a job before I would get bored. I worked as a cleaner at Anthony Hordern's, then I worked for the Sydney Woollahra Council in a road gang, and then delivered bread for Tip Top. That was the worst job of all, actually. And each of those lasted almost exactly six weeks. So it was a fantastic opportunity at Channel 7; and as it happened, it was just the best channel I could have gone to because they were starting really aggressively to plan Australian drama.

Shirley: This was under Jim Oswin?
Weir: Yes. It was the last days of the *Mavis Bramston Show* [a revue program of blackout sketches].

Shirley: And The Battlers [a 1968 drama series produced by Channel 7] was happening as well?
Weir: Yes, and plus the odd pilots of things that didn't surface. And *Beauty and the Beast* was one of the shows I worked on. That's when I got to know Pat Lovell.[1]

Shirley: You were a staging assistant still at this time?
Weir: Yes, I worked as a stagehand through '67 and '68, two years basically.

Shirley: And was there anyone at Channel 7 who particularly impressed you?
Weir: Rod Kirk, who became or was the key director on the *Bramston Show*. And he loved film. He had the job I got eventually, which was doing the film sequences for the *Bramston Show*. We'll call it that, since I forget the other titles it went under. He was doing that I think when I first went to the channel. And then in '67 he got promoted to be the Director

of the show, the key job, the Tape Director. And he had seen my *Count Vim* movie and suggested that I get the job of doing the film sequences for *Bramston*, which were basically shot at forty-eight frames per second. The show was really running low on creative energy and the fastest way to get a laugh was to either shoot anything at forty-eight frames or backwards, which got a laugh because people just had to laugh.

Shirley: So all of them were literally shot at that speed?
Weir: No, I kept trying to keep away from it, but two out of three or just extremely high camp stuff. But I was always putting in more ambitious pieces, suggesting more elaborate things that the cast loved.

Shirley: I think the initial injection of energy had come from Michael Plant. I spoke to David Cahill, who said that Michael Plant was the *Mavis Bramston Show* to begin with. And he had this wonderful unique sense of humor, which worked. When he went, the whole thing started to sort of roll downhill.
Weir: That's interesting, he must have been before me. When I went overseas in '65, that was the show then. The twin influences on me as far as comedy went were the *Bramston Show* and on stage, *Barry Humphries*. So when I did a live program on the ship with two other guys, we did five half-hour shows we called *The Bilge Water Show*, which you can see was really very much influenced by *Barry Humphries* and *Bramston*. There were interviews with fake passengers and whatever, but that was the inspiration. And so it was interesting and I found myself working on that show in '68. I had gotten married at twenty-two. I had so much energy and time to think. I think it's one thing that you often find with young marriages in the creative area—it sort of frees you enormously to pursue your work. I was always working. Every weekend you'd be working on something. Grahame Bond and I would sit around with a tape recorder like this for two days and make sketches up and throw things to each other. And, you know, really it was a fantastic kind of training to think on your feet. That's how literally we would work on a sketch. He might start off with a line of dialogue, and I don't know where it's going. And I take it or I'd pass him a prop of some kind and say, "What do you think of this? What are you going to do with it?" Then he would become a character, and he was going to do somebody who was going to do something with it.

Shirley: And this is for stage work, film work?

Weir: The idea was it could go in any direction. I mean essentially the stage, at first. But then it also was television.

Shirley: There was also *Man on the Green Bike* [a science fiction comedy drama for the Australian Broadcasting Commission].
Weir: Yes, that was some time later, that was '69.

Shirley: How did that come about?
Weir: Through our connection with the Pact Theatre. The guy there was the head of the religious department at the ABC—Robert Allnut—and he had sort of been with another older guy who had really seen something in us and given us this facility of Pact to rehearse, which was the aim of Pact, a little stage, a small theatre. We didn't think it was suitable for our show, but we used to work there and use their stage to rehearse. And then we got *Balloon to Bloom* up and mounted and that prompted Bob to say, "Well, I'd love you to do something for us at the ABC."

Shirley: How did you find the experience of appearing in *The Man on the Green Bike*? It's a huge production.
Weir: It was enormous. Does it exist?

Shirley: It does exist.
Weir: Great!

Shirley: They've got it on tele-record.
Weir: Oh God, I'd love to get a copy.

Shirley: I haven't seen it since it first went to air, but it is there.
Weir: We weren't quite up to it. I think it was a shock the first day of turning up to work to realize that it was a fully professional crew. And I sort of always felt that we were just behind our abilities and our knowledge and didn't take· the right kind of advantage. It was a little too early and I don't know that it helped anybody, or that it helped us in any way.

Shirley: But interestingly, you had Geoff Malone as the *Little Man* who would be brought back in very much the same sort of role for *Homesdale*. Were you thinking in terms of Geoff Malone as a character that you would come back to?
Weir: Yes, I was fascinated at that stage with this sort of Little Man, this sort of worm that could turn. I think the same character was really in the

Cars That Ate Paris, played by Terry Camilleri, it's the same guy. I think that was the end of that particular cycle. And the end of *Cars* is very similar in a way to the end of *Homesdale*. This guy turns and becomes extremely dangerous but also becomes free through facing his tormentors or something. The classic victim type, who fights his way out of it.

Shirley: During that Channel 7 period, *The Flight and Times of Reverend Buck Shotte* was accepted for screening at the Sydney Film Festival. Apparently it was withdrawn. You protested the censorship of *I Love, You Love*. Did you feel that strongly about it?
Weir: Yes I did at the time. (By the way the title is *The Life and Flight of Reverend Buck Shotte*.) I withdrew, it, along with Chris McCullough and one other film. I think it was a futile gesture, and I wish in a way that we could have been persuaded not to do it. I'm not sure that part of my decision to pull out was also connected with the fact that I didn't think that the film was good enough. I don't know. I was delighted to have been accepted. *Count Vim* I put in and David Stratton turned it down but with a very encouraging letter, to his credit. And he was right to turn it down. It was too early and too amateur. But he did say, "I'm really interested, or we are, in whatever else you do."

Shirley: How ambitious was *Life and Flight* compared to *Count Vim*?
Weir: Oh, considerably. I think it was an attempt to inject real professionalism into it. I wanted to put in more interiors, I wanted to have lit interiors. And so there was the studio and we worked there at night, without permission actually.

Shirley: You shot it at Channel 7?
Weir: Yes, the interiors. I didn't even want to ask if we could, because I knew the answer would be no. So we just would plan an evening where we knew nothing was happening. And in fact one night we were sprung by the security guard who said, "What's going on in here?" And I said, "It's a top secret program on youth." He said, "How come I don't know about it?" And I said, "That's how secret it is. It's so secret that they had to even keep it secret from the security." He sort of looked as if he thought, "I don't believe this." But then, who would? But it looked professional. We had our own sets painted and I knew all these guys from working on the follow-up to the *Bramston Show*. I picked flats that suited our set and designed a set from existing stored props and sets, and had them

repainted by Stan in the paint shop. And I think it was Roger Kirk who subsequently did some designs for me.

Shirley: That's right. He went to the ABC afterwards.
Weir: Yes, I still see his credit quite often. And so at night we'd put them up there. And the lighting guys very kindly stayed back for an hour and lit the set for us. We'd shoot on till midnight or one o'clock.

Shirley: And was the *Life and Flight* screened elsewhere, or screened at the Sydney Film Festival? Did it receive any screenings at all?
Weir: I don't recall. The only one I'd know for sure was on television in South Australia, because it won the Young Filmmakers Award in '69 or '70.

Shirley: I think I remember it was available through the Filmmakers Co-Op.
Weir: That's where it went. You're right. Yes, and it went to schools and colleges, but not in the theatre.

At the Commonwealth Film Unit

Shirley: What did you do between leaving Channel 7 and commencing with the Commonwealth Film Unit?
Weir: I was just out of work for a while. I walked out of my job because I had worked for a year on the *Bramston Show* on my stagehand's salary. I went to see them after the end of '68 or early '69 and saw my name back on the stagehands roster. And while I'd sort of accepted that although I didn't get a raise, I was getting experience. But the minute I saw that they'd just used me before moving me back to stagehand the following year, I thought, "I will never do this work." So I went straight upstairs to them in my overalls and saw my boss and said, "This is just grossly unfair." And he said, "Well Peter, something else might come up. We don't have anything for you right now, but you've got the experience." And I said, "I think that should have been paid for." He said, "Well—" And I said, "Okay, I resign." And he said, "Alright, put in your notice." And I said, "No, no. As of this minute I resign. Just give me what I'm due and I'll come and pick it up in a couple of days." I walked downstairs, changed out of my overalls, and I walked out and caught the train home. My wife came home from work—she's a teacher—and I told her what had happened. And she said, "Great!" So she supported me for a while.

I'd heard of the Commonwealth Film Unit so I applied for a job. I remember going to see Frank Bagnall there for an interview and screened my *Count Vim* and *Buck Shotte* and the work I'd done for the *Bramston Show*; and I remember thinking, "I've got to get this job!" As a director. I wasn't going to accept anything less than a director. I thought the interview wasn't going too well and I couldn't understand why. I thought there couldn't be many with this experience. So I kept waiting and just feeling this hesitancy from Frank, and finally at the end I was just finishing telling him of the film idea I had, which was something to do with a guy's suicide off the Harbour Bridge, and he was chuckling away. At the end of it I said, "Is anything wrong? Is there a chance for me to get this job?" He said, "Well there is one problem. I think I may be wrong for you because I've enjoyed this interview and loved seeing the things you've been doing. But I don't think there is anything here that would be interesting enough for you. We do documentaries." So I said, "There's nothing more that I want to do than a serious documentary, I need the experience!" I believe that I was over-qualified. Anyway, I got the job, although they said, "There's no work exactly yet. You'll be paid as a junior director, but you'll have to wait till something comes up." I met Stanley Hawes and then began one of the most exciting periods of my life.

Shirley: You've been quoted as saying, "I knew the only place I wanted to go then was the Commonwealth Film Unit." Why was that? Didn't you have a dislike for formal institutions?

Weir: It was simply to keep working in film, and I didn't want to try another commercial station. I felt, on the one hand, I had got a lot of it. Secondly there was no other station doing as much as they were. I was scarred somewhat by the treatment that was dealt to me at Channel 7. The ABC seemed to be less interesting than the Commonwealth Film Unit. I'd seen a couple of CFU documentaries, their *Diaries*, at the movies. And the thought of possibly working in 35mm. It's hard to believe that then the very sight of a 35mm roll of film with sound was thrilling. To actually touch it was exciting. It was the big time and this was the only institution working with 35mm. I remember going up the first day there. I was on a tour of the building and ended up in the sound department, and there they were mixing *Bullocky* [a 1969 documentary about a fourth-generation bushman]. It was in 35mm and just to hear beautiful crisp sound effects (it was a lovely little film anyway), I felt so excited, I could hardly contain myself. "This is the only place I could be. I'm in the right place." And a terrific bunch of young people there, young directors and production assistants.

Shirley: Who were some of the people that impressed you?
Weir: Arch Nicholson. I remember walking down the corridor, being introduced to him and watching him, and he was cutting a movie, a series of films on *Defensive Driving*, I think it was called. He'd shot six of them and was cutting them and I was impressed by his kind of technical knowledge and his confidence, and the amount of work that he was being given. So he was very interesting. Ian Dunlop, for other reasons. He was already a giant to me.

Shirley: Because of his ethnographic work?
Weir: Yes. I think I had seen his only commercial release.

Shirley: Desert People?
Weir: Yes, *Desert People*. I think it was around about 1969. I'm pretty sure I saw that either just as I joined or just before. He was a star to me. And there he was, walking around in his shorts in the corridor in another room. And there was Brian Hannant, who was a film buff and could talk movies, classic movies and new American cinema (something I didn't know much at all). Bruce Moir, a delightful fellow, was going somewhere. Oliver Howes was more aesthetic and quieter.
Chris McGill and Chris McCullough, too. Chris McCullough was a real dynamo. In fact I worked for him as a camera assistant on a film he was doing, a sort of perennial *What's happening in Australia* thing for the Embassies.

Shirley: Which they were obligated to make every year.
Weir: Keith Gow was an interesting and singular type of man, who was renowned as a great cameraman, and just now moved into directing. I liked him a lot. And then there was, of course, Gil Brealey and Dick Mason, who created the climate that enabled me with others to grow.

Shirley: Was that climate being created when you joined there?
Weir: It was being talked about. They were going to move into drama. And Dick Mason anyway was incredibly impressive to meet. And it was a terrific balance between him and Stanley Hawes. This is all around the time I had the interview with Frank Bagnall that I met Dick. I didn't meet

Stanley until I got the job. But there was something in the air. I was really sensing what I later heard spelt out, that they had plans to take the Commonwealth Film Unit into drama. Not only that but they had some sort of overview—with others as I later learned, Phillip Adams and his recruits, Barry Jones and certain politicians—that there was a generation like myself. It was like we were pilots who were flying on instruments. We couldn't see beyond the cloud. They knew about Bruce Beresford or Fred Schepisi in Melbourne coming through Film House, and the young cameramen that were coming up. They could see a possibility for a film industry. I'd never thought of it.

Shirley: Of course, that climate had been generated by the Vincent inquiry much earlier in the decade and the Producers and Directors Guild's constant campaign to get the Vincent inquiry on the table.[2] And also at the ABC there seemed to be a fair push among directors to get things going.
Weir: That was true. And then they lagged behind, they lost a great opportunity in that period.

Shirley: The ABC did?
Weir: Yes, I know because I applied for a job with the ABC as a freelancer when I finally left, after having done *Cars*. And it was a very cool reception. Their Drama Department I think lagged in that period.

Shirley: A cool reception after you'd done *Cars*?
Weir: Yes, with a proposal to do tele-movies. And I think I sent a couple of storylines to them, and got a very cold letter back. From whoever was then Head of Drama saying, "It's not our policy to do films about 'little green men' or something. We're not encouraging people to get dirty water off their chest." I mean, I was astounded.

Shirley: Just going back to your beginnings at the CFU, what were your initial assignments as a production assistant and/or assistant cameraman?
Weir: It was to assist on this Chris McCullough movie. That was my first job and the cameraman was very reluctant to take me, understandably! I had no experience with the camera, I was given a quick crash course before we took off all around Australia. And he ended up doing most of the work himself because, you know, I would bring the wrong lens or learned slowly as I went along. But it was really very unfair to him. It was

fascinated to watch Chris working as a director because he was fast, very single-minded, had a terrific eye. And he had some of this confidence and certainty that Arch Nicholson had. He knew what he was doing and I really didn't. Despite what I'd done, I really didn't know what I was doing, and had always just jumped in the deep end. This was wonderfully timed to let some technical areas be understood and to catch up with my ambitions in terms of comedy or drama.

Shirley: So, were you still continuing some of your outside work, then?
Weir: Yes, still working on weekends. Wondering where I'd go from here. I mean I had made those two films at Channel 7 for a grand total of ten dollars.

Shirley: What about acting?
Weir: There was a sequence in a film which was meant to be during the Korean War in which I played the central character. At this stage I was also thinking that I was not sure that there might be an acting career for me. There seemed no reason not to act, write, and direct, do everything. That was in fact my last appearance on screen. There was this one scene where they needed a Korean soldier for this face-off between Buck, the American soldier, and the Korean soldier. So I went to a Chinese restaurant and picked the most likely looking young waiter and said to him, "Do you want to earn some money?" And amazingly he turned up and I gave him ten bucks for a day's work. Otherwise, we'd got stock and cameras from Channel 7 through the Social Club's influence.

Shirley: Did you try to get them to distribute any of your earlier films?
Weir: I remember when I went in to see them about distributing *Buck Shotte*. I can still see their faces. We were in a subterranean room somewhere with black walls and bits of film everywhere, and a screen and a projector with about a six-foot distance from projector to screen. And they said, "What is this exactly?" And I said, "Well, it's based on a book that a friend of mine wrote in London which was never published." I told him the plot line. And I said, "It's already shot. Would you be interested?" And they said, "You've made a film from a book? It sounds like Hollywood!" They thought it was very funny. It wasn't exactly a mocking laugh from them so much as an incredulous reaction that anyone would think to do this or would want to—a story film about American Evangelists coming here.

Shirley: This late sixties and early seventies period has been described as the "Young Turk" period of the CFU. Was it obvious to you that it was something like that?

Weir: Oh, yes, anything was possible! It was thrilling. To begin with, I dramatized training films and pushed to get sponsors to do more teaching through drama.

Shirley: What was the collective title of these public service films?

Weir: I only ever remembered my title which was *Stirring the Pool* and starred Judy Morris, which was about office politics. The interesting thing was that Gil really kind of gave us a very quick training program in structured shooting, which was based on his travels in America and visits to studios and production companies. So for a period of a week, we would go down to the stage and he would have sets constructed, for whoever's film was in production. We had make-up and we had continuity, and we had things that I'd never had in a short film.

Shirley: Was he there personally training you?

Weir: Yes. And he would set a scene up and say, "Right, okay, now this is what happens first. You've rehearsed the scene. You block it, then you work out your angles, or you've already got a plan of that. And then you take the actors through that and any contributions from them." Really basic stuff that was fantastic to get at that time. Then they discussed things like "crossing the 180-degree line." What you do, how to work eye-lines out. And then within a couple of weeks I was shooting my first film, and they were very happy with it. It wasn't a bad little film, for what it was. I forget who scripted it. I don't think I did but I did put a lot of touches into it.

Shirley: Was all this in the absence of a proper film school?

Weir: Yes, oh absolutely. I was living from project to project. And I still do, I think. Still today, I generally work on one film at a time, at the most two. No I just always make the film as if it's my last film. I always feel that this is the last one, I've got to get it right. And then wait and see what turns up, which way things go. To a degree it was like that then. The only continuity was working at the Commonwealth Film Unit, which I loved. I couldn't wait to get to work every day. It was a way of life. A tremendously stimulating atmosphere. It was fantastic. However, already the unfortunate choice of the Australian office setup was in operation. That is, on the top floor the best offices were occupied by producers. Below that, the directors were the equivalent of cameramen. We were considered broadly, in a way, as technical people who worked with actors. It was something that could be learnt and mastered, more a Hollywood model than a European model. And I think that wrong move is something that we carry with us today and it severely harmed the industry. It was the failure in a small industry to not realize that it is the director who is the key figure, not the writer and not the producer. It was increasingly frustrating to sit down with producers who knew less than you did, were less experienced, but had the office, had the control of the budget and control of the project.

Directing *Michael*

Shirley: How did you come to direct *Michael*?

Weir: After this series of public service training films, I was called to Gil's office and he said he wanted to give me one of three short films that were going to make up this feature called *Three to Go*.[3] I don't know if they had the title then. I could go and write anything about youth. It was a thirty-minute time limit. I just floated home, "What could I do?" It was just this lovely blank sheet of white paper so far; but it was so exciting. The only thing I ever wrote and wanted to make and never did, in my life, was something called *Rebellion*, which was set during the Vietnam time. It opens with a movie-within-a-movie, about a rebellion in Sydney. I wanted to shoot the troops in the middle of Sydney during a student uprising on New Year's Eve, in which they took over radio and TV stations. I had written it during the period I was working on the *Bramston Show* in '68. So I borrowed some of that for *Michael*.

Shirley: Why was your segment the only one on 16mm rather than 35mm?

Weir: I think originally, if I'm not wrong, that it was all supposed to be in 16mm. Mine came first, and as they saw the dailies coming through, I don't think I got as far as the cut when they said, "There's more in this than we thought." They said, "This has got a lot of potential." So Brian applied for 35mm, and they said, "Why not?"

Shirley: And what was the CFU's reaction to *Michael*'s success at the 1970 AFI Awards?

Weir: It was overshadowed somewhat by a real clash with Gil during the editing. He was very upset about my first cut. He was the producer, and I showed him really quite an early cut about forty to fifty minutes long. I thought it was going fine but a lot needed to be done. But he was apparently shocked by it. I think he was frightened by it.

Shirley: What sort of things was he frightened by?
Weir: Rhythm, pace. He came up with a list of notes from the screening. They were really a demolition job on what he'd seen. I just had to just sit there, which is something that I've never, ever, done since before I'd done the work. This was a short, sharp lesson. For all of his energy and his vision, Gil had this severe shortcoming, which was that he could lose patience very quickly and get very, very angry. And that's not the way to deal with creative people. You don't deal with actors like that. And if you're a producer, you can't get the best from your director by tearing strips off him. It simply makes you obviously very angry yourself, and inhibits those important ideas from coming forward. Fortunately, there were a couple of points that Gil made that were very good, so we made the next cut. When he saw it next time he said, "Yes well, that's better." Anyway, to my surprise and delight it won the AFI's Grand Prix, as it was then.

Shirley: Mike Thornhill wrote a really stinging review in *The Australian*. [Peter laughs] What was your reaction to that?[4]
Weir: I was absolutely staggered. But then I thought, "The film can be seen like this." In fact it was never very well reviewed by anybody, but I didn't care. I suppose because I wasn't expecting the award. You know, suddenly newspapers were there photographing.

Frictions at the CFU

Shirley: Were there aspects of working at the CFU that you resisted?
Weir: Well, they introduced a system where directors had to sign in and out, when they arrived for work. All the staff did. To make sure you weren't shirking, I guess. Then I went and spoke to whomever and said, "Look, this is unreasonable for us directors, because we often work at home." You'd never stop. I'd come in at ten o'clock. I might have been up at six working on the script or had worked on Sunday. There's no way that you can really clock in or clock off. We're creative people. They said, "Well that's the rule." And I said, "Well I'm not going to sign it!" And I never did. And I was asked many times to sign it. They would say, "Peter, look, just get someone else to sign it." But then, I said, "No, I'd rather them fire me." And there were other things: There were no expense accounts for directors, so you couldn't take someone to lunch in a research

situation in a country town, getting information, and you couldn't buy them lunch. It was against all this period of enormous social change in Australia that was seeing the artistic life of the country for the first time spreading out wider than just single individuals, when the only thing before that was to go to England. I remember it had been quite a major decision for me to come back to Australia in '66 with my wife-to-be. It was really almost on the toss of a coin to go back to Australia. It was that close. We'd argue one day to stay and argue another day to go home. I think if I'd been on my own, it might have been a different decision. But I think being together, we felt we could deal with the shortcomings of Australia. But, you know, there was something in the air. And it was true, there was no better place to be than in Australia in the late sixties. Swinging London was over, and it was elsewhere. It was certainly in San Francisco. Sydney was great in those days.

Shirley: When did you start looking at films—I mean, really studying film history?
Weir: I think Keith Gow started a lunchtime film club at the Commonwealth Film Unit, and we would get features in once a week during the lunch hour. That's where I first got to really know Kurosawa's films, we had two or three of them. And everybody got excited and suggested their favorites to be run at the Commonwealth Film Unit. I remember I was so excited when I knew *Seven Samurai* was coming. I'd never seen it. And I waited all week for it at the CFU. And in fact I was so excited, I dressed as a Samurai to go to the screening!

Shirley: Did you?
Weir: Yes, I had full swords and helmets and stuff like that. Just a sort of spontaneous thing.

Shirley: Did anyone else?
Weir: No! [Laughs]

Shirley: What about the National Film Theater? Were you tempted to attend any of their screenings?
Weir: Richard Brennan said, "Look, you know Peter, you must go. Do you know any of Renoir's work?" I said, "No." He said, "My God!" He mentioned a couple of others. "Do you know the early Hitchcock's?" No. He said, "You've got to go. Sign up and learn about what you're clearly going to have a life in." I thought about it. And in fact shortly after, some

interesting programs came up. But I decided I wasn't ready to look at the past work.

Shirley: Why not?

Weir: I instinctively felt it would be too inhibiting. And I was right, I know. Because I did then look at these movies after I'd made three features. And after *The Last Wave* in Adelaide when I living there in '78, with a year off, they had an excellent 16mm library. Of course, this was all pre-tape, so I looked at hundreds of films; and I made up my own program from their catalogue. And I started obviously with silent movies and looked at the great Russian masterpieces. I discovered Pudovkin, you know, because I knew about Eisenstein; but I loved Pudovkin's films. Then went on to the early Hitchcock's, and then Chaplin and D. W. Griffith and then whatever else leading up to the advent of sound. And as I watched through that year, I knew I'd made the right decision. If I'd seen them too early, it would have inhibited me. I had to feel like everything that I was doing was new. So when I would look at something Hitchcock was doing, I mightn't know how he did it but I knew *why* he did it. I had a chance to learn rather than sit there just being astonished, which I would have been. In a way, I think, in a curious way, I invented a kind of imaginary past. In other words, I think I kind of pretended that cinema was just discovered. And really my first films are almost silent movies. Because, one, I couldn't write dialogue; two, even if I could, I couldn't afford sync sound. But particularly too, the actors couldn't say the lines. Young people you had some chance with. Older actors were so hammy, and you couldn't afford at that stage to get at a John Meillon.

Shirley: You just mentioned actors. Why were you preferring amateur actors?

Weir: Yes, those early days a lot of professionals from radio or theatre, older people particularly, had a kind of competitive attitude to the young directors. And don't forget, I'm talking about myself. You either had a beard or long hair or something, so you were representative of this new, often pretentious and irritating and opinionated group of young people. And so that mixed with the fact that you were directing and they had to follow your direction. Often they would resist. Or they simply didn't understand what you meant. If someone's acting badly, you can't really teach them to act well. All you can do is take lines off them and reduce their movements. And they knew what I was doing and they resented that. I remember old Eddie Howell in *The Cars That Ate Paris*, who did a fine job as a Councilor on that. But he had about four lines. I removed two of them, for other reasons actually. I remember him saying, "That's two left out of four." Bitterly. And I said, "Eddie, Eddie, it's not about dialogue. The film's not about dialogue."

Shirley: And you found with amateur actors you could sort of tap into something.

Weir: Exactly, they had no inhibitions. They might have had no training but you had a chance to take what they did naturally and adapt to that, which they'd often do. And try not to tell them too much initially. So see what they did and then follow them, or gently add something to it. But beyond all of that, they looked *right*. They didn't look like *actors*.

Shirley: Had things at the CFU changed much when you returned after your trip overseas?

Weir: I had been so impatient to leave, so impatient to get to make a feature, which was in the works.

While I was away, I'd written the storylines for three films. The Unit just couldn't hold me, it was too small. I was really irritated then by the bureaucracy. I was always impatient.

Homesdale and After the CFU

Shirley: About your next overseas trip in 1971. You just said you came back knowing more about what you wanted to do. What had you seen and done?

Weir: Well, the trip started in a particular way. I had a ticket to Europe, but I wanted to go via America, which was more expensive. So I worked out a way to go there by filming some projects. I heard that the United States Information Service was anxious for a positive image of America on film. They could, under certain circumstances, finance you to shoot film there that was of a positive nature. So many images coming out of America at the time on the news were of riots and anti-war protests, plus all the horrors of Vietnam. So why not film something more positive? So I then went to Channel 7 and said I was going on this trip—why not shoot some magazine items in America? I'd do six or eight shows. So for that they financed the crew. And so I got Tony Wallace who'd worked on *Homesdale*, to come with me and do the sound. Tony had his own equipment, so they paid for that and paid for his fares. Then the Information Service arranged accommodation for us at various hotels. I ended up only filming in Los Angeles and San Francisco four little stories about the alternative society and alternative foods there; that is, how the supermarkets were growing organic foods. In Los Angeles I did one on the Fine Art Squad that was decorating walls with murals. And there was one on the growing health industry. So we sent all these things back. We stayed at the Roosevelt Hotel, right in the heart of Hollywood. And then I went to visit film locations in London. It was just to observe. I got a job, non-paying job, at Elstree Studios, and was assigned to a special effects crew and worked on Ken Russell's *The Boy Friend*, with Twiggy. It was a fantastic film to be on. I remember Ken Russell one day had a riding crop he used to slap his thigh with. It had an ivory greyhound dog-head on the top. One day he slapped his thigh and snapped the head in half. So they called for the props department and said, "Go and fix this." At the same time I met Hitchcock.

Shirley: Was he shooting at the time?
Weir: Yes, he was, and I spent a couple of days on his set, both in the street and on the studio. I spoke to him very briefly. It was wonderful to watch him. I remember him saying, "Why are we waiting" in the street one day. They said "For the sun, Mr. Hitchcock." I thought, Wow, even Hitchcock has to wait for the sun!

Shirley: Anything specific you learned from watching him?
Weir: Only that he had to wait for the sun! Also, to my eternal shame, I thought I knew how to do a shot that he was having trouble with. Fortunately, I didn't say anything to him. I was tempted to say, "Why don't you do it *this* way?" Thank god I didn't! Such is the sort of irrepressible would-be director I think I was. I came back knowing it was a world industry, an international medium. To have even been in Hollywood—on these famous streets, recognizing the locations, even doing some shooting myself. I was proud of that. We were doing 16mm black and white, *but we were shooting*. But, you know, when I came back home, I thought the opportunities were incredible here for a world audience.

Shirley: That's when you found out about the Experimental Film Fund?
Weir: Yes, we had been allocated a grant for *Homesdale* of $1,912. It was obviously worth more, back then. But still, the staggering thing was it

was a *grant*. Obviously it was all for stock and processing. I still begged, borrowed, and stole as much as I could from the Film Unit and other friends. No one was paid. Actors, you see, were all my friends. And I didn't realize it, but as we went along they were resenting this. It was an unhappy shoot, one of the few I've had. Everybody lived at my house. We had a couple of tents and things at Church Point and they lived in the house, sleeping on the floor and whatever. People had to use the showers at certain times, and the lights had to go off at certain times. And when it was over I knew this was the last time I could call on my friends to do this.

Shirley: But this must have invested the film with an on-screen tension?
Weir: Yes, that's true. We were living this thing and people were nasty to each other and cruel and manipulative. It was probably the story feeding life, feeding the story. And the house. We were renting this for fifteen dollars a week. It was a deceased estate, six acres, a wonderful old colonial home, which was the first concrete house ever built in Australia, in 1911. People would say, "It reminds me of something, reminds me of South Africa." Or, someone else would say, a Planter's house in Malaya; or, South America. We were living on the set and with the props. So it was a very romantic setting and very moody. You could make of it what you wanted. So it was a tremendously stimulating place to be, and I guess it gave me the movie really.

Shirley: About that Fund. Were you at all suspicious of the scheme of government subsidy for low-budget filmmakers at that time?
Weir: No! Grateful! It was just as I'd reached that point where I couldn't ask friends to do it anymore, and I was facing the question of how I can go on to other film, other than with the CFU. There was nowhere else for me to go. Here was this fund. I just couldn't believe my luck at being at the right place at the right time. I must have been either the first or second intakes of applicants submitting a script and budget.

Shirley: I understand at one point you were due to play in the *Aunty Jack Show*.[5]
Weir: Oh yes. This was a big shock to Grahame Bond when I came back from that trip to Europe in '71. Perhaps it was also part of my impatience with the CFU. I'd been away six months, on a grant looking at film studios, and travelling. And my life had changed: That trip made me

know that my life was to be in films. And I wrote and I observed. I really worked. And I also saw the *Monty Python Show*. And that made me more certain than ever that I was going to give up the writing and performing side, at least with theatre and television, because they were better than we were. Anyway, Grahame met me at the airport and said we had been accepted for thirteen half hours for the ABC television, for the *Aunty Jack Show*, which we'd done as a pilot for radio. They decided they wanted it as a TV show to replace *The Argonauts Club*. But I told him that I was out. He said, "I can't believe this. Right now?" I mean he was understandably shocked. I said "Grahame, they're better. Have you seen the *Python Show*? They're doing what we do but better." And he said, "Well, so what does that matter?" Which was a fair answer. I said, "No, I've decided I want to concentrate on the film side." So I then had thirteen difficult weeks where I was back at the Commonwealth Film Unit working on documentaries and things; and once a week his show came on, and it was good and was well received. I had a moment's doubt.

Shirley: Did you ever consider working with Grahame after that?
Weir: Well, no it took us years to be able to really talk to each other. Yes, it was a bitter, bitter break. I thought at the time he overreacted. But I think in hindsight I can see his point of view. But I worked and burned the midnight oil, writing *The Cars That Ate Paris*.

Notes

1. Before turning to producing *Picnic at Hanging Rock*, Pat Lovell was well-known to Sydney's television viewers for the children's program *Mr. Squiggle* and the early morning news program *Today*. It was Weir who suggested she join the McElroy twins in producing *Picnic*.

2. In early 1963 Senate Select Committee, led by Senator V. S. Vincent, investigated the state of the Australian film and television industry. The Vincent Report documented its overexposure to American culture and underexposure to Australian local cultural production. Native Australian talent was stifled and driven overseas owing to the lack of local avenues for creative expression. Senator Vincent's Report was emblematic of demands for the development and promotion of culture in Australia. Concessions were made by government and stations for local TV drama. The Sydney Film Festival consequently held its 1964 forum around the theme, "The Australian Film Industry: What of Its Future?" in which Senator Vincent spoke of the need for lobbying to implement the report. Out of this forum came another public forum the following year: The National TV Congress. See Brian McFarlane and Geoff Mayer, *New Australian Cinema* (New York: Cambridge University Press, 1992), 146–49.

3. The other two segments of *Three to Go* were Brian Hannant's *Judy*, starring Judy Morris; and Oliver Howes *Toula*, about a Greek-Australian girl.

4. Thornhill predicted that Weir's "razzle-dazzle" would quickly be consigned to "garbage heap of film history." See Stratton, *The Last New Wave*, 60.

5. *The Aunty Jack Show* was an Aussie version of *Monty Python*. It ran on ABC television from 1972 to '73.

The First Features:
The Cars That Ate Paris

Tom Hogan / 1973

Never before published. Reprinted by permission of Tom Hogan and the National Film and Sound Archives, Sydney.

[Editor's Note: Professor Hogan has kindly offered these introductory remarks to this 1973 interview with Peter Weir.]

I do believe I was the first person to interview Peter Weir for radio (or any other broadcast medium, for that matter). We already knew each other pretty well, because in the late 1960s and early 1970s there developed a strong movement throughout Australia that favored the teaching of screen studies in secondary schools, and we became part of it. I was trained as a high school teacher and film/TV producer, and Peter had already made a number of small but interesting films for television. In 1973, Peter and I were working with film critic John Flaus on a project in Hobart, Tasmania, involving the introduction of more than fifty Tasmanian high school teachers to the new subject of screen studies. I worked with the teachers in television and Peter in film. It happened that our work with the teachers coincided with the opening of Australia's first casino at Hobart's Wrest Point. The opening celebrity act was Jerry Lewis and we invited him to address us during a Wednesday at the local cinema. He agreed, with no fee, and gave a brilliant address. We'd all heard of his knowledge of film on an international basis. Mr. Lewis was generous with his time and offered a Q&A session at the end of his address. Peter was in his element and he and Mr. Lewis engaged in an entertaining and informative exchange of views on filmmaking, directing, and acting. Many present also questioned Mr. Lewis on aspects of our craft but Peter stood out as the leader of the group in that respect. It was a memorable encounter and I've always been grateful to Mr. Jerry Lewis for his erudition and generosity of spirit.

For Peter's first feature, *The Cars That Ate Paris*, he asked me to work as Location Manager. There were a number of his other friends with experience in the audio/visual sphere who were happy for virtually no monetary reward to help a person we thought had enormous potential. By the way, you should know that after Hal and Jim McElroy, the producers of *Cars*, had the film shown in Cannes in 1973, Roger Corman was given the print and said he'd release it in the US market through his New World Company.[1] But Corman reneged on the deal and the film was finally released by New Line Cinema in 1976 with the title, *The Cars That Eat People*. There is a poster you can see of that American version. The film was re-edited without Peter Weir's permission and had added narration. [letter of August 8, 2012]

Tom Hogan: Peter, your *Cars That Ate Paris* sounds like a fascinating project. How did the idea first begin?
Peter Weir: Well, Tom, the first time the idea began to come to me was in France. I was driving through France on a working holiday, a couple of years ago [1971]. And we came to a little section of road. And there was a barricade across the road. There was a heavy mist on the road. There were two men, rather frightening-looking characters behind this barricade. They had the highway jackets on with the red cross on them. They stopped our car. And without saying anything, they directed us down a detour. We immediately took it, naturally enough. But there wasn't any sign of road works or anything happening to the road. The ride just went on ahead on good road. And as I was driving, I said to my wife, "Isn't it funny how we just accepted that situation?" I didn't say to the men, "Why do we turn off here?" Or, "I can't see anything wrong with the road." Or, "Where is your permit?" or something like that. Anyway, it was just a funny thing that turned over in my mind and I wondered what lies ahead. My concern was helped by all this mist swirling about. Later it just wouldn't get out of my mind for some reason: roads, roads, cars . . . and when I got onto cars, I began to collect pictures out of magazines about cars. (I never before had had much interest in cars.) Anyway, some weeks later, we arrived in Paris. I'd been there once before. And like everybody, I found it an incredibly beautiful city. But this time I realized it was a beauty with a cancer, if you like—a cancer of cars. The city was choked with traffic, literally twenty hours a day. It was a nightmare

being there, from the noise and pollution and so on. And so it stuck in my mind that Paris has this beauty, but a marred beauty.

Hogan: Have you written the script yourself?
Weir: It was my original idea, and I worked on it with two collaborating writers. I wrote out a little short story, which is the way I usually work. I was having problems with it so I took it to Keith Gow, an old friend, another director, who works at the Commonwealth Film Unit and Film Australia with me. We worked on that story together and got it into much better shape. Then I took it to a third writer, Piers Davies, who had worked on my last film with me [*Homesdale*]. He lives in New Zealand. I went over to see him with this new version, and we reworked it again. I was having trouble with the ending, so I sent him the first half of the story and asked him to write a second half.

Hogan: So, what sort of contribution did he make to the final script?
Weir: Piers is a solicitor, and writing is a kind of sideline for him. He's a poet really. You see, I work in a very flamboyant, outrageous way, I suppose. I always think up incredible amounts of incidents, amazing events, strange people. And he tones these things down for me. He's very good like that. He says, "But why are you doing this; what's the reason for having this thing happening?" He presents a bit of brake on everything I do. So we, I left New Zealand after ten days with Piers with a very good short story of say, maybe twenty or thirty foolscap pages. About a dozen scenes were blocked out roughly with dialogue. And there were ten thousand details in my mind and in my suitcase, from clothes people might wear to a number of different events.

Hogan: Would you tell us briefly what the film itself is going to be about?
Weir: It's the story of a gang of criminals, for want of a better word, who are making a living off motorcar accidents. It's placed in a small Australian town, although it could be anywhere; because, the motorcar, like television, is one of our international forms of communication. This town has a trap, which it sets at night on a road leading into the town. It's a trap for cars. And then when they catch something in their trap, which operates under the blanket of night, they spot it from a tower. And they send out the recovery, rescue vehicles and bring in the wreck and the dead or injured. They take the wreck into a shed and strip it. Now this takes place in a setting of a kind of depression. While the film is set in

the present, there's this weird mood that reminds one of a 1930s depression. There's an awful blight on the land. You get the feeling there's been an awful economic crisis world-wide, and people are desperately poor. There's a feeling that something awful is going to happen.

Hogan: Just to interrupt for a moment—the film will be a thriller?
Weir: It is a thriller with an underlying social comment on both the sort of capitalist way of life and on motorcars and what we have placed importance on in our society. But that is secondary. Above all, I'm interested in entertainment. And I am interested in telling a story.

Hogan: Now, we're back to the point where that the residents trap cars and apparently live off the proceeds. And where do we go from there?
Weir: It's important that you say, they live off the proceeds. It's not the sort of racket where the big boss is in the city or something and they're making a lot of actual dollars. Given it's an economic crisis, what they're doing is in fact stripping these cars. Various townspeople specialize in various parts of the cars. Someone specializes in the electrical equipment, radios and cassette tapes and so on; somebody in rubber, in the tires; others in upholstery; others in chrome and of course the engines. The women go through the suitcases in the boots and sort the clothes out.

Hogan: So, there's bits and pieces actually sold outside the town and the money comes in from that source?
Weir: Some are, but it's rather more a system of barter and of trade. Yes, you do see cars melted down. For example, you see the old blacksmith, a wonderful old figure of our past in fiction, over this blazing forge with his hammer and so forth. He's busily smashing into hubcaps and melting down fenders and things and making nice little ingots, which probably give the feeling they're going off to another local town. Again, I want to have this overall blanket of some awful economic situation. And these people are desperate and living off what they can. But there is a scene in the milk bar one day, in the Eiffel Tower Café, I should say, where you see a man come in with a brown parcel, one of the townspeople, and he opens it and takes out a pair of patent leather dance pumps and a dinner suit. And he holds them up and sees that they roughly fit the café owner. So, instead of paying the guy cash, he gives him bars of chocolate. A couple of cartons of milk. Some sugar. They strike a reasonable bargain and off he goes.

Hogan: I see. Peter, where do thing go from there?

Weir: Well, into this situation comes our hero, the protagonist of the story, who survives the coroner. A few others have, also. He's caught in the trap and his brother is killed in the accident. So, we then follow him through the rest of the film, through his slow realization of what has happened comes on him. He realizes that he has to turn these people in, or he can keep his mouth shut and perhaps get a bribe of some kind. He chooses this course. The mayor, who controls the whole racket, senses that this character has a weak point. You know the old saying, "Everybody can be bought if the price is right." He discovers what our hero's weakness is. It's not anything obvious like money or metal or anything like that. It's an emotional need; he has no family and the mayor offers him a family. I'm telling too much of the plot! [both laugh] You know the town can't survive like this. You know that there is going to be a fall. That the end is coming and there is a particularly amazing scene of action and chaos at the end when the cars themselves turn on the town and the people. By that, I don't mean it's science fiction. There are drivers in those cars. The drivers of those cars are the children. The young people, the sixteen-, seventeen-year-olds are the killers in the town. These young people have been largely ignored in all the film, we've seen glimpses of them busily making up these monstrous stock cars, monstrous hot rods. And they get into a situation or problem with the town council. They have a confrontation with them and they decide to pay the town back, to get back at them. They attack the town in their cars. And in fact, they do to a degree *consume* the town, they *eat* it. They smash into the buildings.

Hogan: This is really where the film gets its title.

Weir: That's right, yes. And also because they paint faces on the cars. Much like Indians painted war paint on themselves.

Hogan: You'll be shooting in the towns of Sofala and Bathurst, I understand. So I guess the people are going to be very, very important in the film itself.

Weir: Oh heavens, yes. Both in front of the camera as extras and behind the camera. Most certainly. You know, in films you use amateur talent; you look for the right kind of faces or people who can just have a natural way of getting in front of a camera. I'll be looking for those people. I'll be holding auditions in Bathurst as I will in Sofala.

Hogan: When will this be, Peter?

Weir: This will be in September. September is our preparation month. Down in the town, our construction and design team, David Copping, from Sydney, is doing the design. We'll be busy with hammer and nails because we have to build certain parts of the town; obviously, the parts we destroy have to be built first! The townspeople weren't too happy about us destroying their town! So I'll be looking for the cast, first; for cars, second; for car wrecks, three; and for places for us to stay, four.

Hogan: I see. Now, it looks then as if in September, you'll be setting up for production, gearing up for production, looking for people, casting, building sets, and so forth. When does that take place?
Weir: In October. After, of course, the big race, the "Bathurst 500," 'cause there's a real problem there, of course, with accommodation and so forth.

Hogan: It's pretty well all booked out for that weekend.
Weir: That's right. So we're looking for a commencing date, the eighth of October, at this point. We'll be shooting for one month.

Hogan: What do you hope is going to happen then? Will it be only for Australian audiences? Is it for television or cinema?
Weir: It's certainly for cinema. We all hope and we do believe it will go overseas and sell well because everybody has small towns, everybody has motorcars.

Hogan: I suppose it's a big-screen, color production; a feature film?
Weir: Yes.

Hogan: Is it proper of me to ask what sort of money it will cost in Australia?
Weir: Yes, I think the figure is published anyway. I might say at this point the large percentage of the budget came from the Australian government film finance fund called AFDC—the Australian Film Development Corporation, set up to encourage local filmmaking, Australian filmmaking. A very good thing it is too. They've invested $125,000 in the project. And, we're looking for private money now, which we almost have; so it will roundup to the $200,000 mark.

Hogan: And that is while it sounds a lot, it isn't, in fact.
Weir: The costs, as you can imagine, are immense because of the

numbers of people we're bringing up from Sydney. They all have to be paid; they all have to have good accommodation. And with the logistics, the number of cars we build up, and so forth, that money is really very small, when you consider that in America, it's considered that a half million-dollar production is cheap. This film is extremely low budget. The only money that goes out is for the actors we bring from Sydney, and of course laboratories and the technical side; and the food, accommodations, props, vehicles, extras, and so forth.

Hogan: Another question coming up. Peter, apart from David Copping, who you've told us is designing the film, there are two other people with you, the brothers Hal and Jim McElroy.
Weir: Yes, they are the producers of the film. I work with the cameraman, of course. We work out the shots we want and I tell the actors what to do and where to go. The producers' job is to keep the overall production flowing, keep a very close watch on the money, and at this stage find a little bit more money for me.

Hogan: Who of all these people have the most experience with actually shooting a film?
Weir: Well, it varies. They're all in different areas. David Copping, I suppose, has the longest list of credits. He's involved in theatre as well as a designer of the opera, *Don Quixote*—

Hogan: —which is opening at the Opera House.
Weir: And *Ned Kelly*, of course. And he's worked with the McElroys before. This is the first job for the McElroy as producers. Prior to that and on this film as well they're doubling up, doing the work of first assistant director and production manager, both key jobs. My own film experience has been in short fiction films. This is my interest and this is where I've worked. I made a film called *Homesdale*, which was made on 16mm and sold to television. It was a one-hour horror film, a black comedy as they call it. As you're probably beginning to realize, that's my interest, along the Hitchcock lines. That's the closest that I can get to is Alfred Hitchcock.

Hogan: I believe you have actually seen Hitchcock at work in the production of the film *Frenzy*, in England fairly recently.
Weir: Yes, that was in the last year. Yes, I stopped there on the set and it was just amazing to watch him. I introduced myself to him, which was

a kind of funny experience because one doesn't *introduce* oneself to Alfred Hitchcock. [both laugh] You are introduced. I had a little speech prepared to say to him, you know, "I am Peter Weir, an Australian director." Something or other. "I'm interested in your work in suspense." But when I finally confronted him, this living legend, my words came out in the wrong order. They were all there but in the wrong order. So I started to say, "Australia—Ah, that is—Weir—Peter Weir—Mr. Hitchcock—how do you do?—I, film—you." [laughs] He looked at me as if I were something out of the zoo. He said, "Yes, would you like to come back tomorrow?" I didn't attempt to answer or sort it all out.

Hogan: And you didn't have a chance to meet him again?
Weir: No, no. As you can imagine, the man's besieged with students, journalists, fellow directors, and so forth. He hasn't the time or the interest, and he's a very old man and obviously very ill, I should say. But the man just keeps going on. There he is, over seventy, amazing.

Hogan: Okay, let's wrap this up. Any last words about *The Cars That Ate Paris*?
Weir: Just that it's 35mm widescreen color cinema. Its intended to be released internationally and maybe for television sale. It will look much like the foreign films that you see or films from America. We can now do this in this country because we have all the expertise. And we hope that this film will stand up to any foreign product as far as the quality. If I call it a "horror" film, I mean, there's not a lot of blood. I don't agree personally with a lot of tomato sauce splashing across all the screens of the world, these days. I rather think that horror lies in what you don't see rather than what you do see. And this is certainly a film in which it is suggested that awful things are happening, but you don't necessarily see them.

Editor's Note: Professor Thomas Edward (Tom) Hogan, PhD (Macquarie University), MA, BA, Graduate Diploma in Education (Sydney University), Teacher's Certificate (NSW Government, Australia), LTCL (Licentiate of Trinity College, London, Voice Training), has worked professionally as a freelance producer and educator in broadcast radio and in universities worldwide for more than forty years. He has also worked in the Australian feature film industry. He has worked for most Australian radio networks, and for the British Broadcasting Corporation's General Features television division in

London, for whom he also worked as a consultant trainer. The focus of his work outside Australia is on the training of development radio broadcasters and tertiary-level teachers of skills-based curricula in less developed nations. As a Broadcast Radio Consultant, he has worked for the broadcasting divisions of governments in forty-one countries in the Southeast Asia and Pacific regions. In regional workshops in Asia, Southeast Asia, the Pacific, and Australia, he has trained people from an additional fourteen countries. His textbook on radio news, *Radio News Workbook*, first produced for the Australian Film, Television and Radio School in 1985, has been translated into five languages. He is also author of *The Broadcast Writer's Handbook* (AFRTS, 1987) and *Micronesia and the West: Avoiding Cultural Collision* (Friedrich-Ebert-Stiftung, 1988, since revised and updated in 2007).

Notes

1. The McElroy twins were born in Melbourne in 1946. They began working in the film industry as assistant directors for Tony Richardson's *Ned Kelly* in 1971. They were responsible for the development and distribution of *The Cars That Ate Paris* before moving on to *Picnic at Hanging Rock*.

"Weir, Weird, and Weirder Still": The Riddle of Hanging Rock

David Castell / 1976

From *Films Illustrated* 6, no. 3 (November 1976): 92–94. Reprinted by permission of the author.

Until the last few years Australia has been off the map, cinematically speaking, since the overnight collapse of their native industry with the advent of talkies. Even with the period of the last two years, much of the international drum-beating has been done by departments of the Australian government who, with a vision and foresight that is at once admirable and self-shaming, have nurtured the seedling industry with patient care and finance. But it is with *Picnic at Hanging Rock* that Australia truly achieves lift-off: apart from the international acclaim and critical praise, it is simply the most financially successful film ever to have been made in that country.

The director is Peter Weir, a slight, gentle man of thirty-two, with just one other feature, *The Cars That Ate Paris*, behind him. He has a facility for film and a cinematic vision, equaled only in his field by that of Nicolas Roeg (whom, interestingly, he admires greatly). Yet, though his films have actually been set inside Australia, there is nothing national in his themes. Surfing, sheep-shearing, and Swan-swilling, the unholy trinity of antipodean cliché, have no place in his vision. *The Cars That Ate Paris* was a startlingly original fantasy about a community that prospers by the ensnaring and destruction of motor-cars; *Picnic at Hanging Rock* is a period atmosphere piece about a seminary for young ladies and the unexplained disappearance of some pupils during an outing.

The latter is an open-ended film, bristling with enigma, of a kind that would never be countenanced for production in Britain today. "We had three investors," says Weir. "Two of them were government bodies (the Australian Film Development Corporation and the South Australian

Film Corporation) whose express aim is to develop an industry, so only one third of the money was of the type you would have to raise here. So, of course, it is a subsidized idea. It's the sort of film that could only come out of the optimism of a new industry."

The previous Australian film industry crashed when the monopoly situation of British-and-American-owned cinemas coincided with the boom of Hollywood product and Hollywood stars with the introduction of sound films. Overpowered by the big guns from the States and starved of an outlet for the exhibition of its native product, the industry died quietly.

"The new industry bears no relation to the old, it's come about for totally different reasons," says Weir. "I find that I have little interest in its origins; I feel embarrassed when retrospectives are held. It all seems to have very little to do with today. The new industry grew out of the western world youth disturbance of the sixties. We're definitely tied to that mainstream of the hippie people, the flower children, the anti-war movement, the massive pop music boom and the whole do-your-own-thing attitude. It was the Vietnam War that provided the greatest stimulus to young people in the arts and allied areas. The country was divided on the war: it was a clear-cut issue and it provided an atmosphere of tension and excitement the country hadn't known since the conscription issue of World War I. It was a quiet country, a remote country. Suddenly there was violence in the streets. . . .

"People from all walks of life were stimulated to take a point of view. Given that, and mainstream world changes, you had young people deciding *not* to go into banks or insurance companies. They wanted to open furniture shops, or grow vegetables, or move to farms. And we who were interested in films said, simply, 'We'll make films.'

"Film was very much the language of the day, so we borrowed or begged or stole 16mm equipment, got some film stock and persuaded our friends to act in what were then called 'underground films.' Nowadays everything is carefully defined. We didn't define it at the time, we were just a bunch of young people making films. Even the word 'underground' was pretty loosely used. Then a filmmakers' co-operative was formed and the films were hired out for screenings. You still couldn't live off them, but you didn't mind sweeping floors or digging ditches if you could make films at the weekend."

Given this resurgence of interest in the cinema, people of influence a generation or two ahead of Weir and his contemporaries started to agitate. They were the ones who had always been embittered that there was so little culture in Australia and, when they saw the vitality of the new film movement, they lobbied Parliament and government bodies, and started getting the ear of politicians. If you jump in now, they argued, finance these people and set up a film school for future generations, you will succeed in reviving an industry.

"The seed was there," Weir agrees. "It was people and product first, then came the money. I had finished two underground films and was thinking I couldn't go through that experience again. Suddenly there was this thing called the Experimental Film Fund, so I got $2,000 from them for my next film [*Michael*]. I did another one [*Homesdale*] through them, and then a bigger fund was established called the Film Development Corporation, and they helped with *The Cars That Ate Paris* and *Picnic at Hanging Rock*. I found that, as I advanced in experience and proficiency, there was a new type of government fund to match it."

Perhaps the more surprising aspect of this governmental altruism was that it didn't stop short of popular entertainment. *The Adventures of Barry McKenzie* was the first feature made with government money. This and its sequel, plus the *Alvin Purple* sex comedies, got Australian films stereotyped in overseas minds.[1] "I tend to be very defensive about them," says Weir. "I'm not interested in making that kind of film myself, but they were one of the ongoing steps in the growth of our industry. If you take the gap between my last underground film and my first commercial feature, *The Adventures of Barry McKenzie* came right in the middle. It made a lot of money and it brought a lot of Australians out of their houses to see an Australian film for the first time in years. So when my more esoteric subject came up in *The Cars That Ate Paris* they backed it. They certainly wouldn't have done it the other way round."

Weir sees the new Australian cinema as a direct parallel to the new American cinema in Los Angeles. "Once upon a time there was a gigantic gap between the art house film and the commercial film. Suddenly there came out of Hollywood this type of film that could appeal to two audiences, that could have an accessible narrative yet could be full of anything, propagandist or simply bizarre. I shall never forget first seeing *M*A*S*H*, because there were two separate groups laughing in the cinema. Some of us saw it as the first real anti-war film about Vietnam: for others, it was just a good, rollicking service comedy."

Like so many of the young Australian filmmakers, Weir has been on extensive publicity tours in support of *Picnic at Hanging Rock*, trying at the same time to forge new deals for forthcoming projects. "It's usually an ordeal sitting through a film time after time. But because this one is so open-ended, you can actually spend the time in the umpteenth screening speculating and constructing new views of it."

According to Lady Joan Lindsay, who wrote the original book, Weir has brought the mystical element to the fore more than ever she had intended.[2] "She just sat down and wrote the book in her early sixties. She finished it in ten days," says Weir. "It is as though she was possessed to write. She was also extraordinarily enigmatic about the reality of the book. She opens it by saying, 'Whether it is true or not, my readers must decide for themselves. As all the people involved are long since dead, it hardly seems important.' We had to make the decision when it came to the film, so we simply said it was true. Certainly all the characters and the settings were true: every one of those characters lived. And there was a scandal at the school—some dreadful, dreadful thing. Whether it was exactly that, I don't truthfully know.

"I asked Joan Lindsay about it the first I ever met her. She just said, 'I cannot discuss it, I will never discuss it with anyone.' I thought of the tremors and the red cloud that she wrote about, so I thought I would give her a little prod. I cleared my throat and said, 'Would it be going too far, do you think, Lady Lindsay, to say that, up on the rock, a flying saucer might have landed?' She smiled and just said, 'Oh, I think it could have been quite possible.' I don't know if she was having me on or not.

"I think I've settled on my own theory of what happened. The description of the things that happened on the rock are like those that occur when a comet passes near the Earth's surface. If you had taken a liner around the world you might have found that it was super-hot in Chile and that watches stopped. You find an earth tremor in Manila, a very minor disturbance around the globe. In fact, whether it was a comet passing or not, the earth in that area moved slightly. I think that rock literally opened and swallowed them. The girl who survived saw something that was so beyond description—to see into the earth any distance and to see her friends falling—that the mind could not possibly accept what it saw and retain sanity.

"Really the film is as good as your own imagination. Some of the best reactions and comments I've had have been from women. With their so-called sixth sense, their contact with the great mystery of childbirth, women seem to have that extra something to bring to the picture."

Although *Picnic at Hanging Rock* features such Australian actresses as Helen Morse (the star of *Caddie*), Jacki Weaver, and Anne Lambert, its major stars, Rachel Roberts and Dominic Guard, are British. Stressing that they are British characters they were imported to play, Weir is nevertheless concerned with the slow build-up of native stars to accompany the burgeoning industry. "We see the very best of your television and I look with envy at the range of talent available, from the one-line extras through to the stars. Our own stars are only going to get better by doing more films, and they bear the brunt of the curse of the English language. A country like Sweden concentrates on the home market, building up stars like Liv Ullmann and Max Von Sydow and then exporting them. But, of course, an Australian setting up a film has a choice of British or American stars without any language problems.

Already, says Weir, there are signs of hardening arteries in the government munificence. "The more films are made, the more successes, the more conservative the investors are becoming. Both *Picnic at Hanging Rock* and *Caddie* are period pictures, so there are a further eight period pictures in various stages of production. We *created* that trend, but my next project is a contemporary story and although the government body hasn't rejected the application, they are very nervous because it is so 'different.' What they mean is that there is no proven Australian success in that area. Surely they must begin to realize that it's the one who creates the category who is the most interesting, not necessarily the ones that follow."

The project is entitled *The Last Wave* and it's about a solicitor in his late thirties who defends six Aboriginals on a manslaughter charge. It turns out to have been a tribal killing but, while he is defending them, the solicitor has a series of premonitions, waking dreams, visions, all centered on Aboriginals and wartime. "It's a shocking thing for him—a man whose life is entirely based on logic, reasoning, argument, to have it invaded by a paranormal event. It turns out that the only person who can help him is one of the men he is defending. For the Aboriginals, dreaming is just as real as waking. Dreams are messages of great importance. So you have a western white man giving legal aid to the black man, and the black giving spiritual aid to the white.

"I generally end up writing my own materials, because I can't find outside material that suits my particular wish." He thinks it unlikely that this famine will take him to work outside Australia for a while. "I know I'll get offers from abroad, but they won't be the right ones. So I'll probably make a lot of films at home and then, in about ten years, if I'm lucky enough still to be working, the good scripts should start arriving. But I would film anywhere in the world if the story was good."

Apart from Nicolas Roeg ("I reckon I could have made every one of his films, and he could have made every one of mine"), Weir's admiration extends to Kubrick ("the teacher"), Francis Coppola ("he has film in his fingertips"), and Polanski. The fact that most of these directors have worked at some time or other with paranormal subjects isn't the particular pull.

"I'm certainly interested in the paranormal, but not exceptionally so. It's the ordinary that I find difficult to accept. Death is the underpinning thing in all my films. Ever since a very early age, I have found the fact that people die, and that we all walk around accepting it, fundamentally and completely obsessive. Someone once said to me during the flower power era, when I was making underground films, 'The trouble with your films, Peter, is that people are always dying in them. Can't you get away from all this melodrama?'

"Have you seen the newspaper today, turned to the obituary columns? Look at all that melodrama!"

Notes

1. The so-called "ocker comedies" presented an image of raw Australian maleness, crudity, and scatological humor. The taste and lyrical beautify of the early films in the Australian New Wave, particularly *Picnic at Hanging Rock* and Bruce Beresford's *The Getting of Wisdom* (1977), marked a stark contrast to their brash and iconoclastic spirit. See Jonathan Rayner, 60.

2. Joan Lindsay's novel appeared in 1967 and aroused considerable controversy about the purported veracity of its events. Although she claimed to cite actual police transcripts and newspaper reports about the mysterious disappearance of the girls on the Rock, her brief preface hinted otherwise: "Whether *Picnic at Hanging Rock* is fact or fiction, my readers must decide for themselves. As the fateful picnic took place in the year 1900, an all the characters who appear in this book are long since dead, it hardly seems important." See John C. Tibbetts, "Picnic at Hanging Rock," in Tibbetts and James M. Welsh, *The Encyclopedia of Novels into Film* (New York: Facts on File, 2005), 325–26.

For an amusing academic exercise in search of an interpretation of the Rock's enduring mystery, see Saviour Catania, "The Hanging Rock Piper: Weir, Lindsay, and the Spectral Fluidity of Nothing," *Literature/Film Quarterly* 40, no. 2 (2012), 84–95.

The Rock and its environs have proven over the years to be a popular tourist site. Visitors are welcomed at the Hanging Rock Reserve, on South Rock Road, Woodend, Victoria, 3442 (visitmacedonranges.com/natural-attractions/hangingrock). There you can purchase a sequel to Lindsay's novel, *Dream within a Dream*, by Michael Fuery (2012).

Years of Living Dangerously: The Last Wave, The Plumber, Gallipoli, The Year of Living Dangerously

Susan Mathews / 1985

Excerpted from *35mm Dreams* (Australia: Penguin Books, 1985). Reprinted by permission of the author.

[Editor's note: In this second part of the interview, Peter Weir reflects on his feature films, from *Michael* to *The Year of Living Dangerously*.]

"*Gallipoli* was my graduation film," says Peter Weir. It was then, he believes, that his technique caught up with his inspiration. Inspiration is central to Peter Weir's filmmaking: his approach is intuitive rather than cerebral. It is almost a point of honor with him.

Weir's first two films, *Homesdale* (1971) and *The Cars That Ate Paris* (1974), were quirky black comedies, developments of the amateur revues he had been staging in his spare time. *Picnic at Hanging Rock* (1975) and *The Last Wave* (1977) were more conscious attempts to deal with the fragility of commonsense reality with the recognition that "within the ordinary lies the extraordinary." *Picnic at Hanging Rock*, based on the Joan Lindsay novel about the unexplained disappearance of a group of schoolgirls in the last century, was a turning point in the development of the new cinema in Australia: it was the first Australian film that was clearly a "quality film." Weir became the first Australian "auteur" as *Picnic* legitimated Australian movies for the middle-class audience still ready to believe in the inferiority of Australian culture.

Picnic and especially *The Last Wave*, about a lawyer who finds himself psychically drawn to a group of Aboriginals he is defending, reflect Weir's interest in theories of myths and dreams. A concern with ideas and experiences that were outside the realm of common-sense everyday understanding was shared by many people in the sixties. Like many young people at the time Weir was very influenced by the new ways of thinking, and was a strong opponent of the war in Vietnam. Weir's award-winning *Michael*, one section of the 1970 film about youth called *Three to Go*, produced by the Commonwealth Film Unit, is a classic statement of some of those values.

A lapsed radical—"I detest dogma"—Weir nonetheless remains faithful to some of the attitudes of the era. "Just because the decade ends doesn't mean we stop wondering about the enormous gap between the Third World and our world; we don't stop thinking about love or about how to construct some sort of moral system," he says. He is profoundly individualistic: "I always marched in the nonaligned section of the antiwar marches," he affirms, and he is emphatic that his interest in mysticism does not extend to cults that demand abandoning independent thought and action.

Though they came to the conclusion by different routes, Weir shares with George Miller the opinion that "greater detachment is ultimately a freedom" for a director. Aside from making you more vulnerable to the sting of critical rejection, working to intuition rather than to plan can threaten the coherence of a film, as the director risks losing control. After some experimentation Weir has moved away from the "exhilaration" of extreme openness and spontaneity on the set. There is the danger, too, of the filmmaker as "God," to use Weir's term, i.e., someone who can become self-obsesses and place himself or herself at the center of the work.

In *Gallipoli* (1981) Weir employed a more structured approach than before, but his distinctive sensibility did not disappear. The luminous shots of the pyramids under which the Australian soldiers camp on their way to the Turkish battlefield are arguably more potent evocations of the dislocation of past and present, the eternal and the everyday, than the more pointed mysteries of *Picnic at Hanging Rock* and *The Last Wave*. In *The Year of Living Dangerously* (1982), adapted from Christopher Koch's novel about the coup of the Indonesian generals that toppled Sukarno in 1965, there is a harmonious integration of the imagery of the traditional *wayang* puppets into the substance of the story. *The Year of Living Dangerously* sets a fine romance in an authentically turbulent Indonesian setting, the great events of the time moving just beyond the grasp of the Westerners who are the film's subjects. As in *Gallipoli* Weir's interest is in the people rather than the events; his concern is with personal rather than political morality. For some it is his most successful film yet; others are frustrated by the diversity of its concerns and the absence of a clear political stance.

Financed by the giant American MGM movie corporation but produced in Australia by long-lime Weir associates Hal and Jim McElroy, *Living Dangerously* represents one way for a director to work with the American film industry without having to move to foreign territory. The 1980 *Gallipoli* also represented a new approach to financing, being funded entirely by expatriate moguls Rupert Murdoch and Robert Stigwood through their Associated R & R Films.

Weir's personality is clearly stamped on his films, yet he appears to be less engaged in the construction of individual shots than some directors; he prefers to collaborate with a trusted camera operator and director of photography. An important contribution to the look of Weir's films has also come from Wendy Weir, the director's wife, who was credited as production designer on the 1979 telemovie *The Plumber*, and as design consultant on *Gallipoli* and *The Year of Living Dangerously*.

[Weir begins with his account of *Picnic at Hanging Rock*.]

Sue Mathews: The way the Rock is photographed is an important part of *Picnic*—how did you decide on all the locations and angles and so on?
Peter Weir: I went down with the executive producer, Pat Lovell, about a year before the film was made and I took photos of the rock. I remember being quite alarmed when I first arrived there that the rock didn't have an impressive distant view. I had expected, with a rock called Hanging Rock, that there would be some fascinating outcrop that gave the place its name. But it didn't look in any sense threatening or particularly powerful and for a long time I planned to do an optical for a wide shot, where I would matte on a further outcrop of rock above the peak, or even move to another location for wide shots. That bothered me for a long time until one morning when we were going to work there was a particular mist across the plain that gave the Rock that element of drama.

Mathews: Did you shoot that on the spot?
Weir: Yes, we stopped all the cars and sent for a camera and anxiously watched the clock as the sun began to heat up the plain and the mist began to rise, but we managed to get the shot in.

Mathews: How important are painters and paintings to you in conceiving the look of a film?

Weir: I find I gather a folio of prints and photographs before each picture and the walls are covered with them prior to going off to shoot. There can be all sorts of odd things. For example, the whole desert in *Gallipoli* was represented in my own scrapbook by Salvador Dali—those desert landscapes with the huge clocks melting. I always saw Frank and Archie in one of those paintings, walking past one of the clocks.

Mathews: What about Australian paintings?
Weir: I can't recall an image that I carried with me from a particular Australian painting. People often talk of a Tom Roberts influence in *Picnic*, but I wasn't aware of it.[1] I think it's a question of sheer chance—I think I would have as many photographs, postcards, and advertisements as paintings. They are particularly useful for framing and lighting. Sometimes you collect them and you don't quite know why. But I carry the key ones with me, and sometimes show them to the cameraman in a discussion. I was very interested in *Picnic* in a book of photographs by Lartigue, the French photographer and his early experiments with color. There's a sort of desaturated look. We did some tests like that, then pulled back from it. I think any time you're dealing with a technique you explore it to its extreme and then attempt to pull away from it, so it's hardly there.

Mathews: A lot of *Picnic* does seem quite muted and softened.
Weir: That was what I wanted. Wendy worked on a monochromatic look. There's something about strong color in a period film that can disturb. I think it's probably exposure to so many black-and-white photographs.

Mathews: A lot of people remark on a pre-Raphaelite look about *Picnic*. Was that something that you were conscious of at the time in the way you made the girls appear?
Weir: Very much. I knew how they had to look from photographs and paintings. The hard part was finding them. Between Pat Lovell and me, we saw a couple of hundred girls in various States, but by chance we found this particular face, this pre-Raphaelite, nineteenth-century look only in South Australia. You can still see it there—perhaps it's something to do with the way of life. I think of the twenty girls, the large majority were from Adelaide.

It was staggering to see the difference in the girls between Sydney, Melbourne, and Adelaide, in one trip. You found in Sydney and Melbourne you had to go younger and younger to find someone who looked right, but that meant other problems. You'd see a fourteen-year-old Sydney girl who might get away with playing a nineteen-year-old nineteenth-century girl, but even then they often looked wrong. It was partly a question of age but more importantly a kind of serenity, or innocence. I think that innocence is in the story and the faces I was drawn to complemented that. Finally, put those faces in that setting, against that rock, and you've got what the book's about.

Mathews: I've been surprised to hear of classes of schoolgirls today dressing up and going on *Picnic at Hanging Rock* picnics: I had the feeling that the film's point of view was that of an outside observer—almost a voyeur—looking at schoolgirls, rather than coming in any way out of a schoolgirl's sense of herself.

Weir: Films viewed at different times and different places can seem very different—shorter, longer, better, worse, didn't ever know it was so funny. This film is obviously viewed very differently now from then, and by schoolgirls with a different view from others. It is a simple and emotive series of images that obviously are still going to touch some people, perhaps young schoolgirls in particular. It is often hard to remember what you intended at the time—the more powerful and ingrained memory is the difficulty you face with each project.

With much of *Picnic at Hanging Rock* it was clearly dangerous ground I was treading on, given the audience's preconditioning, with a mystery that had no solution. I had to supply an ambience so powerful that it would turn the audience's attention from following the steps of the police investigation into another kind of film. I began some technical experiments (which I continued in *The Last Wave*) with camera speeds for example. So within a dialogue scene I would shoot the character talking in the normal twenty-four frames a second, then I would shoot the character listening in forty-eight frames, or thirty-two frames. I would ask the character listening not to blink or make any extreme movement so that you didn't pick up the slow motion, then I'd intercut those reactions and you would get a stillness in the face of the listener. These things were not discernible to the eye, but you would get this feeling, as you sat in your theatre seat, that you were watching something very different.

With the soundtrack I used white noise, or sounds that were inaudible to the human ear, but were constantly here on the track. I've used earthquakes quite a lot, for example, slowed down or sometimes mixed with something else. I've had comments from people on both *Picnic* and *Last Wave* saying that there were odd moments during the film when they felt a strange disassociation from time and place. Those technical tricks contributed to that.

Mathews: There is a scene during the picnic where Miranda cuts the St. Valentine's cake with a huge butcher's knife. Were they things that were added in as you were going or that you conceived in advance?
Weir: Most of them were preconceived. It was part of the challenge to switch the audience's expectations, and I was forever looking for things like that knife which would build up a mood where anything was possible. I had to do that as there was so little plot. It was to take the idea of the red herring and to embrace that cliché and pass through it and beyond it, to make so many allusions and connections with images that they were no longer red herrings, but something powerful and unknowable.

Mathews: The image of the swan that appears towards the end, representing the vanished Miranda, is that from the book?
Weir: I think it is—it was pretty outrageous. I was always in two minds about whether to leave it in. I think it's like a lot of things—you make a decision and gamble on it.

The Last Wave

Mathews: *The Last Wave* was the film that followed *Picnic*. You've said that the origins of that film lay partly in a conversation with the actor Gulpilil, who plays a lead role in the film.
Weir: Certain scenes in the film were all his, such as those about getting messages from his family through a twitch in his arm—those details were added either by Gulpilil or by Nandjiwarra who played Charlie.

Mathews: How did you find working with Nandjiwarra? When you flew up to Darwin to meet him did you find him willing to talk to you about such things?
Weir: I spoke initially with Lance Bennett who was director of the Aboriginal Cultural Foundation in Darwin. Obviously you can't just turn up in tribal areas and hope to sit down and talk about a movie. Lance listened to the story, he read the script and we had several meetings before he would even consider it. At first he thought we'd be better off dealing with detribalized people, urban people, but he read further drafts and came to believe that this was a worthwhile project and that there was only one man who could help and that was Nandjiwarra, who is a highly respected tribal elder and magistrate on Groote Island.

So he talked to Nandji about it and showed him the script and after some weeks a meeting was set up. They were actually in Darwin with a dance group from Groote Island, practicing prior to leaving for a dance festival in Nigeria. I spent all day with them at Fanny Bay, watching them dance on the beach. I was introduced to Nandji when I arrived. He had a very commanding presence. He indicated that I should come and sit with him and we had tea and smoked cigarettes as his people rehearsed and talked in their language about the rehearsal.

In the first break I turned to him to begin the conversation—I was going to ask what he thought of the script and to expand on it further—and I just looked at that magnificent profile and decided instinctively that I should say nothing at all and left it. That was quite early in the morning and I said nothing all day about it. Then he turned to me at the end of the day and said "can I bring my wife?" And I knew he was going to do the film. He had been assessing me all day. I'd brought up a book to show him, a book of Celtic mythology which had struck a chord with me. And he was interested in that. I wanted in the film to show the contrast between the European without the dreaming and the tribal person with the dreaming, and we talked about some of those things. Later, Nandji changed quite a bit of dialogue and asked for certain things to be put in.

Mathews: Anything that you can remember specifically?
Weir: The dinner scene with the family, which is my favorite scene. It is really constructed by Gulpilil and Nandjiwarra. Nandjiwarra put in all the lines about the law and the law being more important than the man, and that is really the heart of the film. It was a marvelous day's filming, one where you call "cut" and nothing really changes, the conversation continues. In lunch break they didn't particularly care about leaving, the conversation went on between Richard Chamberlain and Nandjiwarra.

Mathews: What was it like for the white actors and for you as a director working with the Aboriginal actors?
Weir: Nandjiwarra has such a powerful presence on the set that in a sense everything came off him when he was working with us. You couldn't help but be aware of him and one of the points of the film was quite clearly demonstrated: that very few of us had ever had any contact with tribal people. There were treasured moments when Nandjiwarra was on the set and one was free to sit with him and have a cup of tea and talk. It was quite a unique way to meet, given also the heightened

drama and tension of a film set—a sort of no-man's land between European and Aboriginal. But it was one of those dangerous situations that occur where the making of the film becomes the film, and that can be an important experience for the film crew, but a lot of it may not be communicated through the film.

Mathews: Did you change much from the written script? How important was spontaneity in what we see looking at the picture?
Weir: Anything with the Aboriginals underwent change. Nandjiwarra was the key. In accepting to do the film, he accepted the principle of recreating a lost Sydney tribe and their symbols and tokens. Initially we made the naive request to use some of his tribal symbols to which he said absolutely not, nor should we use any existing tribal symbols, nor should we use any of our collected paintings and drawings of the vanished Sydney tribe. So Goran Warff, the art director, created a fictional series of symbols and Nandji approved them.

Nandjiwarra had completely grasped this difficult idea, given his perception of the world, of what "fiction" is, of what a fiction film is and how it can give you a truth within its own set of lies. Some of these concepts were very difficult to get around—the idea of *mulkrul*, for instance. It was a word Gulpilil used to describe the other white people who'd come here before the Europeans; and Nandjiwarra had another word for those people. That was the fascination of this film—Heyerdahl's theories that the sea is a highway and there have been many groups and civilizations who have crossed to other countries and perished or stayed briefly or whatever. And that led me to what I think was probably too complex in the film: the possibility of a South American contact, and the idea of *mulkrul*.

Mathews: Because it was your own script were you more open to making changes than if you were working with something written by another person?
Weir: Firstly, it was co-written by Tony Morphett. Looking back we should have gone to another draft because I found myself rewriting it during the shooting, which is a hellish experience.

Mathews: It did well in America.
Weir: Yes, on the "art house" circuit. It has its adherents, and there are those who admire it, particularly in America, much more so than *Picnic*. I haven't seen it for many years, I haven't been game to look at it.

The Plumber

Mathews: The next film you made was the TV movie *The Plumber*. Do you see that as a transition?

Weir: I think it was more a case of saying I could go back to something. *The Plumber* belonged way back with *Homesdale*. It was done very quickly and with no fuss, to go straight into television without the attendant excitement of a cinema release with all its highs and lows. It reached an audience and played and I thought that's great, I've got that possibility of working on teleplays.

I have another short story written that I could do in that style at any time I want to. The change I'd make is to have it on a channel that didn't have commercial breaks. I would only do it as a complete piece, or with one interval in the middle. *The Plumber* was made from one end to the other and played much better that way, given the tension that built up in the piece and the claustrophobic setting. If I could control my feature films on television I would. My plan would be to take a lower fee and hold on to the television rights around the world and only sell them to people who make one break. But I don't know if it was any sort of "transition."

Mathews: I suppose what seems transitional is that while there are mythical elements, as in your earlier films, you seem much more distanced from them.

Weir: Well firstly, it was written because I needed the money, which is sometimes a good way of doing things. It is a true story, though that is irrelevant to the audience. The couple were friends of mine and the plumber was based on someone I'd given a lift to once, hitchhiking, and except for the singing in the bathroom and the ending it is pretty much as it happened.

In reality the plumber did leave, but my friend told me, "the strange thing was that it brought out in me a kind of deviousness, a desire for the survival of my mental state that led me to consider doing really drastic things." She was an anthropologist, studying those things, so I didn't editorialize. Her story about the incident in New Guinea when the chap came into her room, performed his ceremony or whatever and she tipped milk on him, was all from her thesis. I always thought of recounting that incident as an overture—to indicate that it was all going to happen again.

And she had found herself treating it as some ritualistic thing. Like the fascination with the head of a weaving snake—she really, for her own self-knowledge, had to go through it. She had a certain pride and strength, she was not going to be forced out by this man. And obviously with a situation like that she swung wildly between that and thinking "I'm going crazy with this whole thing, it is as straightforward as others see it."

Mathews: I suppose it seems fairly obvious, but the water motif and the idea of water going berserk is something that has recurred in your films. . . .

Weir: In *Living Dangerously* there was a pool scene and I thought I should cut it out because people had begun to comment on my recurring use of water images. But it's in the book so I went with it. I love working with Ron Taylor who's shot a couple of underwater scenes for me; I'd like to do a film with him sometime, all set under the sea.

Gallipoli and Year of Living Dangerously

Mathews: There is an important underwater shot in *Gallipoli*, which followed *The Plumber*.

Weir: That came from the fact that when I first went to Gallipoli I did begin a day down at the beach and swam underwater and was struck by the idea that they had this other particularly peaceful world, where you could float underneath the battlefield so to speak. Down there nothing had really changed. Then I became intrigued when some old soldier told me about being underwater when they were shelled.

Mathews: Did you know when you visited Gallipoli that you were going to make the film?

Weir: No, but I knew my next film was going to be on the First World War. Probably France. Had it been set in France, it could have been more fictional because so little was known about it, it would have been an entirely different sort of film. The visit changed all of that and I left the peninsula knowing that the film would be about Gallipoli.

Mathews: Did being there give you a different sense of Gallipoli and what it means for us as Australians?

Weir: Not at the time. I was really quite confused by my own emotion there. It took a lot of thinking about. I felt an overwhelming emotion on the evening of the first day and was puzzled about that. I'd had no relatives there, I'd been in battle areas before—I kept thinking it's ridiculous. I think the only comparable feeling I've ever had was at Pompeii which

I'd visited back in '65. At Gallipoli, you have an archaeological site really, and it is quite untouched. It's a military zone, no farming and no tourists to speak of because it's so difficult to get to. The war graves are carefully tended, and sited where the men fell.

Mathews: Are there remnants of the trenches still there?
Weir: They are all still there. Now they are only knee deep, but you can wander through the key areas and make your way down Shrapnel Gulley, and you do find a lot of relics there. I brought back a few things. There was a bottle I used in the film and some pieces of shrapnel.

Mathews: Why do you think Gallipoli has become so important as a theme in Australian culture and ideas?
Weir: It was "the birth of a nation." Not just the battle and our part in it, but most importantly the referendums on conscription. The troops had landed at Gallipoli in April 1915, and the first referendum on con-scription was in 1916. I think that during that twelve months people in Australia had absorbed what had happened over there. It became part of the "no" vote from the people in the face of the establishment calling for a "yes" vote to conscription in this hour of Empire's need. And they were so obviously staggered at the "no" that they called for the second refer-endum and got another "no." It was the beginning of a turning away from the Empire.

Mathews: The relationship between the two boys is the central experi-ence of the film—was that emphasis something you got from talking to the returned soldiers?
Weir: Yes, given that there are very few firsthand accounts. That and the diaries of the soldiers, as compiled by Bill Cammage in a book called *The Broken Years*. It was a way of looking at "mateship." When David Wil-liamson and I first looked at it, it seemed a kind of taboo subject, almost too worked over to deal with, but the film became a way of understand-ing mateship.[2] That's what must have driven us because the drafts be-came successively less complex as we stripped one element after another out. Earlier drafts dealt with wide aspects of the battle; from Churchill and the meetings of key figures in London, through to the conscription issue.

Mathews: How important to the concept of mateship is the fact that it's exclusive of women?
Weir: It's fundamental. You have to look at the isolation of the outback

settlements with women having to cook and have the children, the men going off to work with other men. Mateship came from the bush. Although the bushmen may not have been the majority in the first Australian Imperial Force, Australia's volunteer army, they gave the AIF its flavor. The songs, the poems in the *Bulletin*, and so on were all drawing from their experiences and attitudes. It's often said of male filmmakers that we don't deal effectively with women. I think what's more to the point is that we don't deal effectively with emotion, with feminine aspects of the personality, which are also contained in the male. In a stridently heterosexual, macho society, these are doubly dangerous things to deal with, because they can be easily misconstrued.

Mathews: Why did you choose to set the early scenes in Western Australia?
Weir: In the final attack scene the wave we wanted the boys to go out in was West Australian. The first two waves went fairly quickly, but that third wave had that twenty-, twenty-five-minute wait to see if the attack would be cancelled. They were West Australian boys and the words of the officers sending them out was very close to the lines in the film.

Mathews: Why was the desert so important as a setting for part of the lead up to the departure for Gallipoli?
Weir: It always felt right. At one point we'd planned to intercut the early outback scenes of Archie with scenes of Frank and his group working in Perth, contrasting city life with the country. But part of the process of stripping it down, refining it, was getting Frank out into that setting. I wanted to give the film that more abstract start—it was an interesting way to approach a great European war. It also seemed more truthful, given the importance of the men from the country in the AIP so I tried to free it from a period feeling to increase that abstract quality. I kept the costumes to things like khaki shirts, avoided scenes of city life with cars, horses and carts, and so on. In a sense the "three acts" of the film took place in three deserts: the Australian desert, the Egyptian desert, then the desert of Gallipoli—and over each was that clear blue sky.

The Year of Living Dangerously

Mathews: Your next film *The Year of Living Dangerously*, was set in Asia. For many people in Australia an interest in Asia and in Eastern ways of thinking began in the sixties. Was that the case for you too?
Weir: No, not really. On my first trip to Europe in 1965 the first foreign

port was Colombo. I only spent a day there but it did have a great impact on me. My interest has increased with the years, and further travels.

Mathews: How did you make the decision to make *The Year of Living Dangerously*?
Weir: I don't know—you're going back to a choice made in 1978, prior to doing *Gallipoli*, when I took the rights out. So it's always a curious thing that you make a choice to do something on a certain inspiration at a time, then you find you're dealing with it two or three years later, with certain changes of perspective. I was excited by the book, that was the starting point.

Mathews: One of the most interesting aspects of *The Year of Living Dangerously* is that it is set very much in an Asian context and yet the sensibility of Billy Kwan, which is so central to the film, is essentially a Christian sensibility. Do you identify with his attitudes?
Weir: Only some of them—I think that's what I found interesting about the character. I've certainly softened him rather—I think he was less likeable in the novel. What I did like about Billy was his talk about the *wayang*, the Indonesian shadow puppet plays, and its possibilities.[3] I feel Billy finally perishes because he gives up his own belief in the *wayang*. It was the Eastern aspects I was drawn to, not the Western, but they are in opposition and that is part of the story. I just altered the balance in the mix. And Linda Hunt, who played Billy, altered it further.

Mathews: Making the Chinese-Australian dwarf, Billy Kwan, an androgynous sort of character represents a real change from Christopher Koch's book where I gather he is a much more unequivocally masculine figure.[4]
Weir: I needed to equal the originality of Koch's creation in the novel. It was an accident or rather sheer desperation that led me to Linda though now it seems to form a sort of pattern. I was dealing with an almost mythical character—something like a Grimm's fairy tale character who had been transformed by a witch into a hunchback, or a frog. Then of course, there's Beauty and the Beast and Quasimodo. I had to ask myself how important was the question of height, because on screen, close up, the height difference would be far less perceptible, so even casting a very short man (which had proved very difficult) would not capture the feeling I needed. I needed something more. I did at one stage contemplate putting a hunchback onto the character, going much further in

a grotesque physical way to make him a prisoner of the body. I got very excited when I began to think of the incredible implications of casting Linda. So I built the film around that and embraced that casting. A risky decision, but it paid off.

Mathews: Certainly many people who don't know that Linda Hunt is a woman read the character as a man.
Weir: I've had all the reactions and they all seem to join up to the same point: finally it doesn't matter. Her performance is what matters.

Mathews: The image of the *wayang* is carried through in the love story and the interaction between the characters. How happy do you feel with the translation of that imagery in the political sphere. Were you trying to develop it in the same way?
Weir: It was an interesting background for me. There was a glimpse of a dictator who had begun with all the best intentions, and a quick sketch of a patriot, Kumar, giving another angle on "communist" which is such an emotive word. But they were quick sketches, they didn't really interest me terribly. I wanted a rather timeless setting in that background. The film was about Asia to me, and the background was to reflect that. I always felt that if you didn't know anything about it, it wouldn't matter. But I don't think you are ever truly happy with a finished film. It was a complex adaptation and over a dozen drafts David Williamson and I were constantly altering the balance of the elements. I think there is enough of the political story there, but you often have to look into the frame to find it.

Mathews: So the specifics of the coup in Indonesia were not of primary concern for you?
Weir: They gave rise to certain attitudes and reactions from the characters, as with *Gallipoli*.

Mathews: You were asked some years ago about the similarity between your work and Nicholas Roeg's and you observed that Roeg uses sexuality as part of the tension in his films where you use other systems. But in *Living Dangerously* you decided to deal with sex directly.
Weir: It was part of the story; it was simply appropriate to use it. I was quite interested to take it on as it was my first attempt at that kind of relationship. I think it is probably there in my earlier work—there is obviously a sexual tension in *Picnic at Hanging Rock*.

Mathews: The character of Guy Hamilton in *The Year of Living Danger-ously* makes a decision that is fairly unconventional in movie terms in that he chooses to join Jill Bryant and leave Indonesia, abandoning the chance of reporting the biggest story of his career. The character of Jill Bryant herself is fairly unconventional—less passive and mindless than many female film roles.

Weir: I made some quite major changes from the character in the novel—I didn't see the Jill of the novel, I didn't like her. And so I worked with Sigourney Weaver on constructing a woman that we found inter-esting—a combination of strength and femininity.

Mathews: In the book she is pregnant when she gets on the plane. It makes a very big difference that she is not pregnant in the film.

Weir: I thought it would be dangerous in a movie: I don't know how one would ever separate guilt from desire in the action of Hamilton in joining her. It is desire not just for her, but to rejoin his own personality. He is like a man who has lost his shadow towards the end; the only way he can ever continue to be a good journalist and a complete human be-ing is to take that plane. It was one of those significant choices, which Hamilton might have found hard to explain to people, those who could not comprehend his leaving the job. It is in those lines of Kwan's: "why can't you give yourself; why can't you open yourself up; why can't you learn to love?" They are from the novel and they seem to me to be true.

Mathews: The filming of the last sequence seems to get a mixed reaction from people who watch it. Had you always had that ending in mind?

Weir: Yes. It never changed. I always knew it was unfashionable. One of my favorite moments in the film is the mid-shot of Mel as he crosses the tarmac. We did several takes and I think the only thing I asked him to do was to smile, which was the only major development in the scene. I said, "I can't describe it, but there's a special smile, a kind of release. Not from getting out of customs, but in a sense of rejoining yourself; it's like two images that come together." And he did that thing of tipping his head back . . . and to me the film was over.

It's what the film has been about. I realize that some people don't fol-low the clues through from the beginning and the danger is that if you expect the film to conform to a traditional genre or to one's own view of life and people, then all the earlier fragile elements will be missed and the result will be confusing. Some of the more didactic critics asked in their reviews "what kind of film *is* this—is it a love story, is it a thriller, is it a political story?" You could say that it unsuccessfully fails to fuse these elements, but to ask why deal with all those elements together, why not choose one of them, reveals a view of life and films that is very different from my own.

Some said "oh yes, here we have the old moral malaise of the Westerner, the dilemmas from the sixties that we're all so familiar with." But I'm sorry, these issues don't just go away—we don't stop wondering about the enormous gap between the Third World and our world; we don't stop thinking about love, or about how to construct some sort of moral system, and all those elements are touched on within the film. Most of my films have been left incomplete, with the viewer as the final participant: I don't like the didactic approach. One is constantly left wondering and I love it when that's done to me in a film.

Working on the Set

Mathews: Do you consciously do things to engender an atmosphere on a set? Do you have established approaches at the start of a film?
Weir: I think it just happens. An extraordinary feeling of the proximity of chaos hovers around a film set. That is dangerous to the director because it is all-pervasive and you can get very rattled. People are under great stress and are very excited and determined to do their best. I presume it's true on every set: the feeling that you have been selected for this position and that you're going to have to prove your worth. And in the early days of a shoot people trip and knock things over—the old jokes about people on the set bumping into lamp-stands are literally true—until the unit is in rhythm, which sometimes doesn't happen until quite late. Then everything settles down, but in those early weeks it can be very chaotic and you need to develop your own approach to combat that, to harness it, or your ideas can begin to disintegrate.

Mathews: Shooting on location must make a difference to the atmosphere of the film, as opposed to being in a town.
Weir: If the weather's good and the period is not too extended it can be wonderful. For example during the week that we shot all the outback scenes for *Gallipoli* we were in a caravan city attached to an old cattle station. The weather was perfect: hot during the day and crisp and cool in the evening. We had log fires and people told yarns or sang songs. With *Picnic* we started off in Mount Macedon where we were billeted in various old guest houses. It was a beautiful area—it was idyllic. On the other

hand shooting in Manila, where we were on location with *Living Danger-ously*, was very arduous.

Mathews: Francis O'Brien, the American executive producer on *Galli-poli*, commented on the degree of democracy in that production, and as a general characteristic of the Australian film industry as opposed to the American. Is that something you're aware of?

Weir: I'm sure its cultural. In Britain, and to a degree in America, they do call the director "sir," and some of the older Australian crew members who'd gone through foreign features here used to call me "sir" in the early days, to my amazement. I said "don't worry about that" at one stage, but then I realized that's as much an affectation as wearing a baseball cap, in the Australian context. In America it's very highly competitive, people have really fought their way up and won the right to be in the position of assistant director or cameraman or whatever, and there can be a much larger degree of compartmentalizing, and respect for those above you. And a keen awareness that you can be fired, which is much more the American way.

That's not been the case in Australia. Obviously we couldn't do it, we've had to inspire each other—in the seventies there was one of everybody. We were all learning together in those early days, so you were pooling knowledge, with that one common desire to make the picture look as good as anything from anywhere else. But more importantly it's probably just part of our way of doing things—you can see it in the army during the war; there was much more negotiation between officers and men in the Australian forces than in the British.

Constructing the Pictures

Mathews: The relationship between the director and director of photography seems to be a very key one. You've worked a lot with Russell Boyd. [See the Boyd interview near the end of this book.] Have you developed a special way of working together?

Weir: Yes. Of course, until *Living Dangerously* there was also Johnny Seale who was a very important part of the camera team as camera operator. He is now working as a director of photography. So it was really very much Russell Boyd, John Seale, myself, and Wendy Weir. Few people realize when you talk about the lighting of a picture you must also talk about what light is falling on. Here two important aspects come into play: firstly, and most importantly, it's the faces that are being photographed, whether extras or key cast; and secondly, the settings into which they are placed. That team interlocked very well. Russell would light those faces very well, would respond to the faces and the setting, and John Seale would move the camera beautifully amongst and through and around them. Wendy has looked after color on all those pictures. Not only the color of the sets and the costumes but the key colors of the film—in *Gallipoli* for example, you have sand, khaki, and blue. And Russell is absolutely superb in exterior situations. You'll find a number of cameramen who are very good with candlelit ambience in a room, but there are very few people who can use a landscape well. To work in the middle of the day in Australia where you've got that harsh overhead sun which is a very unflattering light and to turn it somehow to advantage takes real skill. In the films that we've done together, I think particularly of the actual picnic in *Picnic at Hanging Rock*. That was done over a period of a week for one hour only, I think between twelve and one, when Russell found the light was at its most interesting. He scrimmed a parachute silk or something above them to soften the light. The techniques are well known but the difference is that it took, with a very low budget, an enormous amount of clever juggling of the schedule and Russ's insistence that we shoot only at that hour to capture that look which became a key element of the film. And also, I think of his photographic work in the scenes of the boys crossing the desert in *Gallipoli*, and the way he used the light in those sequences.

Mathews: Where are the decisions about the composition and framing of a shot made? Do you look through the camera much yourself?
Weir: It depends on the operator. When you build up a strong rapport as I did with Johnny Seale—we worked together on *Picnic, Last Wave*, and *Gallipoli*—you don't need to look very often. I don't do a story board because for me a lot of the pages are blank. There are sequences which I know must look a particular way, and those ones are easy: I'd say "I want to do it this way" and Johnny would look through and improve it. But with scenes that were unplanned, I'd throw myself into the rehearsal and Johnny would watch closely and then I'd turn to him and say "what do you think of that? Did you see her when she turned?" and he'd have got all those things.

So, in other words, the ideas would come from me but the framing and realization were often John's. I was constantly impressed with the way that he would take that idea, and with a different framing, he would come up with a new idea. And given that as a director you want to conserve energy and throw yourself into breaches in the wall, so to speak, I could leave a lot of the framing and movement to John.

Mathews: You will actually play music on the set while a scene is shot? **Weir:** Quite often. Though I think it's only a last resort during the actual shooting. And I'll only do it if I know that the music won't disturb the cast, otherwise I'd be imposing a mood on them which might inhibit their performance. But it's a way of blocking out the creak of the camera dolly, the ping of insects on the lights, or the sound of distant laughter from outside the studio. It's a way of detaching them, and me, from the dozens of pairs of eyes that are watching, and it helps me to fight back the overwhelming weight of ordinariness that surrounds you in daily life, to recall the inspiration. For some actors, of course, it's of no particular interest. Mel Gibson, for example, finds it curious that I play odd bits of music, but it's not his music and he's not particularly interested—he doesn't need it and I keep it away from him.

Mathews: How do you measure the success of a film for yourself? How important is it that a film does well at the box office? **Weir:** In the end I look back to see how close I've come to capturing the original inspiration. The percentage of success varies from film to film. As for the box office, it's like they say—luck and timing.

Notes

1. Tom Roberts (1856–1931) was a prominent Australian painter. He painted a considerable number of fine oil landscapes and portraits. Perhaps his most famous works were two large works *Shearing the Rams* and *The Big Picture* (a group portrait of the first sitting of the Australian Parliament in 1901.

2. A thorough discussion of "mateship" is in Marek Haltof, "In Quest of Self-Identity, *Gallipoli*, Mateship, and the Construction of Australian National Identity," *Journal of Popular Film & TV* 21, no. 1 (Spring 1993), 27–36. David Williamson was a Melbourne playwright who worked on scripts for Peter Weir's *Gallipoli* and *The Year of Living Dangerously*.

3. The *wayang kulit* is one of the oldest of the world's storytelling traditions and is still prominent in the Javanese popular culture. Leather puppets are manipulated before a large white screen enacting stories of the lives and fates of gods and men. This tradition underlies *The Year of Living Dangerously*; and the character of Billy Kwan tells Guy Hamilton, "Did you see my *wayang* puppets? . . . If you want to understand Java, you'll have to understand the *Wayang*." Guy himself symbolizes the *wayang* puppet "Arjuna," the warrior"; and Billy sees himself as "Semar," the dwarf who serves Arjuna. See the discussion of the *wayang* in Jonathan Rayner, *The Films of Peter Weir*, 137–41.

4. C. J. Koch's novel was published in 1978. Before that he had been a radio producer for the Australian Broadcasting Commission. For a comparison of novel-to-film, see James Van Dyck Card, "The Year of Living Dangerously," in Tibbetts and Welsh, 512–13.

Interview with Peter Weir

Luisa Ceretto and Andrea Morini / 1999

Excerpted from *I quaderni del Lumière* 30 (1999). Reprinted by permission of the authors. Thanks to Erik Battaglia of Turin, Italy, for assistance in preparing this interview.

Ceretto and Morini: Could you give us a general background covering the influences on you of films and filmmakers?

Peter Weir: Growing up I think my great stimulation was nature. I lived by the water, so swimming, rocks, and all the elements, the landscape itself, became one's art gallery. When I was very young, it was my father who fostered my love of story-telling. He was a master story-teller and he made up tales that in one case ran for a year or more—they were in the form of a serial, fifteen minutes a night before I went to sleep. The best of these was a pirate story, and fragments remain with me to this day. I would go to sleep with my head spinning with giant squid and shipwrecks and doubloons and marooned sailors. This was my film school! As you know, I didn't go to film school. There was no national film school then, and apart from the Sydney Film Festival and regular visits to the movies, I knew nothing of the history of cinema. I'd grown up with a love of movies developed at the Saturday matinee. Westerns were my favorite, followed by gangster films, and I especially loved the Hammer horror movies. When television came in 1956, I was twelve years old and that had a huge impact on me. I used to annoy my father by insisting that all the lights at home be turned off just like a real movie theater, and there could be no talking during the show. My mother opposed the switching out of the lights, as she'd heard you could go blind watching TV without a light on. I was enthralled with the medium, and it was an era of great programs. I loved *Hitchcock's Half Hour*, *The Twilight Zone*, and the Westerns. Also the television plays and the mid-day movie, which I only saw when I was home sick in bed, which was often, as I suffered, conveniently, perhaps, from asthma.

Ceretto and Morini: Later, of course, your career began with television. . . .

Weir: That was a long time ago, and it was a different country, neither better nor worse, just different. Quieter, more conservative, more 1950s than 1960s. The war changed all that. I mean the Vietnam War. We had troops there and the country was divided in its support of the war, and this conflict accelerated change. There was the growth of the "youth culture" that we're all familiar with from this time, but the impact on my own country was profound—suddenly, it seemed, there was a growth spurt in the Arts, in particular in film. The rebirth of the Australian cinema had its roots in this period, further stimulated by the Sydney Film Festival, which brought one of the great periods of world cinema to our doorstep.

Ceretto and Morini: Is this when you began making films?
Weir: We filmed sketches for live stage shows, and I'd direct those. That led me in 1967 to make my first short film—*Count Vim's Last Exercise.* I wanted it to look "professional," and yet I had no money for sync-sound and lights and so on, so I decided to make it look like a government documentary, with a simple narration. I invented a government department called "The Department for the Final Solution to Old Age." They basically executed people, with their willing cooperation, at age sixty-five. That way, the State saved on old-age pensions. It was a kind of comedy! It was also pretty bad, but few people were making films then, so by default it seemed impressive. This was stuff often shot at twelve frames a second, sort of Chaplin style. I also edited the clips, cutting 16 reversal with no security of a negative! Just put on the white gloves and cut the film with trembling hands. A great way to learn the basics, but not without tension as I really had no idea what I was doing. . . .

Ceretto and Morini: What else were you learning that stood you in good stead for your first Australian feature films?
Weir: You have to be sensitive to the differences in environments and cultures. All your senses become so acute when making a film; you hear and see in a different way. It's a kind of trance, I think! You're both "open" and "focused" at the same time. I found myself in another world working with aborigines in *The Last Wave*. Crucial to my understanding of that culture was an initiated tribal member and a magistrate on Groote Eylandt in the Gulf of Carpentaria in the far north of the country. He was named Nandjiwarra Amagula and played the old man. The

aborigines around him weren't professional actors, either. They came from his tribe. It was a complicated process of finding people who were prepared to take part. I had to go through a government agency and many meetings before I was sitting opposite Nandjiwarra in Darwin and talking through the film with him. English was not his first language, of course. He called me a European, not a white man. He was the only tribal man capable of understanding what I was doing. We spent most of a day and evening together. Lots of long silences! It was in those silences that I felt he was "auditioning" me, as it were!

Ceretto and Morini: Did he ask for any changes in the screenplay?
Weir: Only on one point. Nandji was anxious that the white lawyer [Richard Chamberlain] should declare that "the Law is more important than the Man." I realized that for him this was the most important element in the film. The inroads of Western life on traditional culture, particularly on the young aborigines, was of great concern to him. The Law was at the heart of the very Culture itself; and it was necessarily more important than any individual. Without this Law the Culture would not survive. For the Western, liberal lawyer, this struck at the very core of his belief—that the law must *serve man*, and if it did not, it should be altered. Here was the clash of the two cultures, and with the inclusion of Nandji's request (in the scene where Nandji and David dine with the lawyer and his wife) I had the heart of the dilemma raised in the film. In other scenes, where there was a lot of night shooting, we would often sit together, again mostly in silence. Then occasionally in answer to a question of mine, he would tell me things about tribal life and Culture, as they call it, which were startling. These moments were brief, like suddenly tuning in a short-wave radio to a remote frequency before contact was lost. I tried with frantic rewriting to put many of these revelations into the story. I partly succeeded, but for me those conversations were often more interesting that what I was shooting. But there are traces there, particularly within the center of the film, which are unique to this collaboration. Nandjiwarra saw the film in Darwin. "Very powerful," was all he said. But it was enough.

Ceretto and Morini: Quite a different culture from, say, Indonesia, in *The Year of Living Dangerously*!
Weir: You have lines about "becoming children again" when entering the slums of Jakarta. Which brings me to the character of "Billy Kwan." It was the casting of Billy Kwan that caused so many headaches. The

description of him is almost that of a child, not quite five feet tall. The actor I originally cast didn't work out with Mel [Gibson] who asked for a different actor. So I flew to the U.S., since we'd exhausted possibilities in Australia, Hong Kong, and London. I had to find the actor or risk delaying, even cancelling the film. It was like Cinderella's slipper—every kind of short actor tried to make it work, without success. Finally, the casting director read out the description of a New York–based actor who had all the right qualifications physically, who was highly experienced and available. "Show me the photo!" The actor—or actress—was Linda Hunt. We met with Linda in New York. I liked her immensely and we wondered about rewriting it for a woman, but this was improbable in Jakarta in 1965 and anyways presented all sorts of other problems. But, what made it work, apart from Linda's wonderful reading of the lines? Was it the female sensibility inside the body of a man? Was it the deception itself, the mystery of it? I don't know, but it worked, and we both agreed to give it a try. Linda said to me, "I'll do it, but only if your confidence in me never wavers." And it never did. She went on to win the Academy Award for best supporting actress.

Ceretto and Morini: In a way that brings us to your American experiences. More new environments and cultures, as you say?
Weir: Well, after a number of pictures in Australia, I thought I was growing stale and thought it was the right time to go and make a picture in America. I was looking for fresh landscapes; to be, in a way, a foreigner, a "stranger in a strange land." I love what Hitchcock said in an interview in response to a question about being English and working in America—"A film is its own country," and I think that's true. That was in response to a questions I'd be asked at that time by the press in Australia—"How do you deal with the American studio system when they try to make your ideas fit the commercial mold?" To which I'd reply, that no one can influence me in a way I think wrong for the story. In that sense, the challenge lies with you, the filmmaker, whether you're working in Sydney or L.A. You have to push yourself creatively.

Ceretto and Morini: Several of your American films dealt with singular communities. Like the secret cave of the boys in *Dead Poet's Society*.
Weir: Yes, the society in the cave was like some sort of primeval culture. I was first struck by the description in the screenplay of the boys sneaking off at night and making their way through the forest to the cave. My assistant director had planned one night's shooting based on the

description. I asked for more time, because I intended to enlarge it. These hooded figures (I always saw them hooded, like monks) fascinated me. Something primeval, as if they were going back in time, something to do with the cave, and secret societies, ancient rites—all these things came to mind from reading that passage in the screenplay. Another example was the Amish community in *Witness*. Unlike the Australian aborigines, I was unable to film the Amish. This Fundamentalist Protestant sect has many rules at odds with modern life, one being that no photographs be taken of them. You never get used to the extraordinary sight of a horse and buggy filled with Amish in their basically nineteenth-century clothing, out shopping in the streets of a modern American town. The whole area was like a living museum of a way of life we all shared for centuries. They were gentle people, simple farming folk, and very interested in doing business with us! We rented buggies, bought old clothes, and a lively trade developed. This was briefly interrupted when a meeting of the Elders forbad any further contact with the film company. But they're a pragmatic people, and their rules can bend a little under the right circumstances; and a few days after the banning, a knock was heard at the motel door late at night—"Want to hire some more buggies?" I remember the sight of a line of black hats on the horizon, observing us, like some native population keeping watch on the invader.

Ceretto and Morini: We can't close this out without some comments on your use of music. You must have a very eclectic taste. . . .
Weir: Music is the fountainhead of all the arts for me. If you'd asked me one of those trick questions like, "What would you be if you weren't a film director?" I'd have answered, "composer." Take the Pakistani singer Nusrat Fateh Ali Khan. His music is religious, and even though I can't understand the language, there's such power in his voice, so much emotion. I would play him while going to work on *Fearless*, sitting there in the car listening on my walkman, volume turned up. It would fill me completely and then I would come on set and be ready for the day's work. It was like a transfusion of creative blood.

Ceretto and Morini: How would you use music when you edit the film?
Weir: When you begin cutting, you have to accept constant disappointment until you get THE cut. Sometimes it happens very early, although in my experience this rarely happens; usually it's a struggle. The music can help you in teasing out a truth that's not always evident; and it's

one of the tools I use. I watch each cut with the sound turned off to see how the story is coming over through the images alone—an influence from watching silent movies. I often play music, as the combination of pure sound and image is enormously helpful in understanding what the movie wants to be, because by this time it has its own life and you have to try to understand what it needs.

Peter Weir: Master of Unease

Terry Dowling and George Mannix / 1980

From *Science Fiction: A Review of Speculative Literature* 3, no. 1 (1981). Reprinted by permission of the authors.

Peter Weir is Australia's most provocative and original filmmaker. His work would not be conventionally regarded as science fiction, but it does often rest in the broad area of imaginative and speculative work that tends to be pigeonholed under that name. Peter Nicholls's *Encyclopaedia of Science Fiction*, for instance, has an entry for *The Cars That Ate Paris*, describing it as a film that "does not readily fit into any traditional category," and later revised editions will undoubtedly mention other Weir films with equal caution. *Picnic at Hanging Rock* invites a similar classification, especially since it presents the audience with what one reviewer, Scott Murray, has called a "time zone": "Given the rock's ability to warp time around its perimeters, one can view the monolith as a kind of time zone, one that absorbs people into a fourth dimension [*Cinema Papers*, November–December 1975].

While, fortunately, there is no such heavy-handedness in the film itself, this potential is not to be ignored. On the other hand, one could say that *The Last Wave* is quite openly a "science fiction" film. It tells the story of a mysterious lost race called the Mulkrul, whose tribal remains are found beneath the streets of Sydney and whose spirit has "possessed" a young lawyer. His prophetic "big dreams" (to note a pertinent connection with a psychoanalytic theory) foretell of an impending disaster—part of an ancient cycle being fulfilled.

Weir's other major films—the formative early piece, *Homesdale*, and the telemovie, *The Plumber*—by their suggestion of breakdowns in what could be called orthodox reality, their challenging of our assumptions about what is normal, fit easily into the same broad traditions established by everything from *The Twilight Zone* to Guy Green's *The Magus* or Polanski's *The Tenant*.

The following is an interview with a writer/producer/director who, regardless of whatever departures from the genre he might undertake, will always remain a "natural" within the field of speculative and imaginative filmmaking.

Terry Dowling and George Mannix: You have been dubbed a "Master of Unease." How do you feel about that?
Peter Weir: Well, I think it was probably a phrase I plucked out of the air to answer another question or in reply to another kind of categorizing. I would like to be a *master* filmmaker, I think—if you see it in the craft sense. It seems to me one of the things I enjoy from film to film, even doing television commercials in fact, is the pleasure in mastering that craft. To some extent I still think of myself as an apprentice learning the craft of filmmaking or of storytelling.

"Unease" is an interesting word, and I prefer it to other words that have been suggested. That's why I say it was possibly a reply to another type of statement, like the famous Hitchcock "master of suspense"—obviously it's a play off that. Though I've used a little suspense, I'm still learning about it. Unease is something that has come naturally to me, I think, from my earliest films.

Dowling and Mannix: Has there always been this interest in unease in your own background?
Weir: Not consciously, although it crosses over into a view of life, I think. I become uneasy very quickly. [laughs] To give an example: I was in a hotel room in America a couple of months ago, and heard a strange sound in the middle of the night and couldn't work out what it was. I went through all the normal things, you know—it's a rat in the ceiling or it's somebody in the room upstairs, yes, that's it. But what would they be doing that would make that strange sound? It was a kind of scraping sound with almost a breath—something like the sound a possum can make in this country. That's impossible in a thirty-story hotel in New York. But I couldn't work it out, and somewhere in there I had a fraction of a second of deep unease, of not really knowing, of touching something that later on is still very interesting and exciting. That area—somewhere inside that fraction of a second—is where I work.

Dowling and Mannix: Without wishing to force you into any categories, the very fact that you have permitted yourself to be interviewed in

a journal like this suggests that you see your work as having certain connections with what is popularly regarded as fantasy and science fiction.
How do you see this connection?
Weir: Well firstly, I was no good at science at school. [laughs] To me,
fiction and nonfiction are essentially the same thing. I mean, who draws
the line anyway? I remember when I worked for Film Australia and did a
couple of documentaries, I was fascinated by this word "documentary"
because it implied that there was some kind of truth behind it—you
know, actual television. I don't buy newspapers, except, say, the Saturday papers, just to keep up with what's happening in movies or second-
hand cars or something. But I'd reached a point where I frankly did not
believe what was coming through the television or through newspapers.

But I'm just being cute about the term "science fiction." There is an
area of science fiction I've grown up with. Probably there's a lot of my
generation that was into Saturday afternoon pictures. You had lots of
westerns and occasionally crime thrillers and, of course, Flash Gordon
and the science fiction films which were generally not well done but
were always interesting to see. They were something I grew up with. But
it wasn't, I guess, as for many, until *2001* that suddenly that whole category was elevated and placed in a new perspective. Your imaginings as
a cinema-goer could be opened up into new areas. I guess I owe it to that
film that I began to look elsewhere into this category called science fiction for subjects.

Dowling and Mannix: Do you read science fiction or fantasy?
Weir: No. I've picked up a couple of things but have somehow found it
more accessible on the screen than on the printed page.

Dowling and Mannix: I was just wondering about certain authors—
like J. G. Ballard and Philip K. Dick. . . .
Weir: Well, Ballard, I know the name; but no. I've been tempted. Asimov
is another famous one, isn't he? I've seen them on the bookshelves and
been tempted to go towards them, but for whatever reason I've drawn
back.

Dowling and Mannix: If you were asked to list influences from film,
literature, painting, etc., what artists or works would you name?
Weir: I'd just take a stab. It would be just like compiling a "best of" thing.
In fiction it would certainly be Charles Dickens's work that I've been able

to go back to over the years—that has been consistent. Otherwise I've just gone through vogues—you know, I read all of Aldous Huxley's or all of Fitzgerald's at some point. But I've lost interest in those now.

Dowling and Mannix: That was a rather unfair sort of question, really. When someone like yourself has been responsible for so many strong images, it seems very churlish to then try to pin you down about those images. For us it is just a general background question, to get some idea of what you've been exposed to.

Weir: I could throw you on a wrong track by saying, for example, that I've loved Hieronymus Bosch's paintings, because I have. They've struck chords. But I guess my own source of images and stories has come out of me, is something within me . . . personal observation, not strong literary or film influences. I might say, for the record, being in the film area, it has certainly been Kubrick who has been my inspiration. In fact, generally, not European filmmakers. It's been Hitchcock and above all Kubrick that inspire me. But just recently, by the way, I think that *Alien* is a fantastic piece of work. I love that of all the current science fiction films. *Star Wars* I enjoyed and found fantastically clever, but it was *Alien* that really swept me away.

Dowling and Mannix: Because of what, in particular?

Weir: It was a curious situation because I had in fact been offered a very similar story not long before *Alien* was made. It was an old science fiction film which was to be a remake. . . . The original title of the short story was "Who Goes There?" Howard Hawks did it, I think. It was set in the polar ice regions, in the Antarctic or somewhere, and there's an American base there. . . .

Dowling and Mannix: That was *The Thing*, wasn't it? And the original story was by John W. Campbell.

Weir: *The Thing* was the movie, right. John Carpenter's doing it now. He did *Dark Star, Halloween,* and *The Fog.* He'll do a great job. Anyway, I had this storyline sent to me by my agent, but I couldn't crack it. I loved the setting of the story and the finding of this alien vegetable matter. In fact, it's frighteningly close to the *Alien* idea. They take it into their camp, it begins to thaw out, and then it starts slowly killing off all those in the base. And the question is. how to destroy it? I would enjoy the setting up of it, but the minute the creature took on life of some kind, I found I dropped out and found it silly. But I really came back to it like a dog with a bone, trying to find a way to do it. I couldn't and eventually turned the project down. When I saw *Alien* I realized there *was* a way to do it and Ridley Scott and his scriptwriters had found it.

Dowling and Mannix: A project like that would now be pretty pointless, wouldn't it?
Weir: My agent asked if I wanted to go back to it and I said, No, I think Scott's done it. He's just turned what was for me a B picture area into an A area. These terms sound so funny but, in other words, something done well enough transcends its form. But, of course, as soon as you mention Scott, you mention Giger, and since then I've chased round for all the drawings of his I could get hold of. He is dazzling. He's plugged in to some area of the unconscious.

Dowling and Mannix: On this theme of looking inwards, even as you look out, we should mention Surrealism. Your films all build on and reflect the sort of anxiety and sense of imminence which the French Surrealists called inquietude. Your "obsession with rocks"—recalling for a moment the stone Roman head found in Tunisia which you said "became the starting point for *The Last Wave"*—reminds me very much of the *objets trouvés*—the found objects—which inspired and motivated the Surrealists. Your attention to details of light and landscape, the tension you create around commonplace objects being made suddenly outré, all reinforce this connection. To what extent have you been motivated by the Surrealists? The illusionist Surrealist painters perhaps?
Weir: I was absolutely overwhelmed by my first contact with Surrealism. I can't recall specifically where it was, but I was at Sydney University. It was back in about '63, and there was a period of some considerable creative energy. There was Albie Thorns running the theatre group. Bruce Beresford was just starting in movies with Dick Brennan and a number of others who went on to do feature work. Germaine Greer was creating storms in the English Department. And all of them were drawn towards SUDS—the Sydney University Dramatic Society. I was just on the fringe of that and not really involved. It was very cliquey. But I went to their productions. They had a great drama festival there and brought out some things in the manner of Artaud's Theatre of Cruelty, and what have you. I don't know how I'd feel about it today, but the play *Fando and Lis* of his, which was bizarre, and Boris Vian's *The Apartment* (I think it was called that) were the two most powerful.[1] Among them were a number of other plays that were similar in feeling, all belonging, as I say, to the Theatre

of the Absurd, and all obviously drawing off the post–First World War turmoil and so on. And around then I guess I was looking at the painting of Dali's which I still love very much. Dali remains the strongest of that group for me, and influenced my earliest films and revue sketches, I think. I was involved in a lot of comedy, a lot of university-fringe theatre as an actor and performer with Grahame Bond. He and I formed a little team in the late sixties there, making films and doing revues. And glancing back through that material I am embarrassed because they are, in a sense, so self-consciously "surreal." But this was, of course, part of a Western World movement that was going on possibly in reaction to the Vietnam War, I think, or part of the dust cloud raised by that. There was a new movement of Pop Art, Andy Warhol's soup cans, and so on, which I always felt was a distant cousin of Surrealism and rather paler beside the outrage and cry of agony that is reflected in creative work after the First World War. For me, these sorts of movements in art are locked into great social upheavals and particularly war. That's not to exclude what was happening in Europe, particularly France, at the end of the nineteenth century; you know, that fantasy and melancholy or whatever.

Over the years I have tried to divest myself of any tricks or devices, because I began to see that apparently I could be clever by simply being obscure. Then, of course, these films were only reaching a small audience. They had a lot of other things going for them anyway, but I thought, I must strip myself of these props and find the real energy and power within the images, from as realistic a setting as possible. By doing so, I would double the impact and reach a lot of other people.

Dowling and Mannix: Which is what Dali does with his essentially realistic settings. I'll just throw a number of quotes at you, not for you to comment on necessarily, but just to show you how amazing and inevitable we found these connections between your own work and certain key ideas of the Surrealists. For instance, we have Dali saying: Geology has an oppressive melancholy, which it will never be able to brush from its back. This melancholy has its source in the idea that time is working against it. Or again, his remarking that: "Geology is a state of the landscape / The soul is a state of the landscape. . . ." There is a reference to the Surrealist drive to explore "the mystique of chance encounter"; and to De Chirico's desire to "rehabilitate the object," and so put things into new situations which alarm your audience. And lastly, we have Ernst speaking of the need for "the cultivation of . . . a systematic bewildering." . . .
Weir: That's a good one.

Dowling and Mannix: It's close to what you have done.
Weir: Yes.

Dowling and Mannix: Quite often your own audiences don't know what to do with an experience you have given them. They're fascinated, but when it's in their laps, it's easier for them to dismiss it, even criticize it, which is a point we'll come back to in a moment if we may. But all these references are just obvious points for us to mention.
Weir: It reminds me, actually, that when we were talking earlier about literature and influences, I should have mentioned that in the last few years it is definitely Carl Jung who has excited me more than any other writer, though I've read very little. A friend gave me *Memories, Dreams, Reflections*, which impressed me immensely.[2] I reread the book because I didn't understand so much of it on the first reading; it's so extra-ordinarily personal, in such code—it takes some time, I think, to crack it. But he gave a kind of framework to a lot of the ideas I've had which I thought were a bit eccentric or just plain odd. He showed me that other people think this way

Dowling and Mannix: It has a more general application?
Weir: That's right. His famous archetypal images, and the studies he conducted of primitive tribal groups in Africa when he was there, and how these people possessed a different perception of the world. All of this came together for me around the time I was finishing the script of *The Last Wave*, and a lot of that material, I found, could be looked at from a Jungian perspective.

But let me add that I am in no sense an academic or a student of all his work. What I really mean is that I was just looking through a doorway that he really entered, and where he went I don't really know. But I'm still peering after him.

Dowling and Mannix: This brings me back to Hitchcock and later on, Stanley Kubrick. You've said that you have a great admiration for the work of Alfred Hitchcock who has been acclaimed as the "master of suspense." It would appear that you have gone beyond what Hitchcock set out to do. You are far more—it's a bad word but—"poetic" perhaps. Hitchcock seems to be making entertainment more directly, whereas you don't seem to be doing just that. What similarities would you see your work as having to his, and what differences?
Weir: I think it's vastly different. When you say that I am more poetic

or whatever, I think that, in some areas, this would simply be the fact that I had not mastered the narrative to the extent that he had. I think I would love to make a film finally that was totally accessible to a very broad public, that was as pregnant as some of his mass-entertainment films were, with ideas and mysteries and possibilities. In a sense, there is no similarity. He's from another tradition. But you can just learn from him, I think. You can put yourself through a kind of Hitchcock film-school. Mind you, I didn't do that until . . . in fact, it was only two years ago. Right through to the end of *The Last Wave*—to that point I would not look at any classics. It began as a kind of joke. Back in the late sixties, friends would say: "You must come to the AFI, and see the great Renoirs and Kurosawas and Howard Hawks." And I said I didn't want to. In actual fact, the reason was, I think, that I thought that if I realized how far I had to go, I really might hesitate. Somehow it was . . . well, in those days, as filmmakers, we were like street-fighters (and still are to a degree) or guerrillas, working from the hills with very small arms against a powerful military junta of some kind. And I thought, God, if I knew how small we were and what a great tradition there was. . . . And I think I was right. Because having finished *The Last Wave*, I was living in Adelaide, and there was a very good film library there—the State film library—which had all these classics. So I bought a projector and week in and week out for a year I would borrow four or five films a week. I worked my way through from the Russians to the Germans of the twenties; the silent films, the Chaplins, right through. I've still got a long way to go. But my breath was just taken away as I watched some of these things, the early Hitchcocks and so on. And I think I was in a position to understand or to work out what they'd been up to or doing and learn from them, which I don't think I would have all those years ago.

Dowling and Mannix: It didn't discourage you, obviously.
Weir: No! No! It's also given me a kind of confidence to think that I've reached some of those points on my own in fact, without influence. In other words, as filmmakers we're dealing essentially with ideas and with stories which are common to all people. The film is simply a system of recording and transmitting the ideas.

Dowling and Mannix: Which is that Jungian notion again—the idea of things being common to all people. We come back to certain basics
Weir: Very much so.

Dowling and Mannix: I believe you tell a story of how Hitchcock characterizes suspense in its classic form—a story involving a chair in a locked room. Obviously it did something for you, so would you like to retell it for us here?

Weir: Well, I think it locks back into that stripping away of gimmicks and tricks in the early surrealist type of films that I did, where I wanted to reduce the amount of games that I was playing with the audience—to simplify, in other words. Hitchcock was asked in one interview what the essence of suspense was and could he give an example? And he gave this fabulous example in which there was a small bare room with one chair in it, that was all. The chair was placed in the center of the room and clearly marked in a certain position. There was only one way into the room—a door which was locked and bolted. No other way to get in, no windows, nothing. And the room was guarded all night so that nobody could get in. The next morning, the room was opened and the chair examined, and it had moved two inches. When I read that, I felt the back of my neck tingle, a distinct movement of hair.

Dowling and Mannix: On this same subject, you yourself have said that: "Within the ordinary lies the greatest possibilities of things to happen." With the Hitchcock story in mind, do you ever feel that there are only so many ways of exploring such moments of strangeness, of encounter, of possibility? Is there any limitation to the number of ways you could use to provoke your audience, tease them and give them that "back of the neck" feeling?

Weir: Hitchcock was not dealing with people, for example. It was *just a chair*. But the possibilities occur, I think, by the way, as you are making the film more frequently than as you're writing it. In the writing, you're dealing with different things. You've got certain key images that are part of your story, dealing with this kind of moment, and you write them in. As you would, say, for that scene with the chair, if you knew this was pivotal and the story went on from there about why this chair moved or whatever. That's one kind of planned example. But, in actual fact, I think some of the greatest moments of electricity occur during the shooting and sometimes during the cutting. Going back to the principles of montage of Eisenstein, of the actual editing process, you can get some electric moments in the cutting-room that were never planned by putting one image with another. Or one sound with an image. I've done this frequently in fairly ordinary scenes; laid in very strange sounds from all sorts of sources and they've created a particular effect as you view the film. Also, during the shooting, I've sometimes slowed the film down so I've shot in slow motion, though you wouldn't know. For example, sometimes with Chamberlain when he was talking with the Aborigines or vice versa, I would shoot the scene in the standard way, at standard speed, which is twenty-four frames a second. And during a conversation there are times, naturally, where one party's just listening. So, if it's appropriate, I'll bring in a special camera which shoots at super-slow motion, ask the actor not to blink or move his hands or face at all, and film just a quick burst in slow motion. Then, when I've cut the scene at the normal speed and someone's talking, we'll cut to the person being spoken to and I'll cut in a couple of seconds of his face listening. And then back to our original party who's speaking. Sometimes, as people have watched the scene, they've said there was something odd in that face. That's a case of using a particular means. . . .

Dowling and Mannix: In your films to date you are, in a sense, beguiling your audience into crisis—into a "reality crisis" or a crisis of perception. There are unexpected, intruding causes and effects so that the viewer has to reexamine reality. What would you like to think this crisis does for the individual? What benefit does he get from being in such a state of unease?

Weir: Well, I suppose something I simply enjoy when I come out from seeing a film is that you carry the experience outside the theatre with you—you get in a sense something money can't buy, something which comes to mind time and again after viewing the film. It stays with you. And that, of course, ties in with the entertainment value of the piece. I mean, apart from unease or anything else, I see myself primarily as a storyteller, telling stories in my own particular way. My tradition is that— the greatest tradition of entertainment.

Dowling and Mannix: In presenting the *Hanging Rock* experience, for example, or the excessive "it can't be happening" realities of *The Cars That Ate Paris*, the viewer is stranded in much the same way as Kubrick does at the end of *2001*; forcing us to work out what is going on here. Is this a fair assessment of what you're doing as well?

Weir: Yes. To forget you are in the theatre, too. It's a lovely feeling when a film really works and you *are* isolated. The same thing can happen in live theatre and in opera; a lack of awareness of doors and exits and seats. The experience is all around you.

Dowling and Mannix: It's interesting how that affects some of your audience. It sends them scrambling for comfortable explanations. They resent being put in a situation where you are provoking them. . . .
Weir: [laughs] The more pragmatic of them, anyway.

Dowling and Mannix: Yes. Some viewers and even critics feel cheated or resent the absence of easy solutions in what they would see as unnecessary mystery-mongering on your part. As such, your films can almost be seen as provocations. You do seem to be provoking your audience to reassess the nature of the reality around them, to question the basic shared assumptions that hold society together. Is this a fair statement of intention?
Weir: Yes, I think so. Again, sometimes it's a lack of understanding of the craft. Sometimes I've not known what to do with the atmosphere that I've created. It's like making a Chinese meal without any recipe and you really don't know how to do it again or exactly what it was you did. To take another quote of Hitchcock's talking on what could be called rules of audience, *you can be mysterious but never mystify*. He has a point. Sometimes I've wanted to tell the audience more, to share it more with them, but I've not really known how to. As you go on, you really want to master these things so you can make the decision yourself as to which way you will go.

Dowling and Mannix: In this same area, you seem to have a lot of respect for the actual editing of a film. You do regard that as being a definite creative part?
Weir: Oh, absolutely. If you cut the whole filmmaking process into three parts, it's script, shooting, and editing. And who's to say which is more important? They're all part of the whole.

Dowling and Mannix: Do you do your own editing?
Weir: Not physically, no. But I sit with the editor. I prefer to have an editor than do it myself.

Dowling and Mannix: In a recent article in *Cinema Papers* on your "themes and preoccupations," Brian McFarlane speaks of you as "an artist with a vision and a growing understanding of how this vision may be presented."[3] Later in the same article, McFarlane suggests that "horror" is at the heart of your vision. Others would suggest that it involves more the moment of hesitation that a character and a viewer feels when he is caught—suspended—between the moment of disorientation and his placing of it, his explaining it away. Would you like to encapsulate for us, what you see your vision as being?

Weir: Well, I certainly have never had a plan of action, no overall view. Perhaps one of the roles of critics is to find that, if they so choose. But I've certainly never thought of it in that way. My films are just me at that point in time; the themes and obsessions that recur are part of me. I think that possibly a lot of these areas are to do with something else entirely—quite possibly with a fascination with death or with the fact that we all must die. It's an area that's very difficult to talk about and unfortunately it's not an area that we seem to be able to discuss in our Western society. I think that behind a lot of my themes and obsessions is a skirting around the edges of the great final adventure [laughs], the great leap. . . .

Dowling and Mannix: Given your recent exposure to Jung, you may no longer find that death is the great final adversary most people would see it as being.
Weir: No, I'd like to find that.

Dowling and Mannix: Without wishing to pin this on you, do you think there will be Jungian overtones appearing in your films? Are you impressed enough with the ideas and ways of thinking you've discovered to make that a conscious facet of what you will do in the future?
Weir: No. No. I start off firstly with stories that come to me through the mail, if you like, or through agents or friends who bring them to me. And through my own processes of creativity. The beginnings of a story occur and then you get another clue and eventually you write something down.

Dowling and Mannix: But you do feel you impose something of your own onto a story that you are given?
Weir: Oh, absolutely. But that happens later. I think the initial thing I'm looking for is a good story—the "once upon a time" that is full of characters and events and moments. When the material is coming from elsewhere as happened of course with *Picnic* and with my next film, *The Year of Living Dangerously* (which is from an Australian novel), I have to get inside these stories and make them mine—cannibalize them and swallow them and digest them and become part of the pages and part of the process of thinking that the novelists used to write them. I must

totally absorb them in order to bring them back to something of my own. Which of course makes it difficult to find suitable material.

I approach filmmaking as a storyteller. There is no conscious planning. I mean, things do just happen, and sometimes it's very odd how they do. For example, last year I did a documentary on a potter who lives locally—a fine craftsman, a marvelous man who had been a teacher at East Sydney Tech and had just retired from that position. Anyway, it was a very little subject to deal with; the man was not flamboyant, as you would imagine, a quiet craftsman working away at home, teaching a little, but a man of enormous calm and almost Zen-like qualities without putting him into the hippie set. I found it fascinating that he'd been in a Japanese prisoner-of-war camp and yet, after the war, had found his way back to Japan and a love of the Japanese aesthetic, had many Japanese friends, and so on. That was the starting point. Anyway, it made a very simple documentary, showing him working in his house at night with a Japanese friend, another potter; shots of his pots, etc. Very simple, about twenty minutes long. Anyway, end of story. I delivered the film to the Crafts Council and that was it. A couple of friends have since seen it and said it's spooky; some of those shots when he's lighting his kiln, and so on. And they commented on the strange music we found and used. I had another look at the film and—yes—you can see these things in it. There are some eerie moments. Yet it just came along with me; how could I impose it?

Dowling and Mannix: I think you've made the next question regarding reality crisis as a theme rather redundant. One could say that your themes look like being (I have to put it this way because with your storytelling priority this is probably no longer a conscious thing) the isolation and alienation that leads on to a possibility of revelation and hopefully a transformation. But sometimes it just seems to be provocation. I don't see this as being a fair comment any longer because all this is incidental to what you're doing first of all, which is telling a story. But on our viewing of your films, these things recur, whether by accident or unconsciously, and there does seem to be a strong case for saying that these are Peter Weir themes.

Weir: I think Bergman put it very well when he was asked about conscious themes and signs in his films, and he said how much he worked off intuition. He was being quoted various examples that fitted someone's theory and he used the image of an archer firing an arrow high and then down into a forest. Like the archer, Bergman said he too just fires. Then, after the film is complete, he makes his way through the forest and tries to find where the arrow fell and then wonders why it fell in such a way and why it fell where it did. It was an elaborate way of saying that one just works by intuition and does it. That's my approach, I think.

Also, going back to that film history thing, I feel I don't have a burden of film history. I'm not a film buff. I don't reproduce other people's images and approaches. That must be a curse—knowing too much. Sometimes I think that education in any area can, in fact, inhibit that intuition. Because you *do* tend to say: I don't think it can be done, or else it's been done too well before—I must simply follow in the path of. Going further on this point, I have kept myself a primitive; I am to some extent like the primitive painter who has just picked up a brush and learned how to apply it properly, and so on. I think it was, for me, the right thing to do. It kept me free. But, of course, I then had a hard road learning the craft as I went along. Hence my emphasis on the number of times I did not know how to tell a story well enough, and have sometimes hidden in a mist of flashiness.

Dowling and Mannix: The films you have made to date, creating these moments of confrontation and encounter, are really quite fragile things. . . .
Weir: Yes, very.

Dowling and Mannix: They seem to be easily overbalanced and seen as just black comedy, mere psychological thrillers or even portentous posturing. In trying to make images "resonate" within a film, do you feel that as director you are treading a particularly dangerous line?
Weir: Oh, absolutely, yes. Very thin ice. And again, I think it's by further developing the craft that you can be a little more certain where you put your foot each time and not take so many risks.

Dowling and Mannix: Your line doesn't become any narrower, you just become more adept at keeping on it?
Weir: I think so. I mean, there is a danger. I remember what an eighteenth-century French pianist once said; a very famous virtuoso pianist whose name is no longer a part of the history of music. But as a young man he did have a great talent as a composer, and he said that in the mastering of the craft, he lost the art. And so part of the thing, I think, is to develop further your craft and your control of where you want to take

the audience, but not to lose that precious desperation of the art—that madness, that willingness to experiment which to a degree I've kept in all my films. In other words, once could become too safe. So the real line you're walking, I think, is between craft and art.

Dowling and Mannix: It's interesting that you're going to observe these convictions within your storytelling priority. In finding this balance between art and craft, concept and execution, which of your films do you think is the most successful so far?
Weir: I think the last one, *The Plumber*, given what I wanted to do and the extent to which I achieved it. I don't think it was one hundred per cent in any sense of what I wanted to do, but it was significantly higher than with some of the other films. I got a better control of rhythm and structure in that film. Mind you, it was a simpler piece, made for television. It was a short story, if you like, as against a novel. I tried a different system with that film, too, in the cutting. I videotaped it all, each cut. As you cut a film, you start with what's called the rough cut and then go through various refining processes, which might be three or four, maybe more. It's much the same as going through the draft of a screenplay, honing it down, changing scenes in relation to each other, emphasizing characters and de-emphasizing others, whatever. And I kept copies of all the cuts here at home on television, and would just rerun it, late at night or early in the morning, sometimes for friends, sometimes for myself. So I think I got to know the material better. There's a curious ritual about going into the cutting-room and looking at what the editor has done the day or night before. This demystified that cutting-room.

Dowling and Mannix: Would you tell us, in retrospect, how you view each of your major films?
Weir: I think I have an uncomfortable relationship with most of them. There's a kind of moratorium period where you just simply have to stay away from them. It seems to take about three or four years before I can even look at one again. Except for *The Plumber*, which is less painful, I should say. I've heard this of other filmmakers. It's like looking at yourself several years ago. Of course, by the time you finish a film, you're involved with ideas you've probably been working with for at least two years anyway, if it's gone fast. So in a sense you're already two years on from those particular views in some areas. And you change constantly. I think it comes down to liking bunches of scenes and sounds and scraps

of music and someone's face, that sort of thing. It's like a family snapshot album—you can feel a curious mixture of sentiment and embarrassment and regret.

Dowling and Mannix: With the exception of *Picnic at Hanging Rock* and your new film, all your films are based on your own story ideas. Do you ever see filmmaking as your only medium? Or do you see yourself moving into any other, like writing? I am reminded of J. G. Ballard and, I think, Patrick White saying they would like to have been painters. . . .
Weir: No, I don't think so. If for some reason I couldn't work in films, then I think I would find some other outlet—possibly writing. I've done a little bit of sculpting. It's almost in the hobby area, but I've loved that. I have a natural affinity for stone. In fact, I've made my own little sarcophagus. Ever since my grandfather died, and the funeral parlor people came with their brochures about coffins and things, I decided I would beat them by having my own. So I've almost finished a little sarcophagus for my ashes which I cut out of a block of sandstone. [laughs] I had it written in my will. I remember a very Dickensian lawyer with one eyebrow raised as I described it. He said, "Would one describe it as a stone box, would you say? I see. Fine." He put: one stone box. Then he said, "Where are they to place it?," and I said, "Well, I don't want to put them to any trouble. Some appropriate quiet spot." [laughs] I've carved other things, you know, faces and stone blocks in a vaguely Graeco-Roman style or Coptic designs of one kind or another. And that's been another natural outlet for me, rather than, say, painting or something like that.

Dowling and Mannix: *The Cars That Ate Paris* is often cited as being from a short story by Peter Weir. Was that published as a short story?
Weir: No, but I have written most of my films as short stories first—not to be published but just as a way of feeling the ideas out. It's a case of taking on a discipline almost as if you were going to publish.

Dowling and Mannix: But you'd never consider publishing them as stories?
Weir: No. I don't think they're really good enough. It's just not my forte. But I write them up like that, then I tape-record them, often like a little play reading which I'll just play in my car. I'll do that with scripts, too. I'll do all the voices and sound effects. I've got a tape of *Picnic* somewhere with [drums fingers on table] horses galloping like that. [laughs] I'll do all the voices, everything I can. For wind, I'll go [blowing sound].

Anything, so you can make it live in another form. It's great playing it in the car as if it was a radio show. You can listen and think, Oh God, that's bad and I'd better fix that, or that scene's got more potential. . . .

Dowling and Mannix: You start to build the visual behind it?
Weir: Yes, absolutely. Hearing it in all sorts of other ways. And the re-lated way, I think, is music. I'm a great cassette freak. I find that music begins to gather round a story, anything from rock- and-roll to classi-cal music to folk, or all three, which seems to have threads connected to the ideas you're working with. It becomes part of the whole process of getting a film out. I think music is undoubtedly the greatest key to those hidden passageways in your mind. When you're highly charged as in the process of making a film, the light is in a sense switched on throughout the labyrinth of your mind (using that image) and music can take you through many doors, find many things, unlock images. It will often, of course, have nothing to do with the music that's finally put on the soundtrack. In fact, in most cases, I find that at the end of produc-tion you'll go in a completely different direction with the music. But it helps you get somewhere. I always carry a cassette when I'm shooting. I don't play it every day but I'll often play it for the cast or myself. My bag of tapes is like a doctor's bag—there's everything from African music to rock-and-roll. I play them on the way to the set or on the way home at night.

Dowling and Mannix: The soundtrack of *The Plumber*, for instance, is a brilliant use of native music to set up the contrasting images. That certainly contributed to the feeling on the back of the neck.
Weir: Yes, that's a great piece of music—from the Barundi tribe. A friend, Jim McElroy, found it and gave it to me.

Dowling and Mannix: Hearkening back to the Surrealist notion of "found objects" for a moment, and inspiration from what you've seen and heard, would you care to describe the particular images—the con-ceptual starting points—that led you to make your five major films: *Homesdale, The Cars That Ate Paris, Picnic at Hanging Rock, The Last Wave,* and *The Plumber*?
Weir: Well, going back to *Homesdale*, it was the house we were renting at Church Point. It was a very old colonial home that just had mystery about it and which later in fact became the guest house, Homesdale, in the film. It seemed to have a story attached to it. People would come and

see it and say: "This reminds me of something," or: "There's something about this house." It was like a house on a plantation or in the Crimea, and I wonder if it was ever a hospital or if someone had died there. So. the house became the inspiration, in a sense.

The Cars That Ate Paris came from driving through France and being diverted by a man in a yellow jacket with a little barrier, who pointed to a side road. So that was an actual experience that happened. Why did I take the road? Simply because he had on a Day-Glo jacket and had a little barrier? And later in England I was reading about road accidents and noticed a tiny little column talking about ten or fifteen dead on the British roads and then a big article about a shotgun shooting. So I got to thinking that if you wanted to kill someone, you do it in a road accident.

Dowling and Mannix: So you're synthesizing from everywhere really, aren't you?

Weir: Yes. And the automobile was, if you like, the "object" there. *Picnic,* of course, came through the novel itself, but it brought a whole collection of these other things. *The Last Wave* was that Roman head I found in Tunisia. Knowing I was going to find it: it was the most demonstrably psychic experience I've ever had—that foreknowledge . . . a definite premonition. But as I say, I've always had this great affinity for stone, and ever since I first went to Europe in '65, a love of ruins. I never wanted to buy the guidebook and know who built it or who lived there. That was always dull for me. I just liked all that falling-down marble. So it was appropriate in a sense that I found that Roman head.

The Plumber was a different thing altogether. It was an anecdote told to me at dinner by the very woman who'd lived through it. So it was a different experience, really.

Dowling and Mannix: Could you tell us something about your recent project, *The Year of Living Dangerously*? Do you see it as a departure from your usual role at all?

Weir: Yes. It's from a novel of the same title by Chris Koch, whose brother, Phillip Koch, was a journalist with the ABC. A large part of the inspiration and background research has come through his brother's experience. It's a story set in Southeast Asia, centering on one of a group of journalists who are covering a collapsing Asian regime. The story opens with one particular journalist. Guy Hamilton on assignment in Jakarta as a cameraman, and the subsequent events leading down to the collapse of this regime. It's just a very fine story. I've recently been up in Asia and will go again researching it. It's just so exciting to walk through the bazaars and markets experiencing the new light and the new sounds with this story in mind. I don't know where it will take me. It's a fascinating feeling with a film, I think. Each time you start, you really set sail into unknown waters. You leave at midnight in a fog, not quite sure of where you're going. You're on a rough course, and what you'll see along the way, you don't know.

Dowling and Mannix: We've heard about some other projects—*The Thorn Birds* and even *Gallipoli* involving David Williamson. Is this latter project something you were approached about or were you working on it?
Weir: No. No. I thought of it years ago. I've always been fascinated with the First World War and as far back as '75 I was thinking that I might do something on the trenches in France. Then it occurred to me that perhaps I should tackle Gallipoli, but thought it too obvious. And then in '76 I was on my way to the opening of *Picnic* in London and thought I'd detour and visit the battlefields and make a decision after visiting that. That was such a curious experience—as anyone will tell you who's been there—and I thought, yes, I'll make a film about this in one way or another. So I left it there and then wrote a short story—or storyline, if you like—which I gave to David Williamson. And we drove on through umpteen drafts trying to find the right way to handle this material so it wouldn't be too expensive and not too documentary. I think we've found that, and Pat Lovell's to produce it. She's looking for money at the moment.

Dowling and Mannix: That would be after *The Year of Living Dangerously*?
Weir: It would appear that way at the moment, yes.

Dowling and Mannix: What about *The Thorn Birds* project?
Weir: Well, I spent five months with that project, working with a screen-writer trying to bring the material closer to my own style and simply failed. I thought I could do it even though I knew it was going to be tough. I had full support from the Warner Bros. studio people. They gave me creative freedom, given that I couldn't change the actual building blocks of the story—key characters had to remain, and so on. But I

simply could not do it and reluctantly gave it up. It was exciting in that people had loved it and there was a large audience waiting for it. But I couldn't make it fit me; couldn't digest it.

Dowling and Mannix: It's now being done by Arthur Hitler who did *Love Story*. . . .
Weir: Yes. I think he'll do a fine film. It probably should have gone to him in the first place. It's appropriate. I was the wrong man for it.

Dowling and Mannix: That means you're pulling it back down to a local production again, aren't you? *The Year of Living Dangerously* is Australian-produced, isn't it?
Weir: Yes, with Jim McElroy. He's been the co-producer on all the other films, with the exception of *The Plumber*. *The Thorn Birds* was also in a period in which I was opening myself up.[4] I wanted to widen the choice of material, widen my possibilities and not always be locked into this obsessive sort of storytelling. And I found I couldn't do it. [laughs]

Dowling and Mannix: As a general question, how do you see the imaginative scene at the moment—in writing, in filmmaking, here in Australia, throughout the world? Do you still think it's a healthy industry you're working in?
Weir: The current generation of filmmakers is interesting. I'm glad that the strict division between the art-house and the commercial world which existed in the sixties has collapsed. I think that's a very healthy thing. There are those, of course, who still religiously believe that the two types of films are incompatible. I don't. I have too much respect for audiences, anyway. Then again, there are those who will criticize *Alien* and not even go to see it because it's too popular. I've heard people say that, and it's so limiting. It's truly elitist to despise what the general public like. Often I'm quite mystified by what films the public have loved and that I thought were poor films or silly. But they make the decision to go. I don't believe that people's minds are manipulated to the extent that they go because of advertising. I think that you can do that for the first couple of weeks with a film, but the kind of repeat business the big films do is usually because people have loved them.

Dowling and Mannix: There are many "big" films that have failed in spite of advertising.
Weir: Yes, exactly. People won't go.

Dowling and Mannix: You talked earlier about the fact that you don't watch television or read newspapers as a day to day activity, and seemed to suggest that there was a sort of skepticism on your part towards the kind of information that comes through those media. . . .

Weir: I got that out of order. That's probably reason number two. As for number one . . . well, when I was in my late teens, my grandfather, Archie, was living with us. He was a marvelous man, the boy's ideal grandfather; a bit of a pirate really. He would let you climb trees and throw rocks and he was always watching you with a cheeky smile. But he had one period in the day when you kept away from him—when the morning newspaper arrived. Like a lot of older people, he got up very early to get the paper, and you'd find him in the kitchen there having read it for an hour from cover to cover, in a very cranky mood about some revolution in South America or something. And I thought, this is information you shouldn't have. It's not necessary to know about it. So whether that stayed in my mind or not, I don't know. But in sophisticated Western living, I think you do try to keep anxieties at arms' length. It's part of the reason that I would live here, apart from the great beauty and the fact that it's my own country. I would resist the logic of living in Los Angeles, which is really a reasonable point of view which my agent puts to me. Why not move over here?—simply because of all the possibilities of getting films going just through chatting like we are now, you know, from an idea or chance remark. But it does make one anxious. I've read Kubrick saying the same thing of his living in England. And I've found the same with newspapers and television—they're really just creating and promoting anxiety. And you get to hear of the key issues anyway. During the Iran crisis I bought the newspapers to keep up to date with that; it obviously seemed to have relevance to all of us.

Dowling and Mannix: It's interesting to note that the "master of unease" is also subject to bouts of it.

Weir: [laughs] Yes. As far as television went, I think I watched too much of it at home, and couldn't afford one when I left home and got married. Then I just thought: if I get one I'll never do anything. When I go to motels, shooting films or researching something, I tend to watch a lot of it and catch up with casting. Obviously with Australian shows, it's of benefit to know who's doing what. And I'll go out to see the new *Fawlty Towers* or whatever. I have a strong interest in humor.

Dowling and Mannix: Yes, that goes right back to your work with

Grahame Bond and the Architecture Revues, and things like that, doesn't it? Do you intend to follow it through in filmmaking?
Weir: I'd like to very much. I just did a batch of commercials with John Cleese. He and I got on well. We've exchanged letters since then and are looking for something to do together.

Dowling and Mannix: Just to finish up by directing conversation back into our vested interest pocket for a moment. . . . Having noted such themes as isolation and reality crisis, your respect for the work of Kubrick and Hitchcock, and most especially your own major "fantasy" works—notably *The Last Wave*—would you ever consider making a science fiction film as a means of exploring your interests?
Weir: Oh, absolutely. I think that's why I brought up the example of *Alien* in some detail. And I think it has been others who have led the way for me in that area—as I say, Kubrick and Lucas and to some extent Spielberg with his *Close Encounters*. And certainly Ridley Scott. He's a fabulous filmmaker. He really uses light well and knows how to put power behind the images which is something you can't learn at any of the film schools. You've got to find it or know it.

Notes

1. Boris Vian (1920–1959) was a major figure in French cultural life whose wildly varied output included songs, poems, novels, films, and inventions. Writing under the pseudonym "Vernon Sullivan," he published crime novels in the American "hard-boiled" style.

2. Carl Jung was in his early eighties when *Memories, Dreams, Reflections* was published in 1961. It recounts the great psychologist's spiritual and intellectual awakenings, rather than the external events of his life. Descriptions of his visions, dreams, and fantasies fill the book. He considered them the prism through which he could perceive the collective psyche of humankind. Peter Weir refers to the book frequently.

3. *Cinema Papers* was Australia's leading film magazine. It was issued from Melbourne, Australia, from 1974 to 2001.

4. *The Thorn Birds* (1977) was a best-selling novel by Colleen McCullough. It chronicled sixty years in the lives of the Cleary family, brought from New Zealand to Australia to run their Aunt Mary Carson's ranch. After Peter Weir turned down the project, it was released as a television miniseries in 1983, starring Richard Chamberlain and Rachel Ward, and directed by Daryl Duke.

Towards the Center

Tom Ryan and Brian McFarlane / 1981

From *Cinema Papers*, no. 34 (September–October, 1981, 322–29). Reprinted by permission of the authors.

Central to most of Peter Weir's films is the attempt to move beyond the surface strata of behavior, beyond what is readily perceived, to a realm of experience that is equally "real" but less tangible. In this sense his work reveals a strong impulse towards the abstract, towards the collapse of the forms of the everyday into a stream of "sights and sounds and colors . . . closer to music." This impulse generally belongs to the practitioners of a particular kind of experimental film, yet here it is firmly rooted in the methods of traditional narrative cinema. The sense of the strange which is evoked in *Picnic at Hanging Rock* or *The Last Wave* is initially a creation of a narrative arrangement that refuses to explain itself, that denies its viewers access to ready-made explanations. Like Tom (Tony Llewellyn-Jones) in the former film, the viewer might dwell on the old way: "There's a solution somewhere. There's gotta be!" But part of the pleasure of these films lies in the way in which they refuse such expectations of an easy satisfaction.

The apparent realism of their fictions is insistently challenged, and enriched, by the intrusion of incidents which disturb a familiar order. Like his characters, the viewers of Weir's films are repeatedly faced with the mysteries of the moment, experiences that refuse to succumb to the kinds of patterns imposed by conventional understanding. The films seems to hover as if on the edge of a dream-world, or a place of nightmares, and while Weir's work since *The Cars That Ate Paris* certainly cannot be classified in the realm of "horror" film, at least according to the customary use of the label, nonetheless they share this element in common with them. They are pervaded by the inexplicable, by the sense of awe imbedded in a fleeting glimpse of an unknown terrain, an incursion beyond the looking-glass.

The look which guides the viewer is often that of a character—Michael (Dominic Guard) as he gazes in wonderment at the "Botticelli angels" in *Picnic at Hanging Rock*, David Burton (Richard Chamberlain), fearful of his vision of "the last wave," or Archy (Mark Lee) and Frank (Mel Gibson) faced by the floating funfair of the threatening shore in Gallipoli. But the starting point is always the everyday, for without that, the films' "other" dimension would have no context, no point of entrance for the viewer. The characters who inhabit this territory of the familiar seem to exist outside of psychology, archetypes of the common person, their individual features serving as particular aspects of "the greater whole." Their path through the films leads them towards a confrontation with nothing less than their destiny (the rock, the wave, Gallipoli via the pyramids), beyond the repressions of a Victorian education, beyond the comforts of middle-class Sydney, beyond the constraints of an Australia isolated from all but an impression of the rest of the world.

Tom Ryan and Brian McFarlane: Through your films it is possible to get a sense of somebody who is particularly aware of the expectations of his audience and able to play around with those expectations. When you are making a film, how conscious are you of the audience?
Peter Weir: Very conscious. It's very important for me to be constantly asking myself, in the scripting process or during the shoot, what the audience will understand from this or that, and what it will expect as a consequence. I feel at liberty to play around to the extent that I can control what I want them to know or feel at any given point. And I guess I like to keep them a step behind or to subvert their expectations.

Ryan and McFarlane: What you say has echoes of what Alfred Hitchcock used to say about the audience. Do you share his black humor?
Weir: It's difficult to see things in any broad view like that; but no, I don't think so. I've seen reviews of some of my films which have seen them in terms of black humor, but I don't think that's accurate. I suppose it depends on the way you see things. Maybe bizarre or strange, but I prefer words like enigmatic, curious, and fascinating. When I think about humor, I don't break things down into "black" or anything else. I remember the word "sick" being used in a review of a couple of sketches I did in my university days, but that's a long time ago.

Ryan and McFarlane: Would you like to make comedy?

Weir: Yes. I have an idea for a comedy I'd like to do. My beginnings in this whole business really were in comedy, as a writer-performer in university revue-type things. I am a great Monty Python fan and I remember John Lennon saying that instead of being born a Beatle, he'd rather have been born a Monty Python. I wouldn't have minded that. I love their humor. They may not be on the screens this week, but their humor is in the air. I shot a commercial with John Cleese and we struck up a sort of friendship. We talked about doing something together some day.

Ryan and McFarlane: To what extent do you see yourself as an "auteur," as the controlling influence over your films?
Weir: I do see myself as exercising a control, but I am not sure what that really tells us. I think the word *auteur* has become devalued and we must put it aside; it was a very useful word during the late 1950s and '60s, when the cinema was so polarized, but with the great changes in the 1970s and '80s I don't think it is so useful.

Ryan and McFarlane: In a sense, the most anonymous work you would have done would have been, probably, the earlier work you did for television. How did you get involved in *Luke's Kingdom*?
Weir: I was broke after finishing *Cars That Ate Paris* and there was an awful moment when I didn't know if I could get any work. I contacted the ABC drama department and asked if they knew of me; a guarded "yes" was the answer. So I said, "look, I've a couple of short stories I've written. I'd like to talk to you about developing them into something." I got a very quick "no" on that one. They weren't interested. I don't know if things have changed. So, I was very glad when *Luke's Kingdom* turned up. I did two episodes and, once I had accepted the terms of the way it was made, I enjoyed it. There were really two directors: the producer, Tony Essex, and the director of the episode. Tony directly controlled the scripting and the cutting room. I think I accepted that as a challenge: to see what I could do, two hands behind my back. And, of course, I had no control over the casting or the music. I think I was successful in certain sequences, but it was Tony's show. I was able to experiment, however, and Tony encouraged it. He was more a director than a producer and he didn't care about the budget, he didn't care about excess and he even encouraged it. Whether it was a very good thing or not I don't know, but it was his vision and I thought, in accepting the money, I really had to try and execute his intentions. So it wasn't really me there.

Ryan and McFarlane: Much is made of the landscape as a powerful force in the series. . . .

Weir: Yes. I thought he'd chosen a great location on the banks of the Turron River out of Sofala. It was a country I knew of course from *Cars*, which I had shot in Sofala. In fact, I remembered driving to the location with a car full of actors in period costume and passing the rusty wrecks of Holdens in the backyards of Sofala homesteads. It was a pleasure to get back into country to which I had already responded. But Tony also duplicated a location on Smokey Dawson's Ranch in Sydney. I didn't get the same feeling from that kind of scrubby, city bushland on the edge of the city as I'd got from the Turron country. There is something unpleasant about a lot of countryside around Sydney, I think.

Ryan and McFarlane: Several ideas seem to run through your work, like the one of the ordinary man constantly being under the threat of the extraordinary or the one of the rational man being pushed into areas where rationality won't serve him anymore. Are they ideas that interest you?

Weir: They did interest me, particularly in *The Last Wave*. I think my films are a kind of quest for me even though I don't consciously think about it when I am making them. When I face questions about unreality, the bizarre, black humor, any of these areas, I feel the labels are often the wrong way around. The great black joke is that we agree on a certain reality that's to me plainly full of holes, with great gaps of reason.

Ryan and McFarlane: One issue you rarely tackle is the question of sex. Why is that?

Weir: I don't know. I think eroticism has been present in my films and it's an area I find interesting. But I think the subjects of sex is dwarfed by larger questions. I prefer Jung to Freud. I think Freud was a dazzling, original thinker, but I don't feel his theory was ever tested because it was submerged in a moral debate. It was really never fully explored or talked about, because the key issues were lost in the way moral and religious issues were allowed to interfere. But I'm more inspired by Jung. For him, sex was a part of the great whole and, in that way, I think sexuality is in my work. I direct with my body: I use my sexuality to direct. I have explored the masculine and feminine in my own personality to direct actors and actresses, and that's meant they must explore their duality too. In this way I think I've gained from Jung. When I talk about him, by the way, I must say I have not studied the major body of his work. I have only read the popular works, those half a dozen volumes he wrote for people like me. But it was enough to find some computability and to expand my mind.

Ryan and McFarlane: *Picnic at Hanging Rock* is a film which is very interesting in its exploration of a sort of smothered sexuality in an environment which represses it. . . .
Weir: I was never really interested in that side of the film. I didn't see it as a part of its theme. I remember when I went to London for the promotion, that that was the area which most interested the British critics. Comments ranged from talk of repressed sexuality to the less subtle, talking about lesbianism and so on. But it didn't interest me. For me, the grand theme was Nature, and even the girl's sexuality was as much a part of that as the lizard crawling across the top of the rock. They were part of the same whole: part of larger questions.

Ryan and McFarlane: It's interesting that you don't feel it to be more important, because it does seem very intelligently worked out through the film. For instance, there are kinds of contrasts you set up between the attitudes of those influenced by Victorian education—the girls and the teachers—and those of the servant, Minnie, and her boyfriend, Tom. Also, there is the contrast between Albert the groom, who makes fairly crude comments about the girls as they go up the rock, and the inhibited, more "chivalrous" response of Michael. I think you can trace that sort of thing through the film. . . .
Weir: Perhaps, but that kind of approach is quite foreign to me. The words and analytical thinking, which come from your side of the table, represent something I have unlearned. It is a tool that I was brought up with through my education, something I was trained to use and something I have found I didn't want to use or live with. I am not trying to imply something mystical, simply that to use words like this, is very distant for me. I think what I have done in my own sort of personality course over the past fifteen years is what enables me to make films, or to make them my way, and I think this sort of approach gets in the way. Of course, I sat with Cliff Green and worked things out, and that was a necessary process to get something on to paper, something an audience can understand—a blueprint for the film. Perhaps it would have been easy to talk about this closer to the film, but now, as I am left with a horde of images from that film, it's only the way I began the film, or began thinking about it.

Ryan and McFarlane: The scenes that seemed to matter in the film were not the ones of the girls going up the rock so much as those of earthy, more human behavior—like those ones between Minnie and Tom, which give a context to the rest. Here are people behaving like people, and not like those who have been victims of a certain kind of education. . . .

Weir: It's an interesting part of the balance, but it didn't interest me then, just as it doesn't now. In the film, what interested me were other areas: sounds, smells, the way hair fell on shoulders, images—just pictures.

Ryan and McFarlane: One of the things that is said about your films, and you say it too, is that they avoid politics in the broad sense of the term. Yet in *Picnic at Hanging Rock*, you have a very political situation: there is a certain sort of education, a certain class structure, that the film seems to deal with directly.

Weir: I found it very interesting as an Australian whose origins were in the British Isles, to use the film to sort of wander through the ruins of the class system. And then I went back to that from another angle with *The Plumber*: to look at class in contemporary terms, to what we might have become in our society where we don't seem to have such a clear working-class, middle-class, aristocracy thing.

Ryan and McFarlane: David Hare, the British dramatist, has talked about why he thinks it is important to deal with historical subjects rather than contemporary ones, arguing that by looking back, you can see a process of change. You can identify shifts in a way you can't if you look at the present, where you are submerged in this mass of apparently contradictory information. . . .

Weir: Yes, that is if your interest lies in a clear line between the two. Again I think it comes back to concepts, on the way you see things. A question that is often asked is, "Why are you filmmakers so concerned with the past? Why are you making so many period pictures? What we need are contemporary films that are relevant." But to me, that just never was the question. Past, present, or future—they are all relevant, at least as far as filmmaking goes.

Ryan and McFarlane: From *The Cars That Ate Paris* onwards, almost all your films, at least as far as your comments are reported, are conceived from a personal incident, and you seem to have rejected *The Thorn Birds* because you couldn't get involved. How important is that personal incident as a starting point?

Weir: Since I've become aware that I do this, I am attempting to stop. If something becomes self-conscious and you are continuing to do it, you are just acting yourself out. *The Last Wave* was, in a sense, that externalizing a feeling that came from picking up a head in Tunisia, and the bottle [Eno Salts] that I picked up, among other items, at Gallipoli. But now having done interviews where these things have been photographed and looked at, it is as if for *The Year of Living Dangerously* I will have to go and collect something in Indonesia, which is absolutely absurd. Nevertheless, that kind of connection with a story is important for me; a feeling that it is somehow a part of me—that I am part of the process of the film.

Ryan and McFarlane: One of the credits for *The Last Wave* reads "based on an idea by Peter Weir." Does this idea come from the stone head you picked up in Tunisia?

Weir: In this particular incident in Tunisia, we had stopped at some Roman ruins and I had a kind of premonition. The driver was tooting the horn of the car to make us hurry back, but I delayed. I am glad, because I found a little piece of stone with three parallel lines on it. I pulled it up and it was a hand, a fist attached to a head—about the size of a doll's head. It was a marble figure of some sort, cut from some sort of relief. I later got it dated at the University in Sydney.

I then wondered what was the experience I had passed through, and found myself thinking of it happening to a lawyer or a journalist—someone who dealt with the rational, and with "facts." I let that thought hang about for a while and joined it with some other thoughts I'd been having. A pattern formed and a story began to emerge around that of a lawyer who stumbled across areas of the irrational or the unreal.

Ryan and McFarlane: To what extent is this notion of the irrational essential for you as a starting point for a film?

Weir: I think there are all sorts of other things, too. It may have been important at one point, but I like to feel I am moving in other areas now. We mentioned comedy earlier, and in talking to John Cleese we threw around a couple of ideas and a couple of funny situations. So the search for this story is apparently not following that kind of route. But the area of creativity is obviously one that can be approached by various avenues.

You have to leave yourself open. Just as people jog to keep their bodies fit, there is the equivalent mentally. You must somehow have a set of some sort of exercises. I am not talking about some sort of transcendental meditation, because that's not really worked for me, but you must, somehow, have your mind open like a child. Obviously that is not easy.

Ryan and McFarlane: In *The Last Wave*, was your point of interest the details of the Aboriginal culture? Was it important to you that the audience received those, or that it received the experience of a white Anglo-Saxon man, faced with the area of mystery, the unknown?
Weir: I think it was the latter, because there was so much I didn't understand about the Aboriginal people. I still don't understand and I did not want to draw conclusions on their behalf. Also, I had to use the English language when talking with tribal people, and that further opened up the danger of false conclusions. In talking with them, I had to talk about my character, of course, and what I felt. I had to do that in a particular way to try and get round the language, communication problem. With the tribal people, I did that in a very aggressive way; I had to. The tentative approach just didn't feel right to me; the sort of approach at the "white man's burden" level. I had to come in as an equal, somehow, and that was very difficult. I also knew that if I thought about it too much, I would never start anything. So I came in talking about what I felt was my own "missing link" and feeling. I tried to explain my attitudes to my own past and the kind of things that I'd felt on finding the Roman head. I went to meet Nandjiwarra in Darwin. I just steamed in there, not really knowing what the result might be, but just taking a gamble, an intuitive guess, that I was in the right direction. We communicated rapidly, and I learnt things that I wouldn't have through another process.

Ryan and McFarlane: You seem to share many things with Nicolas Roeg. Not only through *Walkabout*, but also *Don't Look Now*, where it seems there is a more or less comparable situation of the rational man being forced to surrender his rationality to come to terms with his situation. Have you ever considered any kind of similarity between your work and his?
Weir: I have loved a number of his films and, yes, there are areas where our paths have crossed. But in other areas we diverge. His treatment of sexuality or sex is different from mine or is more predominant. He uses that as a part of his tension. I use other systems. It's like waving at

someone in the distance and sharing a smile. But that's about as much as I know about him.

Ryan and McFarlane: A comparison of *Don't Look Now* and *The Last Wave* raises two points of disappointment for me in those films and that is when the mysteries are actually unraveled. In *The Last Wave* it's when one sees the wave with David Burton (Richard Chamberlain) in the last shot. I have always wished that film had ended with his look. . . .
Weir: The ending is still a problem for me.

Ryan and McFarlane: In David Stratton's book *The Last New Wave* [*The Last New Wave: The Australian Film Revival*, 1980], he says you wanted to do the ending in a much more lavish way: perhaps streets being flooded and so on. Was the decision to end the film as you did just forced on you by economics or was there an artistic choice?
Weir: Both elements were involved, but I think I have to be honest and say that I didn't find the solution to the problem of how to end the film, there is no ending and I was painted into a corner. I have seen it happen with other filmmakers dealing in this kind of area. You can't end it. You can try to be clever, and I tried a couple of other endings that I did stop short of any wave, but they were just too neat. The ending just plagued me, and it was an extremely unhappy period. Part way through the film we broke over Easter. I remember a terrible few days wrestling with this ending and pretending I had found a solution to it. But I certainly had no plan I failed to execute.

Ryan and McFarlane: Looking at the film now, do you have an idea of how you might end it?
Weir: No. It's just the last chapter is missing. I just have to leave it; don't look back.

Ryan and McFarlane: Do you have a special interest in myths? It seems to be the case in *The Last Wave* and indeed in *The Plumber*, where the Judy Morris character is very interested in New Guinea tribal habits. . . .
Weir: It's something that comes and goes. I mean, I'd say that, as of this moment, I am not interested, but these things don't go away, they are presumably part of your make-up. They come back when you have worked through it.

Ryan and McFarlane: Would you suggest that is the case because myths tend to be a way of coming to terms with things otherwise unexplainable?

Weir: Yes, I think they are an essential part of civilization and it's given us particular problems as displaced Europeans who chose, for some extraordinary reasons, to leave our myths behind. I think our films in this period are, at times, an attempt to rediscover them or to reinvigorate them or even to create them, as the Americans have done. I think that part of their mythology can be seen on the screen. They didn't invent it, but they plugged into something. In this context, the ending to *The Last Wave* becomes less important to me. It was in the center of the film that my interest lay, in coming close to something and failing to achieve it. I think if I did the film today, I would make it less extravagant from the "disaster" element and stay in the law court.

Ryan and McFarlane: You say "coming close to something." Is it possible to be more precise?

Weir: No. I think you can look at it in a number of ways. I think it was dealing with some very powerful truth, in fact, I was working out while making the film. I don't mean like working out a personal problem, but the chemistry of the people involved and the material we were dealing with became more interesting than the script itself. There was a highly charged atmosphere.

As most people know, that's true of any film set, given that the material has some potential in it, and this was particularly true with *The Last Wave*. I have never had one quite like that and others would have taken the material in different directions. But having Nandjiwarra and David Gulpilil in the city, dealing with that material produced tensions that were quite extraordinary.[1] And all I could do is try and hold on to it. It was very exciting, far more interesting than the rules for constructing a dramatic story, even though it may have led me away from finding a satisfactory conclusion for the film.

Ryan and McFarlane: Is *The Plumber*, then, a return to something much safer?

Weir: No, it wasn't that so much as being in a period where I had no project ready to go. I had this short story and needed some money.

Ryan and McFarlane: Your intention was to write the screenplay for *The Plumber*, but not to direct it. . . .

Weir: Yes, I didn't think there was enough in it for me.

Ryan and McFarlane: Yet, in the context of your work, it looks very much like a Peter Weir film.
Weir: In the end I couldn't let it go.

Ryan and McFarlane: Was it frustrating making it for television?
Weir: Only when I saw it come out on television with the commercial breaks and the small screen. There was a sense of some sort of loss.

Ryan and McFarlane: In some ways, it seemed like a return structurally to *The Cars That Ate Paris*, that is probably more tightly put together.
Weir: I always think of it as a companion piece to *Homesdale* and *Cars*.

Ryan and McFarlane: And again, though you may not agree, a sort of black comedy idea seems to go right through these three films particularly. . . .
Weir: Yes.

Ryan and McFarlane: In the period after *The Plumber*, there seems to be a large gap which I gather is taken up with your time in the U.S. and the abandoned *The Thorn Birds*. Do you still want to work there?
Weir: Well, the U.S. to me now, after so many trips and so many projects that weren't right, has really come down to almost a group of people. I have a number of friends there now, in the business mostly, and I would like to work with them or use them in various capacities. But I feel, at the moment, that it is right for me here. Australia is the most exciting film-making country in the world. How long it will last I don't know. These things fade, as film history teaches us. So, my interest is here now, though if I had found something particularly exciting in the U.S., I would probably go. But it wouldn't be going over for a oncer and then coming back.

Ryan and McFarlane: Is it that there are a lot of constraints in the U.S., like what happened to *Cars*, that seem to be constantly holding you back?
Weir: I don't think that's a good example because the McElroys [producers] and I were just extremely naive. Those were very early days and we thought we were in with the right people, and we weren't. We just got ripped-off. But even if they hadn't done what they did with the cut, the film still wouldn't have worked. So I am not worried about that. I think it's just that they are choked with craft over there. There is just too much refinement, too many filters, too much processing of material. Talk about losing the art! They sure have the craft in great quantity, but if

I hear that word "development" again I think I will just cancel the ticket. It's great to put the script through the punishing process they invented, but there is a time when you have to make it or drop it, and both those decisions they will defer as long as they can—to the detriment of the projects.

Ryan and McFarlane: Would you agree that the title *Gallipoli* refers not so much to a place or a battle as to an idea?
Weir: Yes.

Ryan and McFarlane: In the desert sequence in *Gallipoli*, Frank makes reference to Burke and Wills.[2] It makes some kind of contact between their enterprise and the idea of *Gallipoli*. . . .
Weir: Yes, it was a great idea of David's, linking the two failures.

Ryan and McFarlane: Your collaboration with David Williamson seems to have been a very productive meeting of different interests. Is he happy with the film?
Weir: Yes, I think this is evident from the fact that we are going into another one. We had disagreements, but there were only one or two instances where we walked away thinking maybe we won't get over this one. The film and the ideas involved were bigger than we were, so we could always meet again under those terms.

Ryan and McFarlane: There seems to a be a striking similarity between *Gallipoli* and *Chariots of Fire*. They are both set in the early years of the twentieth century and deal with athletes going off to represent the Empire but not really understanding the implications of what they are doing. . . .
Weir: There are similarities but only superficial ones. The tone is very different. I love the music of Vangelis and had planned to use him for some time, and there he is on the soundtrack of *Chariots*.

Ryan and McFarlane: It seems to be a very relaxed film without being loose, as if it's in no hurry to get where it's going although it knows where that is . . .
Weir: I think that's something that I have learnt. It's such a long apprenticeship you have to serve in films.

Ryan and McFarlane: You obviously make a choice not to show very

much blood. You showed bodies, but there's none of that Sam Peckin-pah-style stuff, which would have made the impact of the actual process of dying pretty powerful and bloody. Were you concerned dramatically to work away from that?
Weir: Yes, but I disagree with an aspect of what you have just said. I do think the more you show, the less real it becomes.

Ryan and McFarlane: How do you feel about Frank? In a sense his destiny remains unsolved. . . .
Weir: I think we know Frank. He was a survivor and a type one can still observe today.

Ryan and McFarlane: Do you agree that the film is less the dramatization of an anti-war viewpoint than a study of the idea of adventure with one's mates and of their competitive urge?
Weir: I saw a headline in the paper today saying, "Americans claim neutron bomb will prevent war." So what does "anti-war" mean? Everyone is anti-war. I think the term was invented in some publicist's office. When the war happened, it happened. I didn't really care why it happened. I have heard too much about that. I did it at school and never believed a word of all the explanations of how it happened. My interest was not in the causes of war but in the men who went.

Ryan and McFarlane: The choice of music for your films seems to be just right. Do you add music after the final cut or do you have some piece of music in mind en route to the final cut?
Weir: Both, I think. Quite often I have been surprised to find that music which gives me inspiration during the shoot just doesn't work with the cut. So I have to put it aside; it has served its purpose.

Ryan and McFarlane: Is the choice of Mozart in the garden party sequence by the lake in *Picnic* deliberately there to point to the oddness of the European culture in this very alien landscape?
Weir: Yes. It struck me as very funny. I also liked the music very much. But it's funny how you change with things. At first, my response was purely a visual one—all the people in those clothes by the water—and that pleased me. But as we played the Mozart on the day of filming I just drifted into some other area. I thought, what beautiful music, and who cares about what happened to some British culture and who cares about the point of the British in Australia or the Europeanness in our

landscape. Suddenly it was too obvious and nothing compared to that piece of music. This obviously happens as you are directing. You drift into other areas. You forget trying to be clever. I constantly try to strip myself of cleverness, because I think that old adage is true: that while mastering your craft you lost your art. So many first films have such vigor, energy, and originality, yet later works often gain in craft and lose that fire.

Ryan and McFarlane: In *Gallipoli*, you manage to create an atmosphere that seems just right. A good example is that extraordinary sense of a "ghostly funfair," as I think Evan Williams in *The Australian* described it, when soldiers arrive at Gallipoli. . . .
Weir: Yes. I think it's something that's come naturally to me and it's something I know will just happen. But I don't know how. The scene you mention came from the description of a veteran, a man called Jack Tarrant who came in as a reinforcement. He said "How can I possibly describe it to you? It was a hospital ship and it had its red cross and green lights on. I can't think of the words to describe it. It was just not what we expected." And that was enough of an inspiration. I was so grateful for the experience that came through what he said. He had given it to me. Evan Williams's description was very apt, I think, for it was exactly how I thought of it.

Ryan and McFarlane: But it's not just the images. You seem to spend a lot of time preparing the soundtracks . . .
Weir: I love sound. I work with it constantly. I feel it's the final creative stage that a director has at his command. I have always worked with Greg Bell and Helen Brown, who are a great team. We have very inventive sessions which can change the tone and mood of a scene. They are constantly experimenting, mostly with familiar sounds. They like to work at replacing the natural sound with some other kind of sound: It's part of the secret of creating that atmosphere when a footstep, in fact, is being created by something either electronic or inconsequential—crushing a packet of chips or something. It gives the sound an edge. But you'd never pick it.

Notes

1. David Gulpilil Ridjimiraril Dalaithngu is an indigenous Australian traditional dancer and actor. When he came of age, he was initiated into the Mandhalpuyngu tribal group. His film acting debut was in Nicholas Roeg's *Walkabout* (1970).

2. Robert O'Hara Burke and William John Wills attempted to cross the Australian interior in 1860–61. A film version was released in 1985, directed by Graeme Clifford and photographed by Russell Boyd.

The Swizzle Stick: Peter Weir and Hollywood Genres

Jonathan Rayner / 1993

From *Film Australia*, N. Sydney, June 22, 1993. This interview and related research were conducted with the support of the British Academy.

Jonathan: In your American films, it seems you're aware of genres, you're aware of previous directors, and when you get to something like *Green Card*, you've reintroduced screwball comedy to talk about an issue like immigration or tolerance.

Peter Weir: I don't think I set out even to do the latter. I wanted to get back to work after *Mosquito Coast*, and nothing interested me that was coming through the mail. I felt so frustrated and disappointed by the reception of that film because it was commercially and critically really not a success in any way I could take some heart in. So I decided to get back to work writing myself again, and I thought I'd write something very simple, very commercial, and so I wrote an early draft of *Green Card*, which was for an Englishman at that point, and having looked at *It Happened One Night* and all that, I thought I'd do something along those lines; and I just put it in the bottom drawer because it seemed irrelevant and uninteresting and television and been-done-before-and-better. And it was only when I saw Gerard Depardieu in an umpteenth film that I thought, or it was suggested to me, that he would be a far more interesting immigrant than an Englishman, the Cary Grant I couldn't find. That was enough to get me started again, rewrite it for a Frenchman, and so part of the excitement of that film was really getting Gerard to work in English, and to introduce him to English-speaking people. There are a lot of people who don't go to foreign films, a surprising number, and I was always faintly embarrassed that it was so much a genre piece. Yes, of course, I put my own jokes in or odd comments or things but it wasn't the motivation. It really was an adventure for me to work with Gerard,

148

JONATHAN RAYNER / 1993   **149**

and for him it was the perfect sort of thing to begin to work in English, sort of clear and clean in conception.

Rayner: It struck me seeing *The Plumber* only recently that elements in that film are almost a dry-run for *Green Card*.
Weir: That's true.

Rayner: The complete clash of characters, people who might just as well be from totally different planets, and the same middle-class woman looking down on something she hasn't encountered before.
Weir: I was aware of it and it bothered me at one point that it seemed like I was remaking it, but I thought it doesn't matter. It was truly an exercise in a way and a very enjoyable one, but something I'd moved on from. It wasn't something that I would see myself repeating, it was just fun to do. I wanted to make a commercial film, which is sometimes a motivation.

Rayner: Scorsese's done it, taken time out to do a commercial film in order to have the opportunity to do the films he really wants to do.
Weir: And in a funny way they can become as interesting at the time of doing them, not so much in looking at them later on. *Green Card*, for all its familiarity, the romantic comedy genre, began with the idea in my mind of a woman opening the door to a stranger who was her husband. That was really a synopsis of what I'd heard of the various "green card" marriages in Los Angeles. It just intrigued me, and for a long time I could just see simply that, both sides of that door opening, and how interesting for them to spend an intimate weekend together. That was enough to think about, to just turn over in my mind. But others . . . *Last Wave* was finding a carved Roman head in Tunisia. I just had to think about it, why I knew I was going to pick this thing up and what it might mean. If I wrote a little story about it, if it was a lawyer it would be very different. A lawyer would have to deal with it in a rational way. Even a lawyer telling the story would have a different reaction to a filmmaker telling the story. The strangest textural things become the grit in the oyster. Those I've known who plan things out to make points are what I call in the propaganda school of filmmaking. It can result in some good films—I think it does result in very short careers, because the minute you operate on the conscious side of the mind, I think slowly the unconscious signals are ignored in the process of preparing and writing the film, because you have in a sense loaned your services to the cause and you're therefore into a

conscious area of consideration. "We'd better do this," or "We'd better do that." I often say that to American script writers because they're writing very much from the conscious side of the mind, in terms of what they think the studios and producers will like. And also political correctness, which now has infiltrated through the screenplays in the most awful way. So scenes between men and women are following one or two predictable results, when they get together at night or a romantic scene or something. No one's allowing strange, dark things to come bubbling in and then writing around them or with them. . . .

Rayner: You seem to rely on chance occurrences to stimulate your films.
Weir: Before shooting *Gallipoli*, I remember visiting the peninsula, where the battlefield is preserved because of being a military zone still, so you can wander in the trenches and you can pick stuff up, and there's no one around. You have one of those odd moments where you know that the history that was in the books actually did happen. "Yes," you say, "there had been a First World War, pretty clearly, because there were all these bullets here." It lasts a fraction of a second. It's comparable to those very rare moments—I think I've had probably only one or two of them—where suddenly time bends, and you're outside the measured time, the agreed time calendar and the clock we live by.

That happened to me once at the pyramids, just looking at the name of a Portuguese sailor who had carved his name on the pyramids on three different voyages in the fifteenth century. And just for a fraction of a second, timed moved for me and then closed over. Hard to describe that feeling, but during that visit to the peninsula, I thought the Australians were these young men who'd come and fought and died—in a way the war was irrelevant, the right or wrong of it—I just wanted to follow a couple of these young men, to make them live and then one of them to die. I was even challenged by an article, an interview with Ingmar Bergman, where he said you can do almost anything on screen except kill somebody, and that's where you can't suspend disbelief. So I thought, I want to try and do that, I want to see somebody die; and that death would be even beyond the war. Of course, everyone who makes a war film makes an anti-war film, but I'm sure the enemy makes anti-war films, whoever they may be. No one wants to go to war, they're just forced to go to war, horribly, and so what was interesting to me was a young man who had to die. After all, we were in Turkey, it was their country, they were defending it. I really didn't have a political point of view there, but I did want to see someone in their youth and imagine what it felt like to be that age, to have to give it up, and know you had to. So it made itself, *Gallipoli*, I just went along for the ride and guided it. Some people who didn't care for the film as much as earlier films said, "I missed your style," or "I preferred the earlier films," and I said, "Well, style is just another tool for me." I didn't ever want to be trapped by style: that probably goes back to the auteur question.

Rayner: I think Harrison Ford said he thought you hadn't "got it," or we hadn't got it, with *Mosquito Coast*.
Weir: I think that *Mosquito Coast* was the only film that I took on without having experienced this particular excitement and this unnamable sort of emotion. I just admired the book enormously, and was looking to make another film after *Living Dangerously*, and it had so many aspects that were close to my way of seeing things. It was set up with Jack Nicholson, and I thought—this was dangerous thinking—he will bring a whole quality to this character, because I didn't truly like this man, or know him. Now that's not saying you have to like everybody you do, or your central character. In fact, I thought that was a reason to do it. I thought, "It's a good idea to do something against that traditional way of approaching a film. Maybe this is what I should be doing, get a little distance from it."

  So Jack fell out, as you know, and then Harrison came into it. He was full of enthusiasm, and I coasted along and enjoyed the making of the film, and put everything I could into it. It was very difficult, but I was happy with what I did. It was the film I wanted to make. I enjoyed it in terms of looking at it as a Shakespearean character, one of his flawed heroes, the Macbeth, the Othello, where the quality that has made them great is accompanied by a hair-line crack that will widen with their having gained power, and you watch this once-great person come apart. And I thought, how exciting on many levels, here particularly with Harrison. Here was a classic movie hero who did solve problems who starts off with the hair-crack, which might widen but then is closed over and healed, the John Wayne in many of his films, and I thought, people will love seeing it go in the other direction. Of course, that was not the case, and I think Harrison compounded the problem quite inadvertently, he did a wonderful job but he brought so many expectations of the other type of hero that the film seemed to have a serious flaw in it, a problem in the film itself as if the film was wrongly made. You know, "things don't go that way!"

  And so, to one degree, the thing I loved was the thing the public hated, and the other was that I made it without a passion. I wouldn't like to think I couldn't do it again, and I may go back and do something in a different way. Now whether the missing passion is what Harrison was talking about, I don't know. But I don't like to think I have to make the films always with the same white heat. I think the danger then is that you would manufacture that, and it would become your trick of getting yourself to work and in the end it would just be ersatz passion. I have this instinct to not destroy but turn away from something that appears to be an aspect of one's talent. There was certainly a period when I stripped all that style out. There were only a couple of moments where my touch would be recognized: drifting past Fat Boy in the dawn, the monolith sort of thing. *Gallipoli* was another period when I turned away from any sort of style, attempting to reinvent oneself probably. But it was certainly a disappointment at the time that it [*Mosquito Coast*] didn't find an audience.

Rayner: The film's ending is "open-ended," to say the least. *Picnic* doesn't have an ending; in *The Last Wave*, what happens? Does he see the wave or not? Only in his mind's eye? Perhaps *The Year of Living Dangerously* comes off with a recognizable generic ending, but even then you're having doubts about these characters, and the tragedy which precedes the ending. So perhaps one of the expectations of a Peter Weir film is that you're not going to get what you expect.
Weir: Well, certainly I think the ending is dictated by the story, and I've changed endings to one degree of another as I've been making them. Not often, but I've already changed the tone or emphasis of them according to the mix of elements. Casting is something for those who've not made a film which is a profound change. I've often talked to writers and said, "Some of the changes you'll see it go through will be the result of the casting, because you must accept that it's going to change by giving that person a past, and understanding what they bring."

Rayner: Reading that you were influenced by or liked Kurosawa films, makes me think of his comments, that if you've got only style, and nothing to say with the style, then there's no point.
Weir: Yeah, quite right, quite true. I mean there are certain characteristics you can see but I think they are rather less interesting. I'm all for the subject, the content rather than the form, which puts you out of tune with a lot of film lovers and academics who are really more interested in the style than the content. The content can in fact irritate.

Rayner: And yet you've got, as we've already talked about, such a dense style, so many things go into what you do.

Weir: It makes sense though, don't you think? One individual, if you are not simply going from project to project, if you have to move on to things that inspire you, then it's going to draw out both your current way of seeing the world and certain profound aspects of yourself that don't change. The same fingerprint will be visible to one degree or another. Hitchcock's a very good example, but what I always thought when I was looking for my place in the scheme of things (because here we were caught between influences—American cinema and European cinema, true of my generation of non-American directors), was, where are you going to go? Here there was a lot of talk at the time that we should develop a uniquely Australian style—whatever they might have had in mind, given that we spoke English—but I'd have felt really comfortable in a particular American context which was that of the 1930s or '40s, and I think I would have flourished there. I would have gone over, or been taken over, and worked for one or other of those big people. I once talked to Norman Lloyd, who played the headmaster in *Dead Poets*. He was a man who'd worked with Hitchcock both as an actor and producer, he was co-producer of the *Hitchcock Half-Hour*, and he worked with Orson Welles in the Mercury Theatre, so he knew that generation and those particular giants, and he was a font of information about the period both on theatre and film. So I told him, "I think I would have fitted in this period, now who do you think would have brought me out?" And he said, "Selznick, without question, and you'd have hated him, you'd have had a terrible time, you'd have had one of those seven-year contracts and every time he loaned you out you'd have gone up the wall!" But I liked the idea of the freedom, where you like the idea of being assigned something you wouldn't necessarily have chosen, but it might bring out an aspect of yourself, or something that might have remained concealed where with the danger of choice you might tend to repeat yourself.

Rayner: Something like that happened with *Witness*, that you were directed towards it.

Weir: Very much so, that's exactly how I saw it, and I refused to take any kind of ironic point of view with it, which some critics commented on as if it was something I was unable to do. Of course it's perfectly easy to be ironic. I wanted to make it as if it were the first of its kind ever made, or it was part of the on-going enjoyment of the audience, as it in fact is. It's very difficult to approach something as if it were the first time: a cliché as it was a melodrama, but I enjoyed reinvigorating it. These things often have some sort of truism in them that we like to be reminded of. . . .

I feel uncomfortable in any kind of institution, groups or clubs or organizations, demonstrations, crowds of people where you give up your individual point of view and join in a common event. I think that's probably some sort of generalization about what you might call the artistic personality. I always think that my tradition is really the storyteller tradition. My background is very much Celtic, Scots, and Irish (mainly Scots), and in my fanciful thinking I always think that I would have in another time been that sort of storyteller, the bard or earlier which was the troubadour. You were always moving on, you were always going to another court. You never got mixed up in the politics of the place: go and sing your song and move to the next gig, as they say. To be reasonable, I had a lot of illness as a child, and right through school I would be off up to two to three weeks, four weeks every winter. I think I got into the habit of that. It was very cozy to stay at home with bronchitis and asthma, things like that, and my mother would indulge, and say, "Stay at home, son," and "Why not take another week to be really sure you're recovered." Of course, I missed so much key schooling, and I was pretty lazy, so when I went back to school I would fudge over what I'd missed, and it all came to a head with my final year at school where I failed what was then called the leaving certificate, the final exam, and had to repeat, and I think then that the pattern began again at university, and so I probably to a degree made the schools the villains too. It was partly not being temperamentally suited and partly that pattern of being behind with the work and not wanting to admit it and do some hard catch-up.

Rayner: In an interview previewing *Green Card*, you said you see yourself as a storyteller, you take on board lots of things before you express yourself, and you see yourself as an entertainer. That seems to fit perfectly with working on projects as an old-style American director, but as you said before you were caught between America and Europe, and *Picnic* comes on like a European art movie.

Weir: I was aware I was going to use the European system for that particular movie, because here was a movie which had no solution. It's one of those categories where you enjoy the experience of the mystery and then there is a solution. We've grown up with the problem being solved: Sherlock Holmes, to take an obvious example, Raymond Chandler, and in our twentieth century science comes into play. We're used to problems being solved. Now this in fact in America caused the film not to be a success, despite how I'd made it, but it did seem to me to be the only way to approach it was to work in the style of a European film with the slower rhythms, with the lack of exciting developments that lead you to an expectation of a solution, but to try and develop within that approach something verging on the hypnotic. That is, the rhythm of the film would lull you into another state and you would begin to go with the film and drop your expectations. There would be certain indications, certain signposts that you were not going to get the conventional solution, and that seemed to be the way to take the film to a non–art house public. That seemed to be the case in many territories, obviously not all, but certainly in Europe where there's tolerance for this kind of rhythm, but in America it was after *Last Wave* that it got distribution, and then did very poorly except for university campuses. But that was the appropriate style and I enjoyed working "in the style of. . . ."

Interestingly, I sense—and it's too early to know—that I'm moving into another period, of which this film is the first. I don't even quite know where it will lead me or in what way. Although it's the fifth American production, it's quite different and I feel differently, and I'm quite excited to see where it leads me, because this picture is playing around with American conventional structure, not in a particularly radical way but in a fairly subtle way, that in the previews I've seen bothers some Americans, again for this expectation as to the way a story will be told from a mainstream source.

Rayner: It's interesting that you talk of this new film as a new phase, because *Green Card* has been seen as a full stop, like you mentioned the design elements persisting from *Picnic*, and the genre characteristics of your American films, it seemed as if everything so far had gone into *Green Card*.
Weir: That's interesting.

Rayner: So, you don't know where you're going now?
Weir: I feel as in some strange way I'm drawing back towards those earlier films. You know, you can never go back, so it's not a case of repeating yourself, but the freedom I felt with those earlier films I feel is back, and yet obviously the bag of tricks has grown. Not that that will make a film work, no amount of craft will, but some sort of ambition has dropped away. Perhaps it's just simply having made a number of films, having gone through the American experience while always living here, which is an interesting difference to some of my colleagues from the same

generation who did move there for one reason or another. I think it's been very valuable in enabling me to go to this third phase, because I haven't lived an American life, and I'm intrigued to know just what that might mean.

But it certainly is that I feel in the mood for exploring more deeply the potential of the medium. I feel that I've reached that level, and that doesn't mean in a sense any kind of new techniques. People talk about the fact that we haven't really explored the medium, and I think often older directors are saying this, and that's not unreasonable. If you're going to go on and explore it yourself, I think it's awful if you reach the end of your career and say, "cinema's in its infancy." That'd be depressing. Perhaps really what you're saying is, "I am creatively in my infancy," and it's certainly embarrassing when people refer to commercials or MTV or something as some indication of a way we could free ourselves up. I don't think that's the point. It's not necessarily technique or style, it's not scientific development in any way. People are going to see *Jurassic Park* it seems, from the impression I'm getting, to literally see dinosaurs walk around, and that's enough for the price of admission, which is fine. But for me it's something about the power of the close-up, and of people: one person looking at another person or looking at an object. It is the hypnotic area, it is the psychic area, that I find is suddenly of interest to me again. I've crossed past it, I've gone through it, I've seen it, I've used it. I mentioned in *Picnic* working in that way and even using certain devices to increase this feeling. For example on that film, slowed down earthquakes, which just register on the optical track, repetitions of certain kinds of sound. Sound's very important for that, but also the pictures, and I've experimented a little bit on this film, enough to whet my appetite and begin to feel that there's plenty of room to push the boundaries further with cinema. Instead of looking out, ahead, perhaps the trick is to look back, to look at the ground that's been covered and what has simply been put to one side as part of the development of film.

Maybe I was beginning to research this by going back after *Green Card*. I began to look at the way they told stories without sound, looking for I don't know what, but for what might have been passed by in the rush, with all the developments in this century. And so I find myself interested in the close-up and the power of the individual who is cast to play the part. In other words, when you cast somebody, they're bringing themselves, their soul, their body, their spirit to you to photograph. Who are they? What do they bring? Why did you cast this one over that one? On the stage it's not relevant because of the fact it's a constant wide shot wherever you're sitting, but the fact we can go into the pores of the skin, and into the eyes. Okay, these are superficial aspects of it, but neverthe-less that person is putting out something. There are those who believe in auras and whatever, that may or may not be true, maybe they do see them, but certainly we can influence each other. The old trick of you can stare at the back of someone's head and make them turn around is true. I'm interested in this area whereas I thought I'd left behind my period of interest in ESP or psychic phenomena in the seventies. It seemed to be part of the times, but perhaps now I'm opening it up and looking at it in a different way. This may make no sense as we're talking it out, but I do feel some potential to do with the contacting of the unconscious, in a more planned way than the random way that it has operated for me up until now. Because of this fascinating situation when someone sits to watch a film, it seems there are two streams operating, coming off the person, that is, their conscious and the unconscious. The conscious you have to get past, you have to satisfy the conscious side of the mind in terms of plot and logic and all the rest of it. It's a formidable barrier, and if you can get through it and reach this unconscious, I've left room for them to join in the process of making the film. Therefore we can't be didactic, but the result is extremely powerful and profound, and so I'm interesting in continuing in that area. It's beyond emotion, although that's part of it, trying to touch some true sentiment if you like.

Rayner: And this is the medium for it? I mean, talking about how you feel about writing music now, you wouldn't work in any other medium?
Weir: Well, I would work in music if my life had led me that way. That's the only other direction I would have gone, I would think, if I'd grown up with it as most musicians have. I suppose there are people who've picked it up, but this is where I find myself. Yes, I think music can do it.
. . .

Rayner: Or music and image, for which there isn't really a vocabulary as yet, for how they work on us together?
Weir: I remember the little poem—it's in one scene that's not in the film, in *Dead Poets* anymore, in collecting so much poetry. It was a Tas-manian poet, a woman and a little poem that I had Robin Williams say. It went into a long TV version: "Words can never say, as music does, The unsayable grace, that leaps like light from mind to mind"—something like that—"Leaps like light, From mind to mind." I think film can do that, express this "unsayable grace."

Rayner: And Hollywood? That was another part of the planned development, the move there?

Weir: I think any filmmaker considers it, with reasonable command of English, and some reject it and some find that they can't work or that their approach to the work is simply not something they can do, but from someone like myself to Wim Wenders, they find their way there. Truffaut didn't, and Bergman didn't. As I say there is a difference with those who don't speak the language, but everybody goes there, including those particular filmmakers. There are stories of them there that I'm always interested to hear: "Did you know Bergman?" "Yes, I did." "Did you know he came here and we were going to do something and it all fell apart?" So there is, I think, for all of us who grew up outside the United States, there is the thrill, particularly of my generation, a pre-television generation, that the first movies you saw were American, the first ones you loved and touched you were American, from the matinee B-grade movies to horror films and including British pictures too. I saw a lot of British pictures when I was growing up. There were Hammer Horror movies which I loved, and some of the Ealing comedies. I saw all of them, I think, and loved that, and one was sorry when that particular strand of filmmaking disappeared. . . .

Rayner: I read an interview with Gillian Armstrong in which she said that if people like Fred Schepisi, Bruce Beresford, and Peter Weir hadn't gone to America, would the money here just have been soaked up by them on fewer and fewer, bigger and bigger projects? And that would have been the end, there would have been no opportunity for the next generation of Australian filmmakers.

Weir: Interesting point, I've never heard it put quite that way. And it's a very important point to put into the consideration of the film school, which is something sometimes they find it hard to justify: the amount of money, millions and millions it costs to keep it running, just like those figures they often quote about a fighter pilot in the air force, how much it costs to produce one. I'm sure it's not far different for a film director after three years at the film school. And you think, "Well, they're going to go off and make films in America," but it's not necessarily true. Jane Campion, interestingly, she's doing *Portrait of a Lady* next, she's slowly moving out. I think I have such a different view. I like that Hitchcock phrase, that "film is its own country," really, and the filmmaker is the dictator of that particular country, and you go and visit it, don't you think? I never really knew how the English thought of Hitchcock. . . .

Rayner: Do you see a future for Australian film?
Weir: Very much so. The atmosphere here is charged, which it wasn't two to three years ago. Baz Luhrmann is obviously a real talent, and so is Jane Campion. She is, I would think, possibly the greatest director that will come out of this area, certainly out of the South Pacific to date. I think what I've seen of her films, she has something so interesting because what she does, perhaps unique in the world, is put you inside a female sensibility. People often say her films are so original, and it's often males saying that, but I don't think it's just that. She tells stories, in her own unique way, but the stories aren't significantly different to anything we've seen. She's not creating a new medium. It's that you are sitting there, and everything for a male is through these female eyes and way of seeing the world. It makes you realize that a lot of other films you've seen made by women have been in a way from a masculine perspective. That's the only conclusion I can reach. I feel this is the way a woman sees, same as if a cat could make a film, or an alien would make a film in the way we do it on Earth. She's following a classic European pattern.

Rayner: You recognize a female sensibility when there aren't really that many outstanding female characters in your films. Is that an area you think is a problem—not a problem, is it simply difficult to do?
Weir: I think the answer is yes. When you're creating alone the way I do it, you go into some sort of pocket of yourself, and the deeper and the further you go into it, the more you're inside your masculine self. I think you can contact the female part of yourself. Some of the films I've made had a kind of feminine aspect to them, but that's been dictated by the subject matter, or a way of seeing things that might be more towards a female sensitivity, but it seems virtually impossible. I tried it in *Green Card*. I very much tried to see it from her side, but she's not a strong female character. I think that's where Jane Campion is going to play her part, and understandably it would be disappointing if she were creating strong male characters. I think *Picnic* was probably the nearest one. I mean, I didn't write it, it was written by a woman. Interesting to imagine how different it would have been through a woman's eyes. . . .

I think the challenge is to attempt to keep yourself open, as you get on in years and experience, to new influences. . . . A chance remark by an actor over dinner, or sound heard on the way to the set can alert you. All your antennae are out, but curiously with this music, you know, the *sound* of the film, I remember when I was working on *The Thorn Birds* and I was the third or fourth director who took this project on. This was in '79 and I signed on to do it, and went to work with the writer in Los Angeles, and was very uncomfortable. I was having . . . I think I took it on for the wrong reasons. It was sort of like a way of moving into international filmmaking and working with the Americans while doing an Australian subject, but the truth was I only liked the outback stuff and found great difficulties once I got into the heart of the novel really. Anyway, I thought there was a way to beat it and that working with the writer we'd do something that'd put me at my ease. And that didn't happen, and I was trying to work out what it was that was inhibiting me so much. I remember the occasion I was to meet—can't remember if it was the writer or the producer in a bar at the Beverly Hills Hotel—and I was waiting, I was early, and I ordered a drink which was some sort of cocktail which had a swizzle stick in it, a plastic stick. So I was playing with the stick, I put it in my mouth, and closed my teeth around the stick and then just abstractly tapped the end of it. Well, of course it vibrates, and sends quite an incredible sound through you, heard inside your skull so to speak, and I thought, what a great thing! So I flicked it again and I thought, "That's the sound that's not in the film," and that sound is now in all my films, and it was a tension, a kind of tension.

Rayner: Something under stress that's being struck all the time?
Weir: Then I thought no more about it than it was just one of those illuminating little moments, and I thought, "I can't do this film, it doesn't have the sound of the swizzle stick." In fact I saved the swizzle stick: I've lost it since but I did have it for years stuck inside a diary as a reminder not to get into that situation again. Do the swizzle stick test *before* I go off and do a movie! . . .

The Iceman Cometh: *Mosquito Coast*

Digby Diehl / 1986

From *American Film*, December 1986. Reprinted by permission of the author.

Gracey Rock, Belize, 12:30 A.M. Gracey Rock was nothing more than a wide spot on the Sibun River—unfarmed raw jungle—until it was transformed into the community of Jeronimo for the filming of Paul Theroux's 1982 novel, *The Mosquito Coast*. The set looks like an army encampment dumped in the Central American jungle, and in this hotbed of political unrest, the resemblance is unnerving. In the middle of the jungle, looking like a foreboding Mayan monolith, sits a juggernaut named "Fat Boy." Built by a latter-day Swiss Family Robinson, this huge ice house symbolizes the technological hubris and American ingenuity they brought to the experiment of starting life over, freed from the decadence and disappointments of modern civilization. Fat Boy is eerily illuminated by large searchlights beaming down from the palm trees, but beyond the lighted perimeter of the set, the jungle is black and intense. The sounds of wild monkeys and tropical birds fill the hot, humid air. The crew moves around under the lights, making sure all is ready for a climactic scene.

Paul Theroux's novel chronicles the saga of freethinker and all-purpose handyman Allie Fox (played by Harrison Ford in the film), whose frustration and disgust with life in America leads him to pack up his family and create a garden of Eden in the jungle. Producer Jerry Hellman acquired the rights to the book when it was first published at least in part because he identified with Fox's independence, his anger at modern life. "I understood what he was all about," Hellman says. "His reaction—to get the hell out of here—is a legitimate reaction to modern life, not the only one, but an appropriate one."

"When I first read the book, I loved the bizarre aspects of it," says director Peter Weir, his ever-present tape deck spewing forth Beethoven's Fifth into the tropical Belize air. Weir is dressed for the jungle in safari jacket and T-shirt and takes an obvious delight in his romantic surroundings. Sweating profusely, he never appears uncomfortable, but basks in both the literal and creative heat.

As we drive over the main highway from Belize City to Guatemala en route to the set, Hellman waxes enthusiastic about the project. The two of us bounce along in the back seat with a tape recorder. "A director like Peter never has a 'finished' script," says Hellman. "Most executives in the business think in terms of script. they want to sit and fiddle with 'the script' until they get it right, and they believe they will know what 'right' is. It's foolhardy to think that there is a finished script and then you go out and shoot it precisely as it's written. That's just not the reality. The reality is an ongoing process."

Weir divides the writing of a film into three parts: the conception (the screenplay), the realization (the shooting), and the shaping (the cutting). "There's a lot of overemphasis on the original screenplay," he says. "What you really want is the conception, the clarity and beauty of the initial idea. Then the middle period, the actual shooting, is the struggle to realize the idea, given the enormous problem of logistics. The third period, the cutting, is the last chance to write the movie into decent shape. Few outside the cutting room understand that film editing is part of the writing process. It's always assumed to be a mechanical function, but it is, in fact, writing using pieces of celluloid."

"Eisenstein said that over and over. And I've found that people who best understand that editing is writing are those who edit film and videotape for news programs," he continues. "I've watched television-news editors fictionalize hard news—I learned more about cutting from them than from anybody. You can take footage of an interview with a Druse militiaman in Beirut and make him anything you want to. You can make him an idiot. You can make him a proud hero. You can make him cruel. This forever destroyed the concept of 'documentary' for me. It's the greatest fiction of all."

Directors vary widely in their approach to the filmmaking process; Weir has a reputation as one of the most "open" directors in the business. His method of working would appear to be seat-of-the-pants, if not downright haphazard.

Weir's inspiration for his interpretation of *Mosquito Coast* comes, he says, from the classics, especially Shakespeare and from the opera. "It's taken me a long time to understand where the power was coming from in this story," he explains. In the background, Wagner's *Die Walküre* is the selection on his tape deck. "There's a tremendous amount of emotion in the story. Unless it is harnessed into some sort of framework by me, I'll be stirring the audience up and they'll wander out feeling uncomfortable because they were moved, but without understanding what to do with their emotion. I think I've got the framework in this operatic feeling. In opera, many times you start with everything wonderful, the songs bright and positive, and then the complexities arise and you end with tragedy."

In the living room of the house Weir occupies in Belize (right next door to the production office), he has ample evidence of his thematic motifs spread out across every available surface. On a large bulletin board he keeps postcards, pages from magazines, and other items that embody the look or the visual impression he wants to give various portions of the film. "A letter sent to me, a snapshot of a child in a village, a pressed flower, a match box, colors . . . they all have a meaning. It's a question of texture, a kind of mosaic of inspirations. If you look carefully, you'll see that almost every key scene is represented by something or other. That's how I've always done my films. I like to have these things around me and let them have their influence as they might."

Weir realizes that his approach is not without danger. "I like to open the door to chance. That implies enormous risks. You presume on the muse visiting you, but at the same time you don't count on it. Driving to work you see street scenes—a face, a hat, a detail—that you often end up putting into the film that very day. I saw a man with a plastic bag on his head with just the face part cut out and a straw hat on top of that and said, 'Let's do that.' But it won't help the drama itself. You've got to have good acting and good thinking."

From Harrison Ford, Weir says he gets both. During the filming of *Witness*, the actor and director established an extraordinary partnership. Ford, the logical man and self-described "technical" actor, is the perfect complement to Weir, the improvisational visionary. "I supply him with something, he supplies me with something," Ford says. "We both benefit from the exchange. Peter has a vision and it's not always articulatable, if that's a word. I'm a person who calls for logic and even a plodding kind of determination to have all the cards on the table. I'm the assistant storyteller."

Ford found the eccentric character of Allie Fox a welcome change from heroic roles. One night, while waiting for the gigantic generators from Miami to be repaired so that shooting could resume, we sit in his air-conditioned motor home/dressing room talking late. He is exhausted, at the end of a long, hard location shoot, and he is beginning to take on the character of Allie Fox in earnest. "I had none of the difficulties that other people had expressed with the character being too irascible, too unconventional," he says. "I found him more often right than wrong in what he was saying. There is also the complexity of the family story, the relationship between a father and son and between a husband and wife. There is humor and pathos, a real range from antic comedy to gut-wrenching stuff. The simple exercise of emotion is something that people don't get very much. At the moment, most films depend more on kinetics for their effect than on having any emotional resonance."

Ford also welcomed the opportunity to work again with Weir, who is gradually gathering his own "repertory company" of crew and actors. And small wonder—Weir is known for running a happy ship. The crew in Belize is a pastiche of Aussies, Brits, and Yanks that number about 150. And key personnel such as director of photography John Seale and film editor Thom Noble, are veterans of other Weir films. "This crew is a combination of people from *Witness* who I found exceptional, mixed with the old crew that go back to my early films in Australia," says Weir. "Here on location, we have that kind of intimacy that only comes on a set. It doesn't exist in peacetime, you might say. On location in the jungle you don't have the nine-to-five mentality that you have in city shooting. I like the concentration that results from everybody being at hand and from the ideas that abound in the surroundings. The atmosphere of the film is within the setting all around you. You disappear into the film." He gestures toward the crowded bar of the Villa Hotel, where the *Mosquito Coast* company is drinking, dancing, and laughing with the locals. Weir frequently holds court there, staying late into the night after a day's shooting. In the background, the music of the Turtle Shell Band, an Afro-Caribbean group from the Belizean coast, issues forth from Weir's tape deck.

"Belize *is* the Mosquito Coast," Hellman says. Although Theroux was unaware of it at the time he was writing the story, the fictional Allie Fox turns out to have a number of factual counterparts. "Central America is full of Allie Foxes," says Weir. "I've heard of four of them since I've been here in Belize. Many of them came down here in the late sixties. Belize is one of the last places in the world where you'll find the drifters, the travelers. No one is down here just on a holiday. If someone says they're here on vacation, you know they're CIA or they're drugs."

For the people who live in Belize, however, the filming of *The Mosquito Coast* is the biggest story that's come their way in a long while. The making of this movie was practically all I heard anyone talking about from the moment I arrived at the rustic, dilapidated airport. Whether I was in a fishing boat or a taxicab, the natives quizzed me about the movie-making. No wonder they were fascinated: In a tiny (population 148,000) agricultural country, the filming employed about three hundred local residents, spent seven or eight million dollars in foreign exchange, and made executive producer Saul Zaentz, for a time, the third largest industry in Belize.

Despite Belizean government cooperation, the logistics of the production have been awesome. The company had to build roads into the jungle, support an entire small hospital for the emergency help, coordinate with fifty local contractors who were accustomed to a leisurely Caribbean pace of life, and stay out of the myriad political skirmishes among the Belizeans, Guatemalans, Salvadoran refugees, and native Indians. In Mexico City, a convoy of catering trucks met up with the motor homes (to be used as dressing rooms) and portable honey wagons, and meandered down the so-called highways of Mexico and Central America to Belize. Shiploads of other trucks and equipment, including three huge electrical generators for night shooting, arrived from Miami. And an exhausted team of couriers shuttled film back and forth from a Miami lab for dailies. (The local airline, TACA, was quickly dubbed "Take A Chance Airline.") "The Miami connection has been a godsend," says production coordinator Judi Bunn. "You have no idea how crazy people get when they can't buy the right American shampoo or deodorant. It's wonderful to have the *New York Times* brought in on Sunday. Of course," she adds with an emphatic British accent, "I had to wait until *Tuesday* for the *London Times*."

At the main jungle location in Gracey Rock, a bulldozer begins clearing an area where the main house for Allie Fox and his family will be built. Ninety feet into an anticipated one-hundred-foot space, the bulldozer hits a twenty-foot-high mound of rock. *The Mosquito Coast* has made an archaeological discovery: an unrecorded Mayan site, probably a minor temple or residential building. Weir modifies their set location plans, but is using the Mayan temple mound as a camera platform for the final Fat Boy sequence.

At 1:45 A.M., first assistant director Mark Egerton signals that all is finally ready for that scene to begin. Harrison Ford, looking quite deranged in wire-rim glasses and slicked-down hair, is sprayed with "sweat." Jerry Hellman swats a mosquito and sprays himself with Deep Woods Off. Peter Weir, grinning puckishly, gets a laugh from the assembled cast and crew as his tape deck blares out Gladys Knight's "I Heard It Through the Grapevine." He greets them by saying, "OK, ladies and gentlemen. Welcome to the late night show. Now, let's do it!" Shortly thereafter, red horns of fire sprout from Fat Boy's head and flames belch forth from its eyes and nose. Civilization has its revenge on Fox and his family as the technological monster rocks the jungle in a series of violent explosions and destroys their dream of Eden.

Fearless: The Poetry of Apocalypse

John C. Tibbetts / 1993

Interview conducted October 10, 1993. Previously unpublished. Printed by permission of the author.

Moments before impact, the plummeting airplane starts to break up into pieces. Passengers, crew, luggage, and fragments of the cabin bounce off each other, spin out of control, and hurtle off into space. At the center of the vortex, however, there is a strange, quiet peace. A serene melody sounds out of the void, enfolding the scene in a loving embrace. Silhouetted against a brilliant circle of light stands one of the passengers, Max Klein, tears in his eyes and a smile on his face. Slowly, deliberately, he moves away toward the light. But then—a still, small voice is heard: "Come back . . . come back." He turns around, uncertainly; he stretches out his hands—

The climactic scene from Peter Weir's *Fearless* may be the most terrifying airplane crash ever filmed; yet it transpires in a preternatural calm. In director Peter Weir's hands, it is not a disaster but a benediction. It is not the moment of Max Klein's death, but the beginning of his life.

"As long as you enter my world, or allow me to throw you into my world," says Peter Weir, "you find yourself where nothing is quite as it seems."

It's a mild Saturday afternoon in 1993 in Los Angeles at the Four Seasons Hotel. Australian film director Peter Weir appears promptly for our interview. He's dressed casually, his beige trousers slightly rumpled and his gray shirt open at the neck. His soft-spoken and retiring manner are deceptive; and as he gets into the flow of our conversation, he quickly brightens and speaks rapidly and directly, with just a trace of an Australian accent. He looks rather like an elf. When he grins (which is often), the corners of his eyes crinkle agreeably and his thick brows rise to sharp peaks under the thatch of straw-colored hair. His hands are always in motion, choreographing the conversation with balletic gestures and graceful arcs.

John C. Tibbetts: You seem to have a reputation for disliking interviews. Why is that?

Peter Weir: That's not really true. I just hate the sort of thing that goes on for several days, with somebody following you about. I lose control then, and I'm a control freak. I can't control the editing of the interview and all of that.

Tibbetts: Let's begin with an image from *Fearless*. When we first see Jeff Bridges, he appears to be emerging from a tropical jungle. But in a moment we see it's only a cornfield. Right away, viewers are caught off balance.

Weir: We wanted to create a certain mood at the outset, that's true. I could have stayed in that cornfield for several days! We had planted eighty-five acres and had lots of smoke and wind machines to create that odd kind of look to it. You may have noticed we didn't have the title and credits here, which is the usual thing to do, but moved them back until after the picture had started. I wanted to throw the audience into the situation, into the images, immediately; and not distract viewers with printing on the screen.

Tibbetts: Do you grow crops on your own ranch back in Australia?

Weir: I have a property north of Sydney, quite a bit of land, but not a farm. My wife and I do keep a tropical garden, though, and we call it our "little piece of Bali."

Tibbetts: I'd like to imagine some pretty exotic plants growing on that land! It would fit. Anyway, your films seem to be driven more by images than by words, now that I think of it. And I'm thinking of the Botticelli angels in *Picnic at Hanging Rock*, for example, and now the Bosch painting in *Fearless*.[1] There's an unworldly kind of implication, something rather menacing, each time, isn't it? I mean, the girls disappear mysteriously in *Hanging Rock* and now the character of Max in *Fearless* withdraws after the plane crash into his own trauma. Or are we talking about some kind of ecstatic state or condition in each case?

Weir: It hadn't occurred to me to match them up until now! But it's interesting that you pointed them out. When I look back into my screenplays I'll find images I've saved at the time—things torn out of magazines, art books, whatever—that have been inspirational to me. And one of those images I kept for this movie was the Bosch picture, *The Ascent into the Empyrean*, which depicts figures coming up to Heaven to some kind of tunnel of light. I found it in a *Life Magazine* article about near-death experiences. I loved that picture. So much so, I thought I had to get it into the film, somehow. And so it got into the series of paintings that Max keeps on his desk. That's a scene, incidentally, that's not in the script.

You know, I've just come back from a fantastic pilgrimage to see that picture. It was about three weeks ago and I was in Venice at the Film Festival and had been told that it was hanging in the Ducal Palace (which seemed odd to me!). Initially, when I asked people, they said they knew nothing about it; but later they admitted, yes, I was right, it is here, but it's off limits. I would have to get special permission to see it. Which I got and then I was taken into the Palace through a series of rooms that had been the Inquisitors' chambers. It looked as if the Chief Inquisitor had just left the day before! Which is what had happened, in a way, after Napoleon arrived and the place was turned rather quickly into a Museum. So I was led through the Inquisition and Torture rooms, where I saw a device where a prisoner was pulled up and held above the ground while he was questioned. Finally, in the room beyond were these seven or eight panels of the Bosch "Heaven and Hell" series, including the one I used in the film. It looked as if it had been painted yesterday. Bosch had worked so hard to get that light right—an effect more powerful than you saw in the print used in the movie.

Tibbetts: It's been two years since you made *Green Card*. Where have you been?

Weir: I had done two films back to back. *Dead Poets* was wrapping up and I was also rewriting the script for *Green Card*, which involved a lot of work with Gerard Depardieu. I needed a rest. I'll be taking a rest this year, too, after *Fearless*. Don't forget, as a film director you can lose that fresh stimulation. For example, you stop reading. Everything you read could be a film, you know? Or already is about to be one! So you get reading back—especially the reading that may have nothing to do with your work. Last year I started reading about Greece and I got everything I could about the "Golden Age." Fascinating.

Tibbetts: What led you to decide to make *Fearless*?

Weir: I had been sent a bunch of so-called "A-List" scripts from Hollywood, and what I saw made me want to see another list! These were all green-lighted pictures, finished and polished and just waiting for a big director and name star. What I wanted was something not so far along, something that had not been through that process already, something I could help develop myself. I wrote the studio heads and said, "What have you got in the bottom drawer, what have you got that you wouldn't send me? What have you got that's broken?" I think I used that term. Not long after that I got a script from producer Mark Rosenberg for *Fearless*. The novel by Rafael Yglesias had only just been published and he had already written on spec a screenplay. I got the first draft, liked it, and was on a plane to Hollywood within two weeks.

Tibbetts: What kinds of changes were made after you took on the story?
Weir: For one thing, I didn't want the story to take place in New York City. That would have meant shooting in New York in August, and I didn't want to do that! Besides, I had already shot *Green Card* there and I needed a change. We decided on San Francisco—which meant that we would have to change the Italian characters in the novel to Latinos and Little Italy to the Mission district. Still, people were surprised at first when I chose Rosie Perez for the part. I guess they were puzzled because there didn't seem to be any precedent in her work that indicated she could do a role like this. It seems like everybody wanted that part, by the way. It was "Cinderella Slipper" time, you know, people coming in and trying to squash their foot into the part.

For another thing, I didn't want to follow the book and have the plane crash at the beginning with the rest of the film serving as just an anticlimax. So I decided to start the film in the moments just after the crash. Then, in a series of Max's flashbacks, we go back to the minutes just before the wreck. Gradually, we lead up to the actual moment of impact. It's not until the very end of the film that we see the crash.

Tibbetts: That scene, like so many other apocalyptic scenes in your films, seems savage and unreal, yet strangely beautiful.
Weir: I spoke to six survivors of Flight 232, which crashed and broke apart in 1989. They kept telling me that nobody ever gets this sort of thing right, and I said, "Well, tell me and I will get it right." What they were saying was it all was unreal, something beyond description. They talked of blinding lights, a sense of slow motion, strange sounds everywhere. Right then I knew I couldn't use a conventional sound track! And I decided to keep the cameras inside—no exterior shots. Plus, the FAA had shown me an excellent film where they had crashed a plane with

cameras inside. I had felt something of these sensations myself, when I flew with some 747 pilots. They took me in a simulator to "experience" the kind of crash in *Fearless*. First, they took out the hydraulics—switch-switch—and said, "Now feel the wheel." There was nothing. No control at all. Now the only way we were staying in the air was with the throttle. No flaps, no way to keep the nose up. You had to accelerate either the right engines or the left engines, and each time the wings would tilt sharply, like this, first one way, then the other. So you had to sort of corkscrew your way along. We crashed from 400 feet—just dropped out of the sky. A great thudding noise. I freaked. Then I sent Jeff and Rosie to experience the same thing! Funny thing, though, I've lost my own fear of flying. When I was young, flying a lot in and out of Sydney, I never thought of it. But during the last ten years or so, it was a problem. I'd be unable to sleep. I would sit there and listen to all the noises—the engine noises. Any change and I would sit up and think, What was that? I had researched near-death experiences before, you know. During the preparations for *Gallipoli* I had read all about the experiences of soldiers who in combat would be cut off from the rest of their units. They knew they were going to die. But then, miraculously, they would find themselves alive, like Lazarus, back from the dead.

Tibbetts: *Fearless* is your tenth film. I don't know anymore whether to think of you as an Australian filmmaker or a Hollywood filmmaker—or does it make a difference to you?
Weir: I think of myself as a character in "Jack and the Beanstalk." I'm Jack and I have my farm in Australia and we have a cow, so to speak, and there's this beanstalk, my career, which I've climbed and which has taken me to the land where the Giant lives, which is Hollywood. And I go there every now and then, am given the Golden Goose, play the Golden Harp to amuse the Giant at dinner. And the Giant always says, why don't you stay? Why do you want to go home? You've got your own room here! But no, I keep returning to the farm.

I like to be a foreigner here in Hollywood! To remain a foreigner! I have an agreement with Immigration about this. If I had lived back in the thirties, though, I might have come out here as one of those émigré fellows—come out here and stayed. But this is a Global Village now, and I can be in either place within twenty-four hours. But seriously, Hollywood's just a state of mind, anyway. It's everywhere. Anytime I want I can find as many "Hollywood types" in Sydney as here!

Tibbetts: Still, Australia is where you got your start. Do you find that we overdo our enthusiasm about the "Australian Renaissance" in the late 1960s? Was it really that wonderful? What were things really like then?
Weir: No, it was fantastic. It was a wonderful time. I was in the thick of it. I was making short films from 1969 on until my first feature in 1973. What's most important (and not usually mentioned) is the exact context of it all. We were at war in Vietnam, too. We were involved in our own student demonstrations. It was the long hair, father against son, the music, the dope, the whole upheaval. In some ways, the conflicts were maybe sharper than in some parts of America. Australia was a very sleepy country that was very homogenous in every way, and the war was therefore more shocking.

There was this incredible contradiction: in a period of social upheaval it was exciting, too. Out of control, this excitement is a dangerous thing; but with a direction, it can be very positive. So, we had lots of theater, clothes shops, restaurants, the film industry—people shooting film. It was an era where you filmed that policeman backing into the crowd. This is evidence. The camera became the AK-47 of young people during that period. The truthful eye. So, cameras were about and people were making films; and I was caught up in this tremendously exciting period. And I'd come back from London in 1966 not sure if I'd made the right decision, although "Swinging London" was just about swung out. My family wrote me off as a complete disaster: Married, no money, sort of just gone off the rails, really; wanting to make films. And out of this sort of ferment came the films we made. We made them by hook and by crook. And the government people saw what we were doing and said, "Look, let's back these guys and get the industry going again." The money was really needed to finance the features we wanted to do. My god, it was great! That feeling for me lasted until the late seventies. By that time, I was needing new stimulation and I came here to do *Witness* in 1984. Much as a painter will change location to get fresh stimulation.

Tibbetts: You work in a business with a lot of hype about directors being artists and working for creative control and all that sort of thing. But you've said before that you don't see yourself as an artist at all. What do you mean by that?
Weir: It's like the tale told about the Japanese potter. The potter is content to work as a craftsman. If the gods choose to touch his hands, that is the action of art—not that the artist decides to make a work of art.

Tibbetts: But you do make conscious decisions about some things, like the use of certain kinds of music in your pictures, a wild mix ranging from Beethoven and Grieg to Penderecki, Gorecki, and African tribal drums.

Weir: On the set I always have music with me. I always carry about a boom box with music that seems appropriate to what we're doing. I guess I'm a sort of "director deejay." I find music can say things that words can't. As a director I have to be careful not to talk too much. It's really not about talking. Sometimes you'll see a director at work and he's talking and talking and explaining this and that and something or other. I find that sort of thing is just inhibiting.

Tibbetts: But can you pin down how you see yourself in this regard? In your earlier years as a filmmaker in the mid-1970s, for example, with *Picnic at Hanging Rock* and *The Last Wave*, how did you regard yourself—as a craftsman or an artist?

Weir: I hesitate to go too deeply into questions like that. All I can say is that I think I was just trying to find my place in the scheme of things at that time. I grew up with the twin influences of the European cinema, through the film festivals, and American cinema and television. I loved both and wasn't sure yet where I fit into that scheme. *Picnic* has a European look to it; *The Last Wave* seems like an American picture made by a Frenchman.

Tibbetts: Do you take a secret delight in the sometimes baffling ambiguity of your pictures, particularly in the endings to *Hanging Rock* and *Last Wave*? While we're all racing around for meanings, do you sit back, snickering through your fingers?

Weir: No, I've probably got my fingers firmly on my brow, thinking is this the right ending?

Tibbetts: Are you going to take to your grave the truth about *Hanging Rock*—whether or not it's really based on a true story?

Weir: I guess so. Or maybe I should leave behind a letter or something . . . ?

Tibbetts: Finally, back to the cornfield in *Fearless*. What are we supposed to think—are you giving us a message—that the exotic jungle is only just a commonplace wheat field; or that the wheat field can be a pretty terrible jungle, after all?

Weir: As long as you enter my world, or allow me to throw you into that world, which begins in that cornfield, it's where nothing is quite as it seems. Therefore, even a cornfield could be threatening.

Notes

1. The "Botticelli angel" refers to Botticelli's painting *The Birth of Venus* (1484–86). The goddess Venus arrives at an earthly shore.

Poetry Man: *Dead Poets Society*

Nancy Griffin / 1988

From *Premiere Magazine*, July 1989. Reprinted by permission.

On the last afternoon of 1988, Robin Williams is being much too funny. It is not the first time this has happened on the set of *Dead Poets Society*. Wholesome as you please in a retro tweed jacket and tie, he is sitting behind a table in the dining hall of St. Andrew's School near Wilmington, Delaware. Williams plays John Keating, an eccentric and inspiring teacher at the Welton Academy for boys, circa 1959. Standing quietly by is director Peter Weir, who has been thumbing through a volume of Shakespeare in search of a verse with which to supplement Williams's scripted lines in the upcoming scene. Someone has just suggested a soliloquy from *Hamlet*—and Williams, who until this moment has behaved like a choirboy, cannot resist the opportunity to lighten things up.

"To sleep—perchance to *cream?*" he wonders aloud. Then he rips into a monologue, mimicking everyone from a patient at the Betty Ford Center who loves her Folger's crystals to an Aussie film director, mate. As crew members prepping the shot place plates of mashed potatoes, meat, and gravy in front of him, Williams's eyes go wide. "Oooh, I was enjoying the movie until that giant piece of chipped beef ruined my evening!'" By now the set is paralyzed with laughter, and when Williams wraps it up with a Shakespearean-death-scene kicker, pretending to stab himself in the neck with a fork, the cast and crew is gasping for breath and holding onto chairs.

Five minutes later, Williams is sitting calmly again with hands folded, his expression the picture of innocence. As entertained as everyone else by Williams's outburst, Peter Weir has restored equilibrium on the set—but hasn't yet found the verse he needs. Then a stand-in hands him a couple of lines of poetry that he has scrawled on a brown paper bag. Weir loves them. As the cameras roll, Keating passes a bowl of potatoes to his straitlaced colleague, McAllister (Leon Pownall), who criticizes him for encouraging freethinking in his classroom. "Only in his dreams can man be truly free," says Keating. "'Twas always thus and always thus will be." McAllister asks if Tennyson is the author of those lines. "No, Keating," is the reply. "Print!" cries Weir.

It is hardly the norm for a stand-in to make a creative contribution on a film set. But it is far more extraordinary to ask a star who gets paid around $4 million a picture for being one of the funniest people in the world to recite poetry instead of crack jokes.

But there is very little that isn't unusual about *Dead Poets Society*, the wild card in this summer's shuffle of films. A two-hour-plus drama, it is a maverick for Walt Disney Studios' Touchstone Pictures, defying two commandments of the studio's development catechism: no rural settings and no snow. The title scarcely conjures up the sort of escapist entertainment that generally means hot-weather box-office bucks. (Weir's two-time collaborator Harrison Ford jokes darkly that the film would be harder to sell only if it were called *Dead Poets Society in Winter*.) Using a strategy that has Williams and others on the "Poets" team more than a little bit nervous, Touchstone chose to release this hard-to-summarize film in June. "I can't describe it in fifteen words or less," says Williams. "It would be like saying the Bible is about a young boy."

Then again, if Disney had wanted high concept, it wouldn't have hired Peter Weir. The man who made *Gallipoli*, *The Year of Living Dangerously*, and *Witness* is a master of strong, multi-layered dramatic narrative. His style combines the visual lyricism and mysticism of an art-film maker with a commercial sensibility. "*Dead Poets Society* is accessible," he insists. "It's a popular Hollywood entertainment. I've always seen myself as a commercial filmmaker, a Hollywood filmmaker—if one takes Hollywood to mean large audiences, not a syndrome."

The only true auteur among his generation of Australian directors, Weir has only once before agreed to take on a studio assignment, *Witness*. Both times, it was Jeffrey Katzenberg who dangled the offer he couldn't refuse. Last year, Weir met with the Disney boss. As the director was on his way out the door, Katzenberg said, "I've got just the film for you," and slipped him a copy of *Poets*. Weir was hooked at once by Tom Schulman's script: "It's the finest piece of writing I've worked with," he says. And he thought Robin Williams, already attached to the project, would be superb as Keating.

Just as his work is renowned for its depth of penetration into a milieu, so does Weir himself become immersed in a film's culture. This was readily apparent on the *Poets* set, where the director strode about like some

Scottish poet of another era in jodhpurs, riding boots, and tweed cap. "I don't know if it was symbiotic," says Williams, "but when we were picking out clothes, he picked out one school scarf for me and one for himself. He would wear the scarf like I wore it."

Gracious and soft spoken, Weir reigns by exhilaration rather than intimidation; he is not one for macho displays or barked orders. "Peter operates creatively from his female self," says Nancy Ellison, a special photographer on *The Mosquito Coast*. "The subliminal message is one of yielding: 'Seduce me with your performance.'" During *Poets* dailies, Weir practically flew out of his seat and cried "Yes!" when pleased by the footage. "Robin would be the first to admit that he is not the star of the film," says Robert Sean Leonard, who plays Neil, one of the students. "Peter is the star."

The tragic—although ultimately uplifting—story line made the film a crucible for intense emotions. John Keating startles his students into an expanded awareness of life's possibilities through the joys of great literature, challenging them to heed Thoreau's call to "suck the marrow out of life." At his provocation, the boys resurrect the secret Dead Poets Society—a club whose members include the spirits of Whitman, Shelley, and other greats. They begin meeting surreptitiously in a cave, where they read verse in a state of newly inflamed passion. Weir filmed in sequence, so that feelings on the set were running high by the time the moving denouement was played out. "You kind of get a clue that something is working when you see Teamsters crying," says Williams.

Weir uncorked the improvisational volcano that is Robin Williams— then remained vigilant so that he didn't erupt beyond the boundaries of the character. "Keating's humor had to be part of the personality," says Weir. "Robin and I agreed at the start that he was not going to be an entertainer in the classroom. That would have been wrong for the film as a whole. It would have been so easy for him to have the kids rolling on the floor, doubled up with laughter. So he had to put the brakes on at times." As a guide, says the actor, "Peter came up with the name 'Robin Keating' to define what he wanted: the scripted character, shaded with an additional 15 percent of Williams's own off-the-cuff dialogue."

The star knew as soon as he saw the dailies when he had gone over the top. "It was like clown makeup on a Kabuki dancer. It didn't fit." Weir did cut Williams loose for what he calls Keating's "creative radiation bombardment" lectures. For the first time Keating faces the seven young poets in the classroom, Weir asked Williams to read a bit of Shakespeare aloud and wing it from there. "I had two cameras going, obviously, and

I just said, 'Boys, this is not a scripted scene. Treat Robin as your teacher and react accordingly, and don't forget that it's 1959.'"

Although Weir admits that at times Williams's impromptu perfor-mances caused shooting delays of precious minutes—as in the dining hall—he let the comic fly. "When he's inspired, it would be a terrible thing to interrupt him," he says. "And he did keep everybody in a very good frame of mind."

Williams finds it as difficult to verbalize Weir's special charisma as he does the film they shaped together. "I rank him up there with the best of people I've worked with," he says. He praises Weir's intuition and "in-credible sensitivity about how far to push someone." All in all, he found Weir an inspiration. "He was, in essence, Keating," says Williams, "for all of us."

Had Peter Weir's own scholastic career been more auspicious, he would not have braved Delaware in December. "I hate school," he says. "That's why I could do this film. I would have been a member of the poets club." The son of a real estate agent, Weir was born in 1944 and raised in Vau-cluse, a harbor-side suburb of Sydney.

By his late teens, Weir felt increasingly uncomfortable in his con-stricted world. "You know, I used to see the ships on their way to Eu-rope," he says, "going out through the harbor. I knew I'd be on one one day, somehow. And so I was, at twenty."

It was a fateful five-week voyage. On the high seas, Weir met both his life's vocation and his wife of twenty-three years, Wendy (who worked as *Poets'* production designer). To chase boredom, he and a couple of mates wrote and performed satirical revues for the ship's passengers. "I felt a tremendous excitement about what I was doing," he says. "Sud-denly, this was very natural to me." After hitching around Europe, he rejoined his friends in London. In Hyde Park, they performed a sketch about American evangelists. "The cockney regulars in Hyde Park were so clever," recalls Weir, "that we could only survive about ten minutes."

Eighteen months later Weir returned with Wendy to Australia, where they were married in 1966. In 1971, the couple traveled back to London and considered settling there. But Weir discovered that Europe's rich cultural soil dried up his own creative instincts. When he walked down his Hampstead street, he couldn't bear the sound of clacking typewriters that seemed to drift from every window. "I couldn't get back to Australia quick enough," he says, "to a more barren cultural environment. It had become part of the process of making something: I will make something in this barrenness. Scripts and films would be my way of reinventing the escape that the ship was in '65."

Weir became a bright light in the Aussie cinema's New Wave. He wrote and directed his first feature in 1973, *The Cars That Ate Paris*, a macabre comedy about an outback town with a high incidence of car accidents. The following year he traced the disappearance of three Victorian schoolgirls and their teacher in *Picnic at Hanging Rock*. And in *The Last Wave* (1977), he immersed Richard Chamberlain in the netherworld of aboriginal culture.

Picnic and *Wave* established Weir as a true spellbinder. Both contain passages of pure imagery, often shot at a slower-than-normal speed (the camera operator was John Seale) and heightened with mesmerizing music. Weir now says that his signature style evolved out of adversity. In his early films "the scripts, including my own, were often so poor that you had to tell the story through the camera. It was a great way to learn about movies. We went through a self-imposed silent-film era in the sixties and seventies."

Despite the political overtones of *Gallipoli* and *The Year of Living Dangerously*, Weir says he is more concerned with probing human behavior than with making specific statements about contemporary society, "That's what I always loved about movies," he says. "They didn't belong to anybody. They were a separate country." When overseas opportunities beckoned, he had no qualms about crossing the Pacific.

Witness, his first American feature, was an Academy Award nominee for Best Picture in 1985 and a solid box-office winner as well. John Seale, this time serving as director of photography, says that during filming, Weir was determined to make even a murder a lovely thing to watch. "He drowned someone in wheat," says Seale. "Peter walked around the farm looking for a way to kill someone beautifully."

Weir's most recent picture, *The Mosquito Coast*, was less successful critically and commercially. He guided Harrison Ford through a bold performance as Allie Fox, the fatally obsessed father. Ford now says of the 1986 film, "I'm not sure we cracked it." But Weir concedes no artistic regrets. "What intrigued me was the very thing that turned the audience off—to take a figure of heroic proportions for whom the story opens up a weakness." He believes that viewers could not stomach the tragic ending. "The tradition of the American narrative is the reverse." He could feel, in the first preview, "the audience hoping for Allie Fox to survive and become president of the United States."

After *The Mosquito Coast*, Weir retreated to his rustic home overlooking Pitt Water Sound in Australia's Palm Beach, north of Sydney. One hot summer day in 1987 he was lying on the sand with Wendy when he spotted a familiar figure emerging from the waves with a surfboard under his arm. "I went over and said, 'Robin Williams?' And he said, 'Hi, good wave on today.'" Weir invited him to his house for coffee. "Little did I realize," says Weir, "that we'd be working very intensely a little over twelve months later."

One week before the film's November start date, Weir installed his seven young actors—handpicked for dramatic talent and classic Anglo-Saxon looks—in rooms along one corridor of a Wilmington hotel. "The infamous floor seven at the Radisson," he says, laughing. "Go there at your own peril. I don't think they ever slept." His strategy for working with his ensemble was basic: "To create an atmosphere where there was no real difference between off-camera and on-camera—that they *were* those people."

Before principal photography began, the boys played soccer together and ran through simple acting exercises, which allowed them to form a group identity naturally. Once shooting started, they were not permitted to see dailies, "so that they would live it rather than make a movie." Utterly dedicated to Weir, the young actors vied for his attention like a litter of pups. "Sometimes he had to enforce just a little bit of discipline," says Williams, "but he never snapped at them."

A veteran of seven Weir films, cinematographer John Seale communicates with the director through osmosis. Seale and his crew averaged twenty-two setups a day, maximizing the speed and spontaneity that Weir loves. For the classroom scenes Seale lit the whole room so that Williams could roam about, leap onto a desk, and play with props. Weir, Seale maintains, "is the only [director] I've worked with who can think solidly on a set. One of his favorite sayings is 'Where is the audience? Are they out buying popcorn, or are they floating six inches above their seats?'"

One typically impetuous script change occurred in a scene in which Todd (Ethan Hawke) learns of the death of Neil (Leonard). As written, the scene was an interior shot of Todd running into the dormitory bathroom and throwing up. When the appointed day arrived, a blizzard enveloped St. Andrew's. Weir goaded the actor to run out into the school yard in grief and sent the rest of the poets after him. On film, the boys are shivering in the snow in their pajamas, heightening the scene's pathos.

Weir also uses music as a directing tool. On the set his big portable tape deck is always at his side. On *Poets* Weir played a lot of Irish music, which fit the Celtic-boarding-school atmosphere, during scene preparations and dailies. "I use the music mainly to psych myself into the company of the muse, really," he explains, "as a weapon against the overwhelming ordinariness that surrounds the film set. And I've found over the years that music helps others."

When Neil's father forbids him to appear as Puck in a production of *A Midsummer Night's Dream*, the boy defies him—and commits suicide later that evening. Leonard remembers that "it was terrifying to get up at 4:30 in the morning and face the cameras to do Shakespeare at 6." As he was preparing to speak Puck's "If we shadows have offended" epilogue, he heard the strains of an Irish tune called "Stray-Away Child" emanating from the boom box. Weir knew it was Leonard's favorite. "I felt as if I could fly after that," says Leonard.

The suicide scene got the classic Weir treatment: ethereal images, slowed-down camera, no dialogue. "It was very interesting to see the boy prepare himself for death," says Weir. "You never see him shoot himself; I didn't even want to hear the shot. But I had to see the preparations and then find the body. So it was one of those sequences that I love."

The only disagreeable aspect of the shoot for Weir was pressure from Disney's budgetary watchdogs. The notoriously thrifty studio had under-scheduled the film, and Weir drove himself to exhaustion in a bootless effort to stay on time. "I got worried that he was going to burn out," says Williams. Weir finally blew up and called Katzenberg. "Jeff says, 'Why didn't you call me sooner?' Anyway, it was fixed up within twenty-four hours." Weir says his relationship with Disney "adds up to a very good experience."

As for the future, Weir says he has left behind any inclination to deal with overt mystical or spiritual themes in his films. "I've tried, to some extent, to disassemble my style, to fight against my own signature. Because I've observed that the great postwar directors from Europe, the great stylists—eventually, their horizons began to narrow. And I found myself tuning out their films because the subject became less and less important. So I decided I would try to be unpredictable and just look for good stories."

Nevertheless, Weir expects that the mysterious undercurrents that make his films distinctive will continue to surface. On the *Poets* set, "there were a lot of different levels going on—without sounding like we're gonna put the Windham Hill records," Williams says. "It's been powerful stuff, working with him. I'd go back again."

It is eleven o'clock on New Year's Eve in New Castle, and a *Poets* party is raging at production manager Duncan Henderson's house. (Robin Williams is in Washington, D.C., but he has already phoned.) Peter Weir bounds in with a schoolboy grin. He is wearing a Welton Academy blazer and carrying his boom box which he puts on top of the refrigerator. He slips a Beatles tape into the machine as the poets gather around. When the opening chords of "Twist and Shout" fill the room, he grabs a kitchen mop and strums it ecstatically. At midnight, Weir is holding a beer bottle as a microphone, into which he and his young friends sing a ragged version of "Please Please Me" at the top of their lungs.

On New Year's morning, John Seale wakes up, looks out his window, and sees that it is snowing heavily. He and Weir have been waiting for some white stuff to shoot a scene in which a bagpiper walks around the Welton campus. When the phone rings, Seale knows who it is before he picks up. "John, you probably know why I'm calling." says the voice on the other end. "Did you have anything special planned for today?"

Weir's Worlds: *The Truman Show*

Virginia Campbell / 1998

From *Movieline* 9, no. 9 (June 1998): 64–68, 88–89, 97. Excerpts reprinted by permission.

Australian director Peter Weir's new film, *The Truman Show*, is about a man named Truman Burbank, who, at the age of thirty, begins to suspect that the neatly arranged life he leads in a shipshape island town in sunny Florida is some sort of elaborate setup of unknown purpose. The truth is more outrageous than he could possibly guess: Truman actually lives on a gigantic soundstage and is the unwitting star of the hit TV program *The Truman Show*, which has broadcast his every move to viewers around the globe ever since he was a baby. The people in Truman's life—his mother, his wife, his best friend—are all actors hired by the show's godlike auteur, Christof. And all of them are lying to him. In short, *The Truman Show* is not your average summer film. It's funny and poignant with a vividly subversive undertow. It's a tale Kafka might have written had he been born into the couch-potato society now approaching the millennium.

Virginia Campbell: Since *The Truman Show* is a sort of seriocomic nightmare fantasy about the ultimate voyeuristic, exploitive television program, it suggests that you take a fairly jaundiced view of the role of media in our daily lives. Is that true?
Peter Weir: It's a broad question, and I hesitate to answer, because modern life is changing so rapidly. It's so puzzling, particularly to someone like me, who is both part of the media and at the same time, between films, very much outside of it. I do a film every couple of years, and then I drop out and go to a house that's well outside of Sydney and live a very simple life. I only look at a newspaper once a week and see very little television.

Campbell: What do you watch on television?

183

Weir: Documentaries mostly. With commercial television, the problem for me is advertising. Commercials have become so seductive, using so much good music and such clever images. The brainwashing strength of it is considerable. I can't see that that's healthy for a society—you're constantly in a state of mild anxiety about acquiring things.

Campbell: Your children are grown up now, but how did you deal with TV when they were little?
Weir: We didn't have one. We had one for the babysitter that we hid in the cupboard. In fact, I remember my son struggling in with this portable set one morning, so excited with this found treasure, saying, "Look what I found in the back of the cupboard."

Campbell: Your son and daughter watched no TV?
Weir: We eventually got a television, but having lived in a world of books, music, and good movies, they'd developed their own taste by the time television was freely available to them. Now that they've grown up and moved out, neither of them has a television.

Campbell: So you really distrusted television.
Weir: Yes, I remember a friend of mine who was in the Children's Television Foundation saying, "Will you join? We want to make better programs for children." And I said, jokingly, "I think that's the worst thing to do. I think we need more bad programs that will drive them outside into the fresh air."

Campbell: You've said in the past that children need to be bored in order to use their imagination.
Weir: Not just children. That's what I do in between films. What I mean by boredom is just allowing your imagination to revitalize itself and to engage with life rather than be dictated to by images that stop you from thinking.

Campbell: So, when you came upon Andrew Niccol's screenplay for *The Truman Show*, did it strike you as the perfect vehicle for dramatizing every doubt one could have about the age of media?
Weir: I decided early on that because this material was so pregnant with metaphors, I would to a large degree ignore them. They were always going to be there.

Campbell: How did you come to direct *The Truman Show*?
Weir: After *Fearless*, so many scripts seemed safe and predictable. The disappointing commercial reception of that film made me determined to do something even less predictable. I thought, Oh well, I'd rather go out in a blaze of obscurity. It became kind of a joke. When people asked, "What are you looking for?" I'd say, "I'm looking for trouble." The one who responded to that was [producer] Scott Rudin. He sent me *The Truman Show*. Q: What was your first impression of it? A: It was, as I'd requested, unusual and original material. I thought about it, and I went through my usual process, which is to deny it, to say, Well, I'm not going to do this, it's too difficult.

Campbell: What seemed so difficult?
Weir: The suspension of disbelief was going to be a huge challenge, because here's a story set not too far in the future and the audience has to go with extraordinary events. The guardians at the gates of logic had to be passed. The easiest way to go was kitschy, but I knew I couldn't do that. And I couldn't do it hyper-real. Yet figuring out how to do it realistically seemed some kind of torturous puzzle, and if you failed, you'd fail in an awful way.

Campbell: What got you over that?
Weir: As with other scripts I went on to do. I found I couldn't get it off my mind—it began to haunt me. You know—in daily life, going to the supermarket I get lost in the aisles because I'm thinking about the story, or some scrap of music is played at random on the radio and it seems as if it's from the soundtrack of this film. [laughs] It's portents—lions whelp in the streets, a two-headed dog is born. And I think, Ah, I have to do this, it's the only way I can get it out of my head.

Campbell: When did the name Jim Carrey come up?
Weir: When I called Scott Rudin to say I was interested, he said, "Do you know a guy called Jim Carrey?" He was thinking I wouldn't know, because at that stage Jim was known only for *Ace Ventura, Pet Detective*. But by chance I'd seen it. And I'd been struck, as I'm sure other filmmakers were, by Jim's innate talent and his utter lack of fear.

Campbell: How had you managed to see *Ace Ventura*?
Weir: I'd seen a poster in the video store, and I liked the look of the guy in it. I sensed the energy I was to see in the film.

Campbell: You proceeded with Scott Rudin and Jim Carrey based only on *Ace Ventura*?

Weir: Really the first three or four minutes of *Ace Ventura*. From the opening titles it was apparent this man was remarkable. And I thought, How fascinating he's interested in *The Truman Show*. To fly this thing I was going to need a highly skilled copilot. Truman couldn't be played in an ordinary way. He'd grown up on a set inside an extensive lie—he would not be like anybody else. Jim has an otherworldliness, and he radiates energy and makes you wake up. In *Ace Ventura* and then the other things I watched later, he reminded me of the early Beatles. He had that humor and recklessness, plus all that talent.

Campbell: You were sold fast, based on limited information. But there are some difficult scenes in the movie that require straight acting. You had no doubts about Jim Carrey being able to do that?

Weir: Meeting Jim was part of the research I had to do. By then he was a star, and I was afraid he'd changed. Success induces fear and caution, and I thought maybe that light had gone out.

Campbell: The meeting obviously went well.

Weir: Jim was welcoming and interested in all sorts of things. A thoughtful man. And there was a degree of mystery about him. He was in no sense a conventional Hollywood success story. I was ready to work, but he wasn't available for fifteen months, until after he did *The Cable Guy* and *Liar Liar*. I wanted to wait for him because he was the only person I sensed could do this.

Campbell: Dennis Hopper was originally cast as Christof, the arrogant genius-creator of *The Truman Show*. How did Ed Harris end up replacing him?

Weir: I'd cast Dennis Hopper when I didn't have a terribly strong idea of what Christof should be. I liked qualities of Dennis I'd seen in his movies, and he has a very interesting manner about him in person—his legend and achievements are part of his persona when you meet him. But as the months passed, I began to formulate my ideas about Christof more clearly. By the time Dennis came to filming, differences arose. Dennis, being a director himself, was most understanding and gracious.

Campbell: So Ed Harris came in at the last minute?

Weir: Yes, and he did the role wonderfully with very little time for preparation. I didn't know before then that he started out in theater, so he has much more range than you might think from the way he's usually cast.

Campbell: How did you decide on Laura Linney for the part of the actress who plays Truman's wife?
Weir: I'd seen her in *Primal Fear*, in which she had an unpredictability—a thing I always look for in the work of actors. She did a splendid audition. I like to play the other part in auditions when the real actor's not available. It gives me a chance to be the character briefly, which is wonderful preparation for directing, and to feel the words in my mouth that they're going to say, which often points up deficiencies. And I learn a lot about the person I'm opposite—I get to look at them in the eyes, in a way I can't if I'm standing back by the camera. I felt she just was the character.

Campbell: As you were waiting for Jim to get free to do this project, his price jumped from $8 million to $20 million. Did your heart sink?
Weir: *The Truman Show* was not going to be typical of the films he'd made. That was my only concern about his price. But then, it wasn't my responsibility, it was the studio's. And he did negotiate down, taking everything into account. He wasn't paid $20 million.

Campbell: How did you get such a restrained performance from this characteristically unrestrained guy?
Weir: He'd try a scene broader, then subtler, and we both felt free to explore the humor. He enjoyed the experimentation—because there was no research he could do, no book he could read called *I Was Born on a Television Show*. We were making it up. As I did with Robin Williams in *Dead Poets Society*, we planned experiments. On *Dead Poets* Robin and I worked out that he would teach Shakespeare and Dickens to a class for half a day with two cameras running and he would do whatever he wanted. Some of that made it into the film. I did the same sort of thing with Jim.

Campbell: This was the first time Jim put himself in the hands of a director whose judgment was going to reign. How did you get him to trust you?
Weir: Jim and I haven't discussed this, so I don't know how he saw it. But by the time he was fully available, I'd had enough time to construct

Truman's world—literally and in terms of ideas. It was obvious to him I had done this preparation—I had nothing else to do—and that I was half-crazy with all this Truman trivia. I had to be careful not to overwhelm him.

Campbell: How half-crazy did you go?
Weir: I wrote an elaborate fictional background to the movie. The movie itself begins in the last few days of the television show *The Truman Show*, but for my own purposes, to get my own mind clear, I needed to construct the twenty-nine years of Truman's life that led up to this point. I began with the back story of Ed Harris's character, Christof, and how he created *The Truman Show*.

Campbell: And this stuff is not in the movie?
Weir: Right. It's just background to explain what Christof was doing with *The Truman Show*. Christof was very cunning—he knew there was a moral question about having taken over Truman's life, but like a politician he saw this as being for the greater good of the world. His vanity was such that he believed he was creating the ideal human being, the True Man. And at the same time, he was going to make a lot of money.

Campbell: How much of the temptation that you know faces any gifted director did you feed into your concept of Christof?
Weir: Christof's scenes weren't filmed till the end, so I was always talking about him and thinking about what he would do. I began to get this awful feeling that there was a lot of me, or the profession, going into it. Christof is very much a movie director. At one point, I toyed with the idea of playing the role myself. Thank God, I didn't. [laughs]

Campbell: Everyone in Truman's world is acting twenty-four hours a day, which is an interesting reflection on late twentieth-century life, where half the people around you seem to be acting in some movie of their own all the time.
Weir: It reminds me of a journalist who told me how popular action movies were when he was covering the civil war in Beirut. He said, "You can't imagine what it's like to sit in a theater watching a Rambo movie or something with a bunch of guys who've got AK-47s between their knees, being thrilled and excited, then all filing back out talking about the movie as they sling their weapons back over their shoulders." You could see it on television—some of them had bandannas a certain way.

They were definitely acting. A lot of terrorists have acting in their backgrounds. It was true of some terrorists in the seventies. I read an article that said a disproportionately high number of them were failed actors. It was a kind of street theater.

Campbell: You did substantial reworking of the original script for *The Truman Show*. What sort of rewriting did you do on, say, *Witness*, for which you had far less time?
Weir: Having started in filmmaking by writing my own material—which I did because I had to, it was not my strongest suit—I've always needed to tailor material so that by the time it comes to shooting it has become mine in a profound way. I used to joke with writers when I started with them by saying, "I'm going to eat your script, it's going to become part of my blood." And I'd ask them to help me. This is the only way I can do it. On *Witness* I gave my notes to the two writers and it wasn't working the way I've described, so I rewrote it and sent it back to them to "put through their typewriter." They were shocked at what I'd done.

Campbell: What had you done?
Weir: I put more Amish ambience in it. And I took out the overt part of the love story—I thought it was rather tacky. I lessened the violence at the end. The writers thought I was so destroying the piece that one of them said to me, to my astonishment, "Don't you want to be walking up the steps at the Dorothy Chandler Pavilion to get your Academy Award?" On all my other films, there was no problem.

Campbell: You often use silence instead of dialogue to make emotional points. I'd guess many of your script changes are just deletions of words.
Weir: On *Witness* that caused more waves than any other changes. At the end of the movie, when Harrison came to say good-bye to Kelly McGillis, the original script had him explaining why he was leaving and she explained how she was feeling. I cut the two pages and said, "If I've done my job, they should be able to just look at each other." The writers and producer were concerned the audience wouldn't understand, and Jeffrey Katzenberg, who was the head of production at Paramount, flew out to talk about it. Jeff asked me to explain the scene, and after I did, he said, "That'll work."

Campbell: And speaking of short, *The Truman Show* is almost revolutionary these days in being well under two hours.

Weir: Every film has its proper length, and you find that out in the editing room. It's a struggle. But one aspect of television that is instructive, once you get past the bombardment, is how much information people can take in in a short time.

Campbell: Did you ever consider moving to Los Angeles, or was it always part of your plan to keep your distance?
Weir: My wife and I did consider it at one time. But we had young children, and we wanted to bring them up Australian. We realized that if we stayed in America they'd be Americans by the time they finished school, so we decided on another approach, which was educating them in Australia and having them travel with us when we did films. That all worked only because I could do postproduction in Sydney—that was built into my contracts.

Campbell: Your way of life seems to protect your creativity so successfully that it looks designed to do that.
Weir: It's like anything in life—it doesn't seem to be deliberate initially, but you look back and you think, there was a plan there. But now, of course, Sydney is turning into Hollywood, so you really can't get away from it.

This Is Your Life: *The Truman Show*

Eric Rudolph / 1998

From *American Cinematographer* 79, no. 6 (June 1998): 74–76. Reprinted by permission.

In *The Truman Show*, director Peter Weir and cinematographer Peter Biziou, BSC, tell the imaginative tale of a hapless man whose very existence has been turned into a television show.

In today's media-saturated world, cohabitating strangers are ceaselessly documented in vivid detail on MTV, continuous video feeds from the bedrooms of young women are available to anyone with Internet access, and an unending stream of people seem willing to reveal sordid aspects of their lives on tabloid television talk shows.

This alarming set of real-life circumstances has inspired accomplished director Peter Weir (*Witness, Dead Poet's Society*) to "broadcast" *The Truman Show*, an endlessly inventive feature film about a man whose entire life, twenty-four hours a day since birth, has been televised to the world without his knowledge.

The unwitting star of this wildly popular program, Truman Burbank (Jim Carrey), is selected from a group of unwanted children by producer Christof (Ed Harris), a domineering auteur who hires actors to portray young Truman's parents, friends, co-workers and, eventually, his wife.

Truman is raised in an island town painstakingly assembled on the world's largest soundstage—an enclosed, county-sized, and completely artificial bubble with its own fake sun, sky, and weather. Unable to overcome his crippling fear of water (a condition produced during his youth when a boating mishap claims the life of his "father"), Truman is a prisoner of his surroundings, but eventually adjusts to—and even revels in—the town's relentlessly cheery environment. His every move is recorded by five thousnd hidden television cameras which are manipulated from Christof's central control room, located high above it all in a

191

bogus "moon." The effort is all worth it, because *The Truman Show* is a worldwide smash that earns a tremendous fortune for its creators.

However, the oblivious Truman is not completely untouched by reality. As a youth he becomes smitten with Sylvia, a young female "extra" with a forthright manner and strong, unusual good looks. During a stolen nighttime rendezvous at the beach, she begins to tell him the big secret, only to be cut off by her "father," who zooms right up to the shoreline in the family automobile. Stuffing his daughter into the front seat and slamming the car into gear, the man shouts out that the clan is moving to Fiji.

Truman is so haunted by this brush with real-life infatuation, and so uninterested in his bland "Stepford Wife" spouse, Meryl (Laura Linney), that he begins a touching daily ritual: purchasing fashion magazines and using the photographs in them to try to piece together a simulacrum of the absent Sylvia's face, police Identikit-style. When not trying to re-create Sylvia's haunting beauty, Truman unsuccessfully attempts to contact the island of Fiji. He soon begins to discover other chinks in Christof's artificial world, but his attempts at escape are invariably foiled in set pieces reminiscent of the surrealistic sixties television show *The Prisoner*.

Weir says that he was attracted to this unusual project because of the quality of the screenplay, which was penned by fellow director Andrew Niccol (*Gattaca*). The esteemed Australian filmmaker explains, "I was intrigued by this complete world that Andrew had invented, because I knew that I would be involved in creating everything from the ground up, a world within a world."

To assist in the building of the story's bright, clean fantasyland, Weir chose director of photography Peter Biziou, whose resume includes such stunningly photographed films as *Richard III*, *In the Name of the Father*, and *Mississippi Burning* (for which he earned an Academy Award for Best Cinematography). "I was taken with the way Peter uses light, his choice of lenses and his overall look," the filmmaker says. "I loved his work with [directors] Alan Parker and Jim Sheridan. He takes chances, yet one always sees what one needs to see. I also knew that Peter is selective and only takes on films to which he feels he can offer something unique."

Weir further sensed that Biziou "was a man you could talk to, and he had a great interest in light and how it fell in relation to the story. The way the light falls in our images is a major part of a director's storytelling ability, followed only by dialogue. Here was a case where a hell of a lot of the film's story had to be told with the light."

He continues: "All of the light in Truman's world is artificial. We were after a heightened reality, an artificiality, and we needed to devise a way to convey that feeling without it being too disturbing to the audience. If it looked too odd, then the audience might feel that Truman should have caught on to [his situation] sooner. It had to look, at least at the start, like a somewhat regular movie; we have to believe it as much as Truman believes it. Then we can allow it all to come apart." The result of this thinking was Biziou's masterful use of a high-key lighting style which is the polar opposite of film noir, yet somehow achieves a similarly eerie emotional resonance.

In searching for the right look, Weir also studied old *Saturday Evening Post* covers by hyper-realist painter Norman Rockwell. He found inspiration in the "idealization" of Rockwell's renderings of an America that had already largely vanished by the time the artist created many of them.

Along with production designer Dennis Gassner (*Waterworld*, *The Hudsucker Proxy*) Weir and Biziou even researched the field of covert video surveillance. It was determined that while the various lenses and systems used in that field created an effective look, "Most of them were too strong and obvious for us," Biziou explains. "Peter wanted us to use the simplest methods to imply surveillance, so that he would be free to be as dramatic as he wished in telling the story."

To suggest the "surveillance" feel, Biziou used "slightly unusual camera angles and positions, and framing foreground elements in a stronger way, which seemed to support the uneasy feeling" that was inherent in the story.

Weir saw *The Truman Show* as a chance to utilize the long-abandoned silent-era cinematic technique of vignetting the edges of the frame to emphasize the center. He used this technique to suggest that the cameras watching Truman were indeed hidden behind or contained within various objects. He offers, "I had become hooked on vignettes, as used by people like D. W. Griffith. I love the technique purely on its own, as a simple but highly effective cinematic device. It was somewhat surprising to me that vignetting hadn't yet been revived."

To create the vignettes, which Biziou says also helped convey "a more obvious, menacing feel," the cinematographer used a variety of gobos placed in front of the lens. Some of the effect was also added or enhanced digitally by postproduction supervisor Mike McAlister, whom Biziou credits with "doing a great deal to subtly enhance the look of the film."

Naturally, the overall look of *The Truman Show* was influenced by television images, particularly commercials. Weir offers, "We took a lot from the current vogue for extreme wide-angle lenses in commercials, where characters often lean into the lens with their eyeballs wide open. And we borrowed our high-key, somewhat glossy lighting approach from commercials and situation comedies. We often used a lot more light in interiors than one would normally use, to keep it all sparkly and clean. We were always reminding ourselves that in this world, everything was for sale." The director specifically refers to the story's winking conceit that the fictional *Truman Show* series is supported entirely by advertising revenue generated by in-your-face product placements staged by Truman's friends and associates.

Other influences also shaped the look of the film. Weir notes, "We began to adopt a combination of imaging styles from the bold graphic framing of television commercials to the more obvious, somewhat menacing feeling of surveillance, using static, long-held angles. We combined these with the predictable visual routine of TV soap operas." Subtlety ruled the day, however: "The public is so aware of what is going on with TV that we only had to infer these various feelings."

While interiors showing Truman's domestic life were filmed in a way that was "a little too well-lit and sort of glossy," Biziou didn't want the lighting to be overly brash. Seeking to retain some of the filmic quality that is expected in features, the cameraman saws that he modified the television-style lighting by sculpting it with "a lot of black flagging and drapes, to control the soft light and keep it from being too flat."

Truman's world was created by the filmmakers in the real-life municipality of Seaside, Florida, a "planned community" created by developers on seventy-eight acres of beachfront property on the Gulf Coast. The real town of Seaside (called Seahaven in the film) was designed so it would maintain a distinctly Rockwell-esque look, recalling small-town, pre-suburban America. (According to a report in the *New York Times,* all Seaside homes are required to have a front porch and a white picket fence.)

Needless to say, Seaside was chosen for its slightly unreal, too-perfect look. For Biziou's purposes, however, the town was far from perfect. As he details, "Seaside consists of rows and row of similar houses, all of which were white or pale pastel, and it faces south. That [color scheme], bathed in strong, glistening sunlight all day long, naturally created extremes of contrast and shadows. It was only by putting in a tremendous amount of fill light that we achieved the quality that really suited our needs.

"In adding the fill, we got this lovely bright sunny feel without any craggy harsh shadows anywhere," Biziou elaborates. "It began to take on this very slightly super-real feel, almost looking like a controlled environment, which was exactly what we were after. It is often by accident, perseverance and accepting what you've been given that you do things you never quite expected.

"This huge amount of fill also gave us very good apertures—f8 or f11 on daylight exteriors—and the depth and sharpness added to the hyper-realistic fed."

Producing such an abundance of bright daylight fill was a major technical undertaking. "We used enormous forty-foot-square scrim reflectors and diffusers, several of them at a time, which could be moved into place quickly via cherry pickers," Biziou recounts. "We would aim several 12Ks at or through these scrims, which would produce volumes of lovely, powerful, soft fill. Combined with the bright blue skies, this look helped imply that there was something unreal going on, but one never knew quite what."

Weir concurs with his cinematographer, noting that the augmented Florida light was as important to the look and feel of the film as the town itself. "When we got a clear day, the sky was a sort of aching blue and the houses were gleaming white," the director recalls. "Waiting for clear, windless days and then pumping in all of this fill slowed us down, but I would remind myself when I was getting impatient that this was being done in order to make everything gleam and look like a commercial.

"I think when Peter [Biziou] took his first look at the town, he gulped hard," Weir adds. "You had to wear sunglasses just to look at the houses. But I am thrilled with his work."

To help cope with the extremes of contrast still evident in the day exterior setups despite the enormous fill lights, Biziou chose to shoot these portions of *The Truman Show* on Eastman Kodak's EXR 5248 stock, which is rated at 64 ASA for daylight with an 85 filter. "We used it for its fine detail and excellent exposure latitude," he says. "It was wonderful for handling the extremes in contrast that we weren't quite able to tame."

For day interiors and car shots, Biziou used Kodak's 200 ASA EXR 5293. "I wanted good aperture and depth," he offers. "For night interiors and exteriors I used the 500 ASA [Vision 500T] 5279, which is a great high-speed stock with surprising sharpness and detail."

Throughout the show, the cinematographer worked closely with Deluxe Laboratories, which "gave us consistently good dailies, for which I was really grateful." However, Biziou did extra work to help ensure that his dailies hit the mark. "In addition to the normal lab reports, I sent Deluxe handwritten notes on each day's run, so the timer would be well-informed," he relates. "They said they found these notes useful, as they normally get no such information and don't have any guidance on how to print. Mike Millican, the timer at Deluxe who finished the film, gave us a wonderfully timed first print."

In order to keep the images clear and sharp, Biziou avoided lens diffusion and filtration during initial photography. He reveals, however, that "we did ask for a slight warm tone on the final grading before the release print. We found this tone in one of our daily runs and just loved the way it looked."

Biziou's camera system was a new choice for him: Panavision's Platinum Panaflex with Primo lenses, which "hold [strong light] before flaring very well and take contrast very kindly. I tested them extensively because I had never used them before. This film was an ideal place to use the Primos because of the wide contrast ranges we encountered in the bright sun."

Wide-angle lenses were used extensively to both emulate the style of television commercials and to approximate the super-wide look of the extreme lenses used on surveillance cameras. Aspheron elements were sometimes added to the wide lenses to make them even wider and further emphasize the off-kilter feel of life in Seahaven. Long lenses were also used to mimic images created by stationary outdoor surveillance cameras, such as those now so popular with television news operations.

In a town with five thousand hidden cameras, the devices are bound to show up in some unusual places, and Biziou credits his crew with bringing that concept to life. "Our key grip, Chris Centrella, is one of the most imaginative I've ever worked with," the cinematographer attests. "He would put cameras in the most extraordinary places on short notice. If suddenly we wanted to put a camera in the revolving doors of Truman's office building, Chris would have that ready for us while we were shooting another scene. He was always ahead, always asking bright questions and on his tip-toes all the time, but with a smile!"

Biziou notes that Centrella played a hand in creating one of the more amusing and unexpected shots in the film, in which Truman is seen driving his car from a very unusual perspective. The cinematographer explains, "We were using a car that had been stripped of the dashboard and engine to allow us flexibility in camera placement, so we got a wide-angle lens right in there where the dashboard radio would have been, and added a masking gobo in front of the lens. Mike McAlister later composited in some little liquid-crystal digital numbers to reveal that we're in fact looking at Truman from the *inside* of his car radio."

This scene, like all of the driving shots, was lit with bright diffused light. Biziou reports, "We went to the extra effort of balancing the light levels in the car interiors lo the outside so that we would have the same exposure level for both, to get the look of a controlled environment, and the depth of field to heighten it."

The lenses used for the car interiors were some of the widest on the show, including 12mm, 14mm, 17mm, and 21mm units. Biziou reports that these extreme optics were occasionally pushed even further with the addition of diopters, which allowed the lenses to be placed even closer to the subject than normal to "add to the uneasy feeling we were after."

While Seahaven has the look of a normal, albeit idealized town (occasionally recalling the idyllic suburbs depicted in such television shows as *The Brady Bunch*), its complete artifice leads to some odd occurrences in the film. One hilarious example is an early scene in which an HMI lamp falls from the sky and crashes to the ground next to Truman, prompting him to search the heavens in utter confusion. Adding to the gag is the fact that the lamp is labeled "SIRIUS"—denoting it as *Alpha Canis Majoris*, the Dog Star, and the brightest in the sky after the sun. Biziou recalls, "It was in the script that some object fell from the sky, and the question of just what it should be was going around the set. Peter Weir took great pleasure in asking people what they thought the object should be, and then took great pleasure in deciding that it should be a movie light. We did two shots the lamp falling, but Peter later decided he wanted a high, aerial view, which Mike McAlister put together on the computer using a high-angle shot of the town."

Another combination of in-camera and digital work occurs during a frantic nighttime search for Truman after he somehow eludes the ubiquitous cameras and disappears. Christof tells his staff to bring up the sun, even though it is still nighttime by the show's internal clock. Reports Biziou, "We actually brought up the sun—*physically*. Our key grip and the chief electrician mounted about three hundred Par 36 bulbs into three large banks mounted on a tube frame on a crane hoist. We then jerked these lights up sixty feet in the air in about four seconds."

The dramatic lighting plan was heightened by the use of a false horizon. Biziou continues, "We had an enormous black flag stretched between two cherry pickers just in front of the lights when we popped them into the air. The shadows of the people and the trees shortened quickly, and the horizon line washed across the buildings. It was quite an effect, and it worked well in combination with Mike McAlister's amazing impressionistic digital sunrise."

While the God's-eye view of the HMI dropping from the sky and the shot of the rapidly rising sun are overt uses of special effects, Biziou believes that many of the film's other postproduction enhancements will sneak past almost everyone. "Mike McAlister digitally added a little fill and diffusion in the last seconds of the shots depicting the effects of the rapid sunrise, just to help the fake sunlight look more like daylight," the cameraman begins. "But a lot of the other digital elements look photographic as well. At times, the weather would change and we'd lose the intense blue skies we felt were so important. Mike would put them back digitally. I love it when digital work is subtle and is used without doing bangs and crashes and explosions." Additional extensive "invisible" effects work was added by Matte World Digital, including the creation of Seahaven's false topography, the extension of various buildings exteriors, and the addiction of scope to the surrounding artificial sea and sky (see photos).

The ruse of Truman's life in Seahaven, of course, eventually fails. When our hero finally realizes that something is terribly wrong and that he is unable to leave the town by any land routes, he confronts his aversion to the water by heading out to sea on a sailboat. Biziou recalls, "[After finishing in Florida,] we rushed back to Los Angeles and set up at the Universal Studios tank, where Peter Chesney had built special water clumps, wave-makers, and hydraulic lifts so we could put the boat on its side or turn it completely over."

All of the sailing action takes place over a short period of time in the story, so Biziou needed to have consistent lighting throughout the two-week tank shoot. Toward this end, he explains, "Chris Centrella built a one hundred by sixty foot diffusion scrim and got the largest mobile crane possible, which could go 250 feet up. Chris would literally boom this flag over the tank to keep Truman's boat in shadow. As the sun moved from cast to west, he would move the flag so we always stayed in shadow. It was a real bonus which gave us immediate lighting consistency."

However, Biziou cautions that this bold approach was not without considerable risks. "Chris had to compute and work out his stresses and strains and really know what he was dealing with, because any wind over fifteen miles an hour could have tipped the crane over. You could lift an airplane with that kind of span. Fortunately, we had no such problems.

"The big scrim gave me the soft light of an overcast day, so I then armed in a Musco from the background to add a strong backlight source to all of the various waterworks, such as the rain and waves. Water spurts just have no life without some backlight. The diffused sunlight and the Musco backlight comprised the only lighting we used in the scene."

In an attempt to get the water-shy Truman to turn the boat back toward shore, Christof orders up some nasty weather, escalating the tumult as the undaunted star soldiers forward. Finally, horrendous hurricane-force winds are dialed up from the *Truman Show* control room. To create the tempest, Biziou explains, "We had two jet engines on trucks, as is common these days, which screamed across the water and just took the tops of the waves off and gave them a nice cresting. These engines arc extremely noisy and smelly, but I'd recommend them any time; they're wonderful machines. It was a joy to see a proper thrusting wind. That, coupled with the blasting of fire hoses into the jet engine stream, which would just get energetically strewn across the whole scene, gave us some wonderful storm footage."

The defiant Truman eventually ties himself to the boat's mast, willing to die in his attempt to discover what is beyond the manmade confines of Seahaven. Picking up on that classical element, Weir notes, "The story of *The Truman Show* is not new; it is a love story about a man trying to reach freedom and find the truth. What is new is the state that we find ourselves in during the late twentieth century. With the colonization of the airwaves, with empires being formed by satellites beaming programs down and by the Internet, there are now more people with enormous power and influence in our lives—people who are not elected to these positions. And while they're not necessarily malevolent people, we know how power corrupts. It will be interesting to see how people respond to a story that deals with someone who is misusing that power, someone who is not in the guise of a conventional villain."

He's Fought His Own Way Back to Work

Terrence Rafferty / 2011

"It would have been different," said the Australian director Peter Weir, whose new film, *The Way Back* is his first in more than seven years, "if I'd changed professions during those years, or done nothing but read and hang about." But since his previous movie, *Master and Commander*, he has worked on three different projects that fell through, he said: "So if I can use the analogy of a pilot, for those five or six years I was constantly inside the simulator, doing a lot of writing, thinking about how to make a story work on the screen." He paused. "As is the purpose of the simulator, you create all kinds of difficulties for yourself to overcome, so by the time of the actual flight you've been through it in a sense."

It's amazing to think that a filmmaker as experienced, as respected and as successful as Weir—four times nominated for a best director Oscar—could have been stuck in that simulator for so long. But, as one of his *Way Back* stars, Jim Sturgess, put it, "It's kind of a scary cinematic climate at the moment." And the weather is perhaps especially inhospitable to the ambitious, adventurous sorts of movies Weir is happiest making. (This film, with a relatively modest $30 million budget, had to be produced independently.)

"At this point in my life I want a large canvas," he said by telephone from his home in Sydney. "It's always interesting to look at some important event that's making the characters behave in a certain way. That's a staple of cinema, and that's how the movies I liked as a child always seemed to me."

Master and Commander was certainly that kind of picture, a vivid, tur-bulent ripping yarn about naval warfare in the Napoleonic era, and *The Way Back*, though quieter, is no less consequential stuff. This film, which is based on a memoir by the Polish writer Slavomir Rawicz, is about a group of prisoners who escape from a Soviet gulag in 1940 and trek thou-sands of miles to freedom, across the frozen steppes, across the Gobi des-ert and finally across the Himalayas: the lucky ones make it to India.

"I've always been fascinated by survival stories," Weir said. "Even in circumstances that aren't so extreme, the question of what makes anybody keep going is always an intriguing one. What do you live for? I mean, any human being can just give up. You can lie down and die. There's something we have to have within us to drive us on, whatever it might be."

He said this softly, almost quizzically; he's not by temperament a pon-tificator. But it's a grander statement than any in the film itself, which concentrates on the tactile minutiae of day-to-day survival and leaves the characters' emotions mostly unspoken. "The movie is completely lacking in sentimentality," Ed Harris, who plays an enigmatic American escapee known only as Mr. Smith, said from Southern California. And Sturgess, who was in London, confirmed that the director didn't want the huge moments that so often disfigure the triumph-of-the-human-spirit sort of movie.

"When I first read the script," he said, "I'd come to a scene and think, 'This is a place to use my acting chops.' But in shooting that somehow became false, didn't seem real enough." He continued, "I had to learn to throw all that stuff out, to just be part of the landscape in a way—just be *present* and stop acting."

Weir, who spent his early years in show business writing and perform-ing comedy sketches, became a movie director in the 1970s, at a time when the Australian film industry was pretty ragged and caught-on-the-fly realism was practically the only cinematic style available. He intro-duced fantastic elements into his first movies, *The Cars That Ate Paris* (1974), *Picnic at Hanging Rock* (1975) and *The Last Wave* (1977), but usually without recourse to special effects. He had to use suggestion—incon-gruous details, spooky elisions—instead. And in some peculiar way the making of those more fanciful films may have sharpened his sense of the importance of visual precision, his highly developed taste for *l'image juste*. You can see it clearly in his first large-scale historical films, the World War I epic *Gallipoli* (1981) and the thickly atmospheric *Year of Liv-ing Dangerously* (1982), about a revolution in Indonesia.

"I tend to believe that a myriad of small details, from wardrobe and costume to dirt under the fingernails, will all somehow play their part," he said. "This may sometimes seem excessive, but I do think that attention to detail affects everybody on a film, particularly the actors and the department heads, gives them the feeling that they've got to come up to that level of reality."

His actors appreciate the pains he takes. "Peter's preparation, the vast amount of research he does, is amazing," Harris said. "Once he decides to do something, he just puts the blinders on and stays focused. And for me as an actor it's exciting to work with someone who pays attention to everything." Sturgess said, "He's so concerned with getting things right, it makes you sort of relaxed."

Relaxed is not, however, a word that springs immediately to mind when you're watching the actors in *The Way Back*—who also include Colin Farrell and Saorise Ronan—grunt and sweat and suffer and drag their weary carcasses through all manner of unforgiving terrain. (The film, which opens nationwide January 21, was shot mostly in Bulgaria and Morocco, with a few scenes in India.) "It's what you imagine making a film was like back in the early days of cinema," Sturgess said. And that's perhaps the real reason Weir hasn't been able to make many films in the last couple of decades: there was a five-year gap between *Fearless* in 1993 and his next film, *The Truman Show*, and then another five passed before *Master and Commander*.

It's hard not to feel, at certain moments of *The Way Back*, that the rigors of Weir's meticulous approach to filmmaking, his patience and his doggedness, have both served him well and taken their toll. The ordeal of getting this movie onto the screen is, somehow, reflected in the story itself. His whole career seems faintly—perhaps illusorily—present in this grim but starkly beautiful trek, kind of shimmering on the horizon like a mirage. A few wistful-sounding remarks of Weir's suggested that he was at least on some level aware of this odd resonance. "I wonder what kind of survival mechanism I may have drawn on for this, what tanks of adrenaline I found I had," he said. "I think because I'd had those other projects that failed to come to light, I was determined that this one was going to happen, and I drew on those reserves of energy."

Harris went further. "He's so careful about what he chooses to do, and he doesn't do anything unless he feels that there's something in there for him to explore," he said. "He's aware that filmmaking is a process of discovery, that you don't just make a stand and say this is what the movie is going to be. You have a gut feeling about something, and you pursue that through the preparation and the shooting and the cutting and then, after all that, you realize why you wanted to do it."

Harris is right about that, and Weir would probably admit it. He would perhaps also acknowledge that this isn't the *easiest* way to make films or the surest path to success. When you set out, you can never be certain you'll get to someplace you want to be, as this movie's weary travelers discover, to their sorrow, when they arrive in Mongolia only to find that it's no safe haven for them and they'll have to keep struggling on.

The Way Back is as stark and unfussy a film as Peter Weir has ever made, and there's a sense in it of an artist moving, step by step, one foot in front of the other, toward the hard-won freedom of simplicity. "Really," he said, "as a filmmaker you spend all your life working on simplification. That's what you aim for if you're lucky enough to have a long career." He's earned his luck. It's good to see him in full flight again.

"I Am Your Eyes": Interviews with Russell Boyd, ACS, ASC

John C. Tibbetts / 2012

Interviews conducted July 9–21, 2012. Previously unpublished. Printed by permission of Russell Boyd and Peter Weir.

A magical and supernatural light stands against the natural obscurity of things.
—Charles Baudelaire

[Editor's note: From his early years as one of the prime architects of the Australian New Wave in the 1970s, to his years working in Hollywood, capped recently by his Oscar for *Master and Commander*, Russell Boyd is in the front rank of today's greatest cinematographers. He belongs to a generation of remarkable young Australian cinematographers who have gone on to global success.[1] Boyd's legendary collaboration with director Peter Weir has to date produced six features during a span of more than thirty-five years.]

Russell Boyd was born in 1944 to a Victorian rural family. After working as an amateur still photographer, he went to Cinesound in Melbourne as a news photographer. Moving to Sydney, he worked on television news and commercials at Channel 7. He shot his first feature film, *Between Wars*, in 1973, for which he won ACS Milli Award as Australian Cinematographer of the Year. A year later he teamed up with Peter Weir for *Picnic at Hanging Rock* (for which he won a BAFTA award for Best Cinematography)—followed by *The Last Wave* (1976), *Gallipoli* (1981), *The Year of Living Dangerously* (1982), *Master and Commander* (2003, for which he won an Oscar), and *The Way Back* (2010). He and Weir, declares Martha Ansara In her history of Australian cinematographers, *The Shadowcatchers* (2012), work "through a process of extensive visual and historical research and consultation to infuse [their] films' closely detailed images with something subtle, something seemingly more than meets the eye" (154).

His American films include titles as various as the two *Crocodile Dundee* entries, Bruce Beresford's *Tender Mercies* (1983), Gillian Armstrong's *Mrs. Soffel* (1984), and two films for Ron Shelton, *White Men Can't Jump* (1991) and *Tin Cup* (1995).[2]

Mr. Boyd has been a member of the Australian Cinematographers Society (ACS) since 1975 and member of the American Society of Cinematographers (ASC) since 2004. In 1988 he became the first of only two cinematographers to be recognized by the Australian Film Institute's Raymond Longford Award, which is given to "unwavering commitment over many years to excellence in the film and television industries."[3] He was inaugurated into the ACS Hall of Fame in 1998.

I met and talked with Russell Boyd at his Newport home on three occasions during my stay in Sydney, July 9–21, 2012. He is the most congenial of spirits and exerts a rugged health and blunt, down-to-earth amiability. Our first meeting transpired in an impromptu fashion on July 16, 2012, when we were joined by Peter Weir. When I realized that their respective work schedules had kept them apart for many months, I suggested they get together for a chat. They welcomed the opportunity to catch up on things and share some memories with me.

I. Interview with Russell Boyd and Peter Weir

Picture the scene: We are in a park near Newport, sitting on a picnic bench in the hot, greening afternoon. Bird calls stitch the air all around us, and somewhere in the distance a groundskeeper is trimming bushes. Boyd's and Weir's greetings stumble over each other. Indeed—

John C. Tibbetts: [breaking into the preliminaries]—You guys are finishing each other's sentences!
Peter Weir: You must have been surprised, John, when you asked, do we see each other often? Not really; but even after a long gap between films we can just pick things up.
Tibbetts: But you're not talking about films at all—
Russell Boyd: Well . . . we're talking about gardens, actually!
Weir: Yeah, Russ is the real thing, you know, a real gardener!
Boyd: His wife is, too!
Weir: I just *labor* in the garden, but I love it. [turns to Boyd] Maybe we should talk about making films about *gardening*! [laughs]

Tibbetts: All right, let's do that—but about your real films, at least. Russell, when did you first meet Peter?

Boyd: He was shooting *The Cars That Ate Paris*. My friend, Michael Thornhill, who had directed my first feature, *Between Wars*, and I drove out to observe Peter's night shoot.⁴ The second time I met Pete was in a car on the way to the airport to scout locations for *Picnic at Hanging Rock*. Believe it or not, there had been no serious conversations or interviews before that.

Weir: One of the producers, Hal McElroy, had recommended him.

Tibbetts: What were some of your concerns about taking on the project?

Weir: [turns to Boyd] The light. The first thing I began to notice about your work was how you handled light, and moody night lighting, headlights flaring in the lens, torchlight in a cave, neon light flashing. But this?—[gestures around him]. But how do you shoot in *this*, in the light of midday, with hard top light? It's great at dawn and great at dusk; but how do you shoot throughout the day? But I had noticed Russ had a terrific look in his day scenes and landscapes.

Boyd: [nods] Australian light is quite harsh. We have a much smaller population and therefore not so much pollution in the air. The bigger cities in the U.S. and Europe and India have a lot more pollution, which has the wonderful effect of softening the light. We have had to learn how to manipulate this harsh light with what tools we have, like filters and lots of "fill" light to soften contrasts; things like that. To work in the middle of day with that harsh, overhead sun takes real skill. And we had only five weeks—

Boyd: [turns to Weir] Was it really five weeks?

Weir: Maybe six.

Boyd: I can't believe how we got through it in that time! And we had limited access to equipment and paraphernalia—not just because it was difficult to get up there on the Rock, but because there wasn't that much equipment to work with in Australia at that time.

Weir: Sometimes we had only an hour or so each day for some scenes—

Boyd: —Around the noon hour. Like the picnic. Remember? It took us a week—

Weir: You insisted on that! I remember that parachute silk you put above them—

Boyd: —To soften the light, yep.

Tibbetts: That reminds me of that magical opening shot of the Rock coming out of the fog. It's got to be one of the greatest rack-focuses in the history of the movies. Who wants to talk about that? [Weir nods toward Boyd]

Boyd: We were all in the car driving to the set one morning, and as we came over the hill, we got our first view of the Rock that day. It was all shrouded in fog. It was pretty sinister. So we decided to shoot that effect right away. We flagged down the camera truck behind us and started rolling. Actually, John, it's not a rack-focus. It's a "locked-off" shot used twice—one with the fog covering the bottom of the rock; the other after the fog had lifted.

Weir: I remember we had to hurry about it. I don't think a film like this would be made today, either because of the subject matter or because it was of its time.

Tibbetts: When did you guys first realize you had something pretty special with this film?

Weir: Well, the dailies were pretty promising. I always wanted to project dailies in as much of a theater situation as possible. Even on location. The phrase I use in the cutting room is, if the fates are kind, "it's working"; which has nothing to do with the expected public reaction, but with the way you intended it. And it's a great relief when that happens . . . sometimes at the eleventh hour. Everything was so new, then. I was in Adelaide when it opened at a house with four cinema screens. I think it was one of the first theaters in the world to have been rebuilt for multiple screens. I think *Godfather Part Two* was also playing there. To see the big marquee and people hurrying in . . . that was a thrill.

Tibbetts: Is it possible to overestimate now the importance of *Hanging Rock* had in the international recognition of Australian films?

Weir: Yes, it is. I think it meant a great deal here; but it was not successful in America, and it took a long time to sell. In fact, my next film, *The Last Wave*, was sold first. But a mystery story without a solution—which was the challenge in making it—and to create a mood where the audience didn't *want* a solution—

Boyd: And viewers knew straight away there was no solution!

Weir: But the Americans thought that was a problem in distributing the film. There's a story that a distributor threw his coffee cup at the screen and said, "There's no goddam solution." But it found a home on college campuses.

Tibbetts: What a contrast the visual "look" of your next film was!
Boyd: In *The Last Wave*, we didn't refer in any way to how we shot *Picnic* in any way; the story was so different. You know, Directors of Photography often get typecast, although we like to turn our hands to different subject matter; and so this was a different road to go down. And in prep, we did talk a lot about the "look" of the film—
Weir: The rain was particularly interesting to talk about. I love to watch rain on the screen.
Boyd: But not *in* the theater!
Weir: [laughs] So I'd talk to Russ about *how* we can get this or that effect. How to get a harder edge.
Boyd: And we had John Seale again as the Camera Operator—
Weir: Johnny was the third member of the team.

Tibbetts: Time is short to have you two guys together, so let's skip ahead to your recent films together. Russell, after twenty years, Peter comes to you about *Master and Commander*. He tells you: "We're going to climb to the top of sailing ships and we're going to the Galapagos Islands"—and you must have said, "Are you talking to me???"
Weir: [confiding] Russ is a sailor, you know.
Boyd: Remember, Pete, by chance we were together on a plane to L.A. to work on different projects. We were sitting at the front—
Weir: —the only passengers—
Boyd: —and you told me whole story of *Master and Commander*; and I thought, Gee, I'd love to shoot that movie! [turns to Weir] And then you called me at my hotel that night and said you were sending around the script—
Weir: —And then we met at a Thai restaurant—
Boyd: —I remember it clearly—
Weir: But it was actually on the plane that the whole thing got started. And it was within "X" number of weeks that we found ourselves on the *New Endeavor*! And we had to get up to the top of those shrouds! And using the Panavision camera with anamorphic lenses. It was a new thing when I had first used it on *The Cars That Ate Paris*. But I burnt my fingers on that one. But it was Russell who encouraged me to look at it for *The Year of Living Dangerously*. He thought it was the best format for that picture. He loved composing for that format—2.35 to 1 screen ratio—
Boyd: —A painterly frame—

Weir: —And he eased me into it; and the screen was *alive* with information. And we used it on *Master and Commander.*

Tibbetts: In 1930 Sergei Eisenstein proposed that a square frame was the best aspect ratio. Would you consider shooting that way?
Weir: —In black-and-white, yes. Put it another way. I think it makes sense in controlling the elements in the frame. I prefer to look through the viewfinder—
Boyd: [turning to Weir]—Unlike some other directors I've worked with in the last decade!
Weir: —Because I grew up with that system. And because I direct from the side of the camera.
Boyd: Right. One of the only directors I've ever worked with who actually stands beside the camera.
Weir: [turns to Boyd] Is that right?
Boyd: Most use the digital monitor. Now we've got video cameras in the film camera that relay back to the director's monitor.
Weir: You're sitting away from the set, your head buried in the monitor, calling out instructions either verbally or through the mic to the camera about the framing. But you're composing for a *theater* space; but here you are with your head *this* big in front of the tiny screen, so you tend to compose too close or too wide. But when you stand back beside the camera, you've got basically a beautiful wider view of the whole scene, and you tend to compose better with the naked eye. But it was different in *Master and Commander,* because I couldn't get in those tiny spaces. We didn't want to build extra room for those cramped ship interiors.
Boyd: The beams would clout your head! [turns to Weir] And there are also the nuances of the *performance* itself. You can't tell that when you're so far away.
Weir: But, you know, I talk about the *"Hindenberg* Balloon Theory." No one ever talks about what the picture format was for the moments when the *Hindenberg* goes down in flames. And think of the Zapruder film. Both tragedies. It's the *power* of the moment, of the film, that takes over.

[The conversation breaks off for a moment. The sounds of a leaf blower in the distance are growing louder. Distracted, Weir shouts to the workman, "Thank you! That'll be fine! We're trying to shoot a film here!" He pulls a finger across his throat. Boyd is laughing. Weir points to me and calls out again in mock exasperation, "This gentleman has come out here all the way from America!"

I can't help but note that off the set, neither of these two master filmmakers have any control over the world at all.]

[Both are laughing.]

Tibbetts: Will we see you two sometime soon in another project together?
Weir: We'd like to . . . but I work so infrequently. The clock is against us, somewhat. But I do know with Russ that we can work for those ideas that are just out of our reach. I may be the leader of the expedition, but I can say to him, "Help me to reach it!" [reaches above his head] If you can just *touch* it, that's what you're after. And that's what Russ can do. [Turns to Boyd] To have worked with each other. . . . You and I were a good match.

II. Later Interviews with Russell Boyd

Two days later Russell Boyd has invited me to his weekend home in Newport, forty-five minutes north of Sydney for the first of his solo interviews. His two grown sons and their families frequently come up here on weekends. Outside the window in the sparkling sunlight lies the Pitt Water Sound, with dozens of white sails bobbing in the water. Inside, we are sitting in the kitchen before a large table piled high with files and photo albums. His entire career lies before us, inviting his comments as he sifts through the papers. Although we talked about his career in America, presented here are those remarks pertaining specifically to his work with Peter Weir.

At this moment Russell has just returned from shooting a television commercial.

John C. Tibbetts: Do you shoot a lot of commercials these days?
Russell Boyd: Mostly, nowadays. As you know, I've been on the road for forty years making films, away for five to seven months at a time. It's a long, long time to be away from family and friends. It's time to spend more time at home. I'm sixty-eight years old now, so shooting television commercials, which I enjoy anyway, keeps me at home.

Tibbetts: And while we talk, looking around, I see some paintings—
Boyd: —That's a painting by an artist by the name of Adrian Lockhart and it's called "The Surfer." I know him, and he surfs nearly every day of his life. He's quite a successful artist who has exhibitions several times a year. But the reason I love that painting is the way it evokes the water.

[He turns back to me.] As you can see, my place is very sparsely decorated, because it's mainly a weekend place. I just love it because of its simplicity and the wonderful view. Summertime is quite hot here. The sun sets out to the west, and at about seven o'clock in the evening, when the sun's just about to set, it comes pouring in here. We've got shutters that we drag across to get away from the heat a little bit.

Tibbetts: Now what's the best time to be out on your boat?
Boyd: Ahh, anytime really. Or around lunchtime when the wind gets up a little bit. It's a twenty-two-foot "trailer sailer," as we call it. It has a keel that drops. You wind the keel down so you can actually be birthed in quite shallow water. My wife named it actually, but I've never had it painted on the side. She named it "Tickle Pink" [laughs], because the hull is a pink, or a magenta color, which was by design. I had the boat made. It's a small yacht, a very small yacht. I don't sail nearly as much as I would like to. Sometimes the garden takes preference to boating.

Directors of Photography vs Camera Operators

Tibbetts: Your credits list you as a Director of Photography. How is that different from a Camera Operator?
Boyd: We tend to work in the English, or the American system here. In the English system the film director works very closely with the Camera Operator, which is how Peter likes it. The Camera Operator is the one who during a take will either turn the wheels on the gear head or operate the pan handle. He will set up the camera and help choose angles and lenses that may be specific to that story or specific to that scene. He and the director and the Director of Photography will have a three-way conversation about how the scene is choreographed for the camera. So the Camera Operator's role is incredibly important; he can be a major contributor to the movie. The Director of Photography's main role really, apart from working on camera angles, the film stocks, et cetera, is mainly in the lighting. Lighting is a whole different department. As Director of Photography, I work with my gaffer, who's a senior electrician, on how we should light a scene after we see a rehearsal.

Tibbetts: In Bristol once, I interviewed David Watkin, a British cinematographer. He almost boasted about the fact he never looks through the camera.[5]
Boyd: Yeah. I've heard that about David. I understand [laughs]—here's my telling tales out of school—I understand that once he'd lit a scene,

he'd sit down with a newspaper for the rest of the take. Look, it's "horses for courses," the way I see it. I like to adapt to whatever way a director wants to work. Either Peter might bypass me to deal much more directly with the Operator, or he might bypass the Operator to go through me. I like to play it either way. I don't let my ego get in the way. I don't have much of an ego, anyway. In the States, Directors of Photography are much more attached to the director. Directors who have come up through the States don't tend to view Operators in the same way as we do. There's a subtle difference. For the films I made in the Hollywood system, I've always collaborated strongly with the Operator anyway. And directors, I think, respond to that as well. But if the director just wants to deal with me, that's fine too. Take Ron Shelton, for example, who I've made a few films with—he likes to work with his DP probably more than the Operator. Like I say, it's "horses for courses."

Tibbetts: It seems like we don't know enough about what you guys do on a film. You don't see many interviews with cinematographers.
Boyd: I think when we do talk we like to pass on information that might be useful to other cinematographers. We don't talk to pat ourselves on the back. I certainly don't. There's a lot of sharing of knowledge between cinematographers, or Directors of Photography in the American Society of Cinematographers and the Australian Cinematographers Society, which is a much smaller organization. At least once a month, they'll have a technical night where somebody will bring some equipment in and explain it to all the younger guys or girls or budding cinematographers. Yes, it's a field of endeavor that's unusual, and it's evolving rapidly now because of the digital explosion. One thing I do know, which strikes me as kinda funny whenever I go to the US to work—is that I get an "O-1 Visa," which is sort of a media or entertainment business visa.

Tibbetts: There is such a thing?
Boyd: It's so I can work legally in the States. When you hit Los Angeles airport, often the immigration are pretty grumpy. So you walk up and hand them your passport and they look at your visa and say, "What are you doing?" "Oh, I'm working on a film." "Oh, what film?" "And who's in it?" "Mel Gibson." "Oh, Mel Gibson!" And they go nuts. It's so much a part of American culture, the movies. The whole movie business is very much in the forefront of the American psyche, I think.

Climbing the Rock

Tibbetts: All right, it's the 18th of July 2012, and we're back again at your lakeside cottage. Shall we call it your "weekend estate?"
Boyd: I guess you could call it that!

Tibbetts: A few days ago you and Peter talked briefly with me about coming together for your first film, *Picnic at Hanging Rock*. Let's get into that some more. What did you know about Peter Weir at that point?[6]
Boyd: I didn't know much about Peter. I probably had seen *Homesdale*. And I certainly knew that he was emerging as one of the fine talents in the Australian film industry. It was during that time when so many young directors were coming from the Australian Film, Television and Radio School [AFRTS], like Phil Noyce, Graham Shirley, John Papadopoulos, Gillian Armstrong, and others. They were all making short films at the time. Michael Thornhill was the first director to give me a feature film to shoot. He wasn't part of that nucleus of people, but he was definitely of that generation, and he knew them all, too. Here was this mix of young twenty-five-year-olds attempting to make films. It was a great time.

Tibbetts: For the cinematographers, too, I would think.
Boyd: Yep. The cinematographers were very lucky, because the directors would make four or five films in Australia, more than likely with the same Director of Photography. So when they later went to Hollywood, as a bit of a security blanket, they took us as well. So we were able to get the proper visas and work in the States. We were incredibly lucky. I was very aware that we were going about raising the consciousness of Australian culture. I don't why, exactly, but I felt it was an important thing to do.

Tibbetts: And so was shooting *Picnic at Hanging Rock*!
Boyd: Michael and I went up to Bathurst, which is in the Blue Mountains, several hours from here, where they were shooting *The Cars That Ate Paris*. Peter was coming back to Sydney for the weekend, so he lent us his room in the motel. So we sort of met, passed like ships in the night. The very next time I met Peter was, I think, when we headed off to Hanging Rock to do location scouts. And we talked, you know, non-stop about the film.

Tibbetts: But it sounds so casual, almost.

Boyd: We in those days didn't have a rigorous way of going about things. Films were almost made by the seat of our pants, to a great degree; whereas, in the States and nowadays here, it's a much more structured way of going about things.

Tibbetts: So at that time, how would you describe yourself as a young artist? Cocky and determined or insecure and ambitious?

Boyd: Ambitious, no. Insecure, yes. Not cocky. It takes quite a while to master the art and craft of cinematography. As you can understand, it's quite technical as well as needing visual imagination. The two separate parts of the craft take a while to harness. And as I said before, even on *Picnic* I was scared shitless on what was going to come back the next night from the lab. 'Cause I didn't know near as much as I do nowadays. Nowadays, I feel much more confident, obviously. I've always felt that getting that technical thing behind you, that's when you can really start being creative.

Tibbetts: But you were a known commodity by that time.

Boyd: In the commercial world, yes. And also in low-budget, weekend films, what you might call student films now. I made a few of them with Michael Thornhill. You know, as you say, I was in the right place at the right time. I was lucky. I actually did something on *Cars*, by the way— shots of one of the wrecked cars. I was second or third camera. Probably uncredited, I'm sure.

Tibbetts: I guess in those days a film like that said a lot about the social protest movement going on about Vietnam?

Boyd: Yep. It was Vietnam and there was a lot of social unrest. But it's more important that Peter loves to get hold of a story that really interests him, whether it's set in the year 1500 or in the future.

Tibbetts: Now, I assume at some point you read Joan Lindsay's book?

Boyd: No. I've never read the book. I tend to steer clear of reading a book, if I already have the script, the screenplay, in front of me.

Tibbetts: Of what I've seen of the screenplay, there's nothing in it that indicates visual effects, like slow motion, or any special kind of lighting set-up.

Boyd: That's something that a filmmaker like Peter would add.

Tibbetts: So, was that the first time you had ever seen Hanging Rock?
Boyd: It was. It was. And you've just been there yourself, haven't you? The Rock really doesn't look as treacherous or threatening as we made it look in the film. We stumbled around the Rock for a couple of days, choosing little locations where we might shoot certain scenes. We found that flat, table-like area, for example, where we could shoot the girls lying down to sleep.

Tibbetts: Did you have a still camera with you as a kind of notebook, to keep track of the locations?
Boyd: I'm sure I did. I don't have any of those photos anymore, though.

Tibbetts: There's a Visitors Center there, now. And in certain places there are steps cut into the rock to help climbers.
Boyd: There certainly was not a visitor's center then! We had to trudge up to the top of the Rock on dirt paths. And driving there was just on a dirt road. I could see right away it was going to be very difficult to get our equipment up there.

Tibbetts: This is a young man's game. It must have been tough for you guys charging around the Rock with heavy equipment.
Boyd: Absolutely. I think I was twenty-nine when we made *Picnic*. Peter's just a couple months younger than I am. So he would have been twenty-eight, maybe twenty-nine. So, we were youngsters really. Not so much in age but in terms of experience, with a lot more experience ahead of us! I guess you could say we were "gung ho!"—but really, we were just given a job to do to the best of our ability. Fortunately, we pulled it off. We set up on a Sunday and started shooting on a Monday. We had a number of lights we wanted to take up to the Rock. There was no power up there, of course, so we had to helicopter in a few small generators, one to the top of the Rock and one halfway down. They were very difficult to manhandle, quite heavy. And the helicopter dropped one of them that Sunday, so the gaffer came to me and said, "We've only got one generator up there." Oh no, I thought, oh god! That's when I decided I had to use more bounce light.

"Into the Light of Things"

Tibbetts: Now, when you say "bounce light," are you talking about big reflectors?
Boyd: I'm talking about big sheets, John, about ten feet by ten feet, or

twelve feet by twelve feet. Often, it was a flat piece of polystyrene. The sort of thing you make coolers out of. They were on metal frames. But also, I often used a hand-held piece of polystyrene, about three feet by three feet, to get in close.

Tibbetts: All the time I was climbing around, I was thinking, "How in the world did you guys find enough space for the cameras and for people holding bounces?"
Boyd: First, we had just one camera. In those days, you only ever shot with one camera, 'cause you could only afford one. What happens is as you go closer in on an actor, you have to bring your light in closer. So on a lot of those close-ups I used only a hand-held piece of polystyrene. I would stand right next to camera and just direct the reflection of the bounce light onto the actors faces. It's a very flattering light and a very soft effect. A small light source is like the sun from millions of miles away.

Tibbetts: And gauze over the lens, sometimes?
Boyd: Yes, always. Entirely on *Picnic* I had gauze over the lens as a diffusion. I used gauze over the front part of the lens, rather than the back. Even up to the Sunday before we began shooting, I was cutting cardboard cutouts of the diameter of the lens and attaching what was like a mosquito cloth. We did very shallow depth of field, otherwise you could see the outline of the net in the shot. I had to open the lens up as much as possible. And I was constantly adding neutral density filters.

Tibbetts: Was John Seale a part of all this?
Boyd: Well, he had to be as operator. Of course he went with it.[7]

Tibbetts: Gosh, the kind of impressionistic "look" of that picture created a sensation on the international scene.
Boyd: Well, you know, that eventually led to my career in America, to be honest.

Motion Control

Tibbetts: The slow motion sequences . . . is slow motion something that can be done in post? Or do you have to shoot it in slow motion in the first place?
Boyd: You mean, like when the girls cross the stream?

Tibbetts: Sure, that and so many other moments.

Boyd: Although we normally shoot at twenty-four frames per second, we can easily switch to forty-eight or fifty or seventy-five.

Tibbetts: Can you switch speeds during the take?
Boyd: Nowadays you can, but what it does is it affects the exposure, so you have to have a link between the aperture of the lens and the speed you're shooting at. It's called "ramping." I did a lot of it much later on *White Men Can't Jump*. That'd start at twenty-four frames and we'd ramp it up to fifty or a hundred.

Tibbetts: But you couldn't do that with *Picnic*?
Boyd: No, but we could set it before the shot. Peter would say, "Let's shoot at forty-eight frames," which is exactly double. So we can dial it into the camera to shoot at forty-eight frames. But don't forget, we didn't have a lot of time. Peter's very efficient. If he's got a performance he wants in take two, or in take one, sometimes, he'll move on. So, he's not a director who does multiple takes and experiments a lot. I think the schedule was just six weeks for that movie.

Tibbetts: Now, if you were shooting that film today, with all of the ul-tra-modern equipment, and crew and everything else, could you have done as good a job as you did then?
Boyd: I doubt it. I don't think I would approach it any differently today. We would have equipment that was light and more mobile, I probably would have had more electric light up on the Rock, because the gen-erators are smaller and more powerful. But, you know, one of the great things about *Picnic* was that everything was fairly *raw* about it, if you know what I mean. The amount of equipment we had, the money we had to spend on it, the time we had to do it in. And don't forget, it wasn't all shot at Hanging Rock. Appleyard College wasn't in Victoria, but in South Australia, in Adelaide. And that was a major part of the film. The school actually was Martindale Hall. It still exists.

Tibbetts: Did you have to use different equipment for the school scenes?
Boyd: You see, when we shot *Picnic*, Panavision hadn't long been in use before that. Their main production camera was quite a big, heavy sort of rehash of a Mitchell camera, which was used in the thirties, forties and fifties. The Panavision camera was too heavy to lug around up and down

the Rock. So, we used the latest Arriflex camera, which was a BL, a sound camera, a little bit noisy in those days, but much lighter and more user-friendly. When we went to shoot at Adelaide, we were able to use the Panavision camera. All the interiors of the school were shot at Martindale Hall. And the exteriors, too. So when the girls came back from the Rock, it might have been three weeks later that we did the scenes where the horse and the cart came back.

Getting back to your question, I would hate to think that if we were to make that film now that I would treat it any differently. I certainly would have treated the visuals the same and hopefully we would have had John Seale there and Peter there as well, obviously. Yeah, I don't think it will ever get remade though. I hope not.

Cast Calls

Tibbetts: Now, a study in contrast is Anne Lambert as Miranda and Rachel Roberts as Miss Appleyard. You must have been working closely with them.
Boyd: Of course.

Tibbetts: So, by contrast, what did Lambert know about the vision you were creating? Did you tell her you wanted some sort of angelic "look"?
Boyd: When Peter cast her, he would have made that very clear to her.

Tibbetts: But did you tell her how you were going to light her?
Boyd: Pretty much. Funnily enough, I had actually worked with Anne Lambert on a television commercial before that. Probably a year or so before that. Then, she was fourteen or fifteen. And she was absolutely beautiful. She still is a beautiful person, actually. But she was absolutely gorgeous and the commercial that she was in was for a soft drink. And she was known as "Fancy Nancy" [laughs] in that commercial. So what I'm getting at, is she had some experience as either a model or a budding young actress; so she didn't come to *Picnic* entirely without experience. She knew some of the ropes for sure.

Tibbetts: And you had Rachel Roberts, a real veteran.
Boyd: Absolutely. She was married to a playwright [Alan Dobie]. She was a strong person on the set. You know, actors sometimes play their roles off screen. They like to stay in character. I'm not saying that she was staying in character, exactly, but she always had that persona about her as the school headmistress. No question of it. And we also had the gorgeous

Helen

Helen Morse as the French teacher, who was a very well known theatre actor.

Tibbetts: Have you had occasion to work with or run into Anne Lambert after this?

Boyd: No, but I've seen her. One evening at the Art Gallery of New South Wales there was a twenty-fifth retrospective of *Picnic*. So it must have been around the year 2000. Anne was there and Peter went and made a speech. The screenwriter was there, the producers were there, quite a few of the other performers as well. It was a good night, actually.

Tibbetts: You would hope an iconic performance like that would not turn out to be some kind of a curse for her, limiting her in other roles. I know she played other parts that were a lot different.

Boyd: She probably may never have been in the sure hands of a director like Peter again, though. I think she did a reasonable amount of television after that, and I think she went to London to make a career there. But around here she disappeared for quite a while.

Tibbetts: Which is appropriate!

Boyd: Yeah, yeah.

Tibbetts: She must get those jokes all the time.

[laughs]

Sounds of Music

Tibbetts: How does the cast react to Peter carrying around a big boom box on the set?

Boyd: On all the films I've ever made with Peter, he's done that. Peter would play music over the first few takes so the sound recorders wouldn't get anything usable; but he'd just play it while the actors are performing. Then he'd switch it off and do another take.

Tibbetts: You would hope that your actors would not be tone deaf! Otherwise they might wonder what this guy's doing, charging around with a boom box [both laugh]. It could be a joke, easily.

Boyd: I know, but I think people take Peter too seriously for that. Actors, particularly. To get to work with Peter would be the high moment of your career as an actor, I would think.

Tibbetts: So . . . when did you guys all begin to realize what you had?
Boyd: Pretty early, I think. Once the film started coming back from the lab here in Sydney. It was two days before we saw what we'd just shot. At night we'd set up a projector and see what is known as the work print. They'd print all of the rushes, all of the negatives we shot and we'd sit and watch it. Pretty early on we realized there was something special about the locations, about the girls, obviously about Peter's direction.

Tibbetts: And you didn't even know about the pan-pipe music yet.
Boyd: No, not at all. Not until the film was in postproduction. But I must say this: I'm often asked by film schools to talk to students or whatever about certain films that I've worked on, often with Peter. And every time I see *Picnic*, I can't help but marvel at the fact that it was Peter's second major film, really. There's subtle things in that film that I still see all these years later that I didn't realize were going on in front of the camera. It's extraordinary to me. It often happens, actually. I'm talking about the way he constructed scenes as well. And the way he manipulated them in the editing to get the story across, to push the story on, if you know what I mean. Peter liked to shoot fewer takes but lots of alternatives. He'd probably change angles after a couple of takes rather than, like some directors who will sit there on the same angle for fifteen takes.

Tibbetts: Is it true that you shot another ending?
Boyd: Yes, we did. We must have done it in principle photography, where we had make-up and hair and all the departments still together. Yes, we shot an alternative ending where Mrs. Appleyard decides to go up to the Rock to find out exactly where the girls disappeared. (You can still find photos of Mrs. Appleyard with her umbrella setting out for the Rock.) And one of the scenes we shot was her body being carried back down on a stretcher. Peter just decided not to use it.

Tibbetts: Are you glad?
Boyd: It would have made no difference to me. I thought the story was well told the way he did tell it in the final cut.

Tibbetts: Did *Picnic* have an immediate impact on your career?
Boyd: Without slapping myself on the back, I did become sort of "the first cab off of the rank." Do you know that expression? It means you take the first cab that's on the cab rank. I think the younger directors considered me that way; first choice to shoot their films. Peter elevated

my career. It gave me the reputation of being able to put something on the screen.

Snapshots

[During our last interview, Russell Boyd leafs through the pages of a splendidly illustrated limited edition of the novel and script of *Picnic at Hanging Rock*, published in 2002 by the Macedon Ranges Shire Council. The photographs bear ample testimony to the luminous beauty of the film. Immediately catching his eye is the famous opening shot of the fog-shrouded Rock.]

Tibbetts: You and Peter talked about that shot earlier with me. Would you elaborate on that now?

Boyd: Okay. We were driving to the set and as we turned the corner and got our first glimpse of Hanging Rock, Peter said, "Ah, look at it, it looks absolutely fantastic!" It was shrouded in cloud and the Rock was menacing but beautiful. And I think it might have been a bit backlit. The camera truck was behind us by ten minutes or so. So he said, "Stop, stop, stop, stop! We must shoot this!" We didn't have the cameras with us, so we waited until the camera truck caught up with us. We flagged it down and grabbed the equipment out of the back of the truck and shot the Rock in that early morning light.

[Boyd turns to another image, the famous "picnic" with the girls and the other characters disported around the grassy area in the soft, golden light. It has all the nuance of a Renoir outing.]

This shot here is nearly halfway up the Rock, actually. When we first scouted the scene, I had known Peter for only about two days! We eventually shot a big long pan around the area, which also ends the movie as well. When we chose the location, I said, "I think we can only shoot for an hour a day here, when the light's just perfect." You see, in the morning, the area was too shadowy from the trees. By late morning, it was perfect, with lots of overhead light. After an hour, it was completely in shadow again because the sun had moved further around. I asked if there was any chance that we could come back every day and continue, one shot at time or two shots at a time? I'm sure they thought I was mad. Actually, I was terrified. As I told Peter the other day, I was terrified I was going to get fired off of the movie then and there! But eventually the producers agreed, Hal and Jim McElroy and Pat Lovell. And the assistant director, Mark Egerton. Mark was a keen photographer and understood exactly what I was talking about. He said, "I think I can make it work." So he would schedule time just before lunch each day for that five or six days; and we'd go and shoot one or two more shots of that scene.

Tibbetts: And the world is forever grateful!
Boyd: Well, I'm forever grateful that I didn't get fired! [both laugh] And if I had, I probably wouldn't be sitting here now talking to you. [looks again at the photo, pausing, remembering . . .]
Here's the lovely hill and moss. That's the backlight on the girls and parasols. See that light on Helen's [Morse] face? I'm sure, that was bounced light from in front of her. It's just beautiful, soft, molded, and rounded. And it falls off nicely into shadow.

Tibbetts: It's hard for us to imagine looking at a shot like that somewhere back behind it all are a camera, crew, and people holding up reflectors. [laughs]
Boyd: It's difficult to tell from the photograph but obviously some of the girls with their white parasols are in shadow, but these girls [points to a detail in the photograph] have backlight on them. The sun obviously was just about to go behind this big rock. We chose to shoot this scene at the same time of day just before lunch. But you can only work with what you've got. I guess that's where the skill comes in; you don't learn that in school.

Tibbetts: Ultimately you are subject to the whims of the sun, aren't you? I mean, you can only control so much.
Boyd: Exactly, you are left in the lap of the gods, totally.

Tibbetts: Did the white gowns and the tops of the parasols serve as reflectors?
Boyd: To a degree, yeah. Although usually, we don't use bright white in costumes. Normally, we dye it down so it doesn't jump out so much; so it's not quite as bright.

Tibbetts: And I guess it was hot at those times . . . and lots of flies?
Boyd: Yep. But you don't see the flies. They stayed down by Catering!

[Russell Boyd turns the pages and gazes at a beautiful color photo of

Miranda's last moments on the Rock before her disappearance. Her head is slightly turned, her right arm is upraised in a tentative gesture—A greeting? A farewell? The shallow-depth image keeps her in focus, surrounded by a foreground and background of a blurred abundance of lush green foliage. A wisp of golden hair falls across her face.]

Ahh, so beautiful. . . . Gee, I haven't looked through this book for a long, long time. I discovered it in an old bookstore not far from home, about ten or fifteen years ago. I grabbed a copy of it. I don't know how far up the rock you got, you probably passed that without realizing that's where Anne—Miranda—disappeared through the cleft in the rock.

Tibbetts: I found so many areas where there are little clefts in the rocks.
Boyd: Yeah, the Rock is littered with them. I'm not sure I could even find that exact spot anymore. [turns the page] That's the girl, Edith, frightened, running down the Rock. I remember the screaming sounds on the soundtrack. That's looking down from a helicopter shot. I remember, Peter and I went up and had only a half an hour to get that shot. He specifically wanted that angle.

The Last Wave

Tibbetts: Let's continue with *The Last Wave*. It certainly kept you and Peter from being typecast as creating another impressionistic, "warm" and hazy look.
Boyd: Well, I don't think you'd accuse Peter of ever making the same movie twice. Which is one of his great attributes. And as far as I'm concerned, cinematographers can also get pigeonholed into a certain type of look, of a certain type of film. One of the great things of working in the industry in Australia is we have a varied choice of stories to tell that require a separate look, a different look. And so it's great for a cinematographer to explore those territories.

Tibbetts: But at that time, continuing to work together in *The Last Wave* after *Picnic* must have seemed the natural thing to do.
Boyd: Well, it's comfortable. It gives any member of that team confidence in what they're doing. Peter's very inspirational to work with, as you can imagine. And he inspires the best work out of people. So, when he's getting the best out of *you*, for example, why not give him another run? People like to stick with him.

Tibbetts: The film's look is quite different from *Picnic*, kind of hard-edged, or something.

Boyd: Because there was going to be a lot of rain in the movie—special effects rain—I thought the picture should have a colder, bluer look about it, to add a little bit of mystery to it. When I say "blue," I mean a technique we often use for night shoots that involves filtering of the lens.

Tibbetts: Somewhere you talked about the fact that you had to do a lot of shooting with available light. That is to say, some of the night scenes, especially outside of the house, where there wasn't any sort of additional light you could use.

Boyd: Well, not so much night scenes, but dusk scenes. There is a scene in *The Last Wave* where Richard Chamberlain drives his Volvo home into the driveway in the pouring rain. In the next shot he goes inside the door and says hello to one of his children. (One of them, incidentally, was little Ingrid Weir, Peter's daughter, when she was about three or four years old.) We often shoot those dusk scenes by the seat of our pants, because there's a very, very critical time where there's very little *ambiance* in the sky, but enough for the sky not to be black, and still enough light to shoot without any additional light whatsoever. And it's a beautiful time of day to shoot and you only get time for one or two takes.

Tibbetts: I think it's called the "magic hour."

Boyd: It *is* called the *magic hour*. So I deliberately changed filters on the camera to make the light and the rain colder and bluer. Yes, it was shot with available light, but we did use those filters. We did the same sort of thing on *Gallipoli* when Archy was about to leave the ranch. His grandfather knew that he was going to sign up for the war, but his mother didn't. It's quite a poignant scene. We shot that at dusk, too, without any additional light, and it's quite evocative.

Tibbetts: You can't emphasize enough how lighting can enhance, compliment mood and story, can you?

Boyd: Well, that, that to me is the role of the cinematographer, to set the mood that the director's created with his actors in telling the story. That's really our prime role, I think.

Tibbetts: Now, about that final shot, with the massive wave engulfing everything . . . was that some sort of image that was turned upside-down . . . ?

Boyd: There's a very well-known underwater cinematographer here by the name of George Greenough. You know, the original ending of the film was going to have a model of Sydney, a complete miniature recreation, including the harbor and the beaches. We were going to flood it. But it proved to be too expensive to build. Then Peter decided to enlist the help of Greenough to create that big, swirling overhead wave. It was put across quite simply to create that effect that Peter wanted.

Tibbetts: Do you see it as an apocalypse, not just as a physical destruction but maybe some sort of a spiritual destruction?
Boyd: Well, I think that film has quite a lot of metaphors in it, doesn't it? Some of them I don't understand to this day. I *can* tell you we were all wet almost the whole way through it.

Tibbetts: And at one point earlier, the sky is raining frogs.
Boyd: Well, as you know, Peter loves delving into the slightly offbeat or unusual. He loves to surprise his audiences with touches like that. Originally, we tried to develop a sequence of black rain falling in broad daylight. But we just didn't have the budget or technical expertise to do it. We abandoned that idea. So somehow we got to the frogs. I remember other strange moments, like the guy crossing a street carrying a palm tree in the pouring rain. At the same time, water was gushing out of Chamberlain's car radio. It's just the little things that Peter's so good at that just throw the audience slightly off.

Tibbetts: But getting back to the frogs. Is somebody out of camera range with a bucket full of frogs?
Boyd: Yep, a couple of special effects guys had a ladder near the side of the camera and suspended between them was a platform out of camera range. I think I remember they just physically threw down the frogs.

Tibbetts: About those underground scenes beneath Sydney and in the caves, were those shot in the studio?
Boyd: We were totally underground. There were two sequences in two locations. One was where Chamberlain was going in to find the cave, and that was actually shot, believe it or not, in the sewers of Sydney, off of Bondi. It was rotten down there. It was rough. Working down deep in the sewers, I mean, it wasn't very pleasant. The other location was where Chamberlain actually entered the cave, where all the mysterious indigenous artifacts were, delving back into Dreamtime, which is our

Indigenous Forebears' way of understanding creation. And that was in a cave, not far from here, just along the coast, looking out onto the Pacific Ocean, not far from where Peter lives.

Tibbetts: Were there any special circumstances working with the Aborigines?
Boyd: You probably should ask Peter that question. Not for me at all. I will say that performances are something that can be difficult to extract from them, only because their culture is so different to ours. We had one by the name of Nandjiwarra, who was actually a tribal elder. He was the older guy, the one who pointed the bone at the window. He was a tribal elder, and tribal elders in indigenous society are the ones who pass on everything from Dreamtime. I won't say it's "mythical," because they think it actually happened. The elder's job is to pass on all of those mores or all of those beliefs onto the younger generation. So when the younger generation gets on to the new generation, the new tribal elders continue pass it on. So all that information goes from generation to generation to generation. I think it's getting harder nowadays, because many Aboriginal societies have urbanized, living in Sydney and other cities.

Tibbetts: You don't recall Nandjiwarra being reluctant to be photographed?
Boyd: He wasn't reluctant to be photographed, but I think there were certain instances when he didn't want to do what Peter asked him to do. For example, I don't think he was very good with dialogue and couldn't remember lines clearly. They were totally alien to him. But he had such a wonderful presence on the screen. Just him being there got the message across.

Gallipoli and The Year of Living Dangerously

Tibbetts: Now we're looking at pictures from *Gallipoli*. There's the pyramid. One of the scenes everybody remembers is the soccer game at the base of the pyramid. Tell me about that scene.
Boyd: It wasn't soccer; this game was Australian Rules. David Williamson, the co-writer with Peter, was a big Australian Rules fan, as I am, because we grew up out of Melbourne. So Peter's idea about a rugby game outside the pyramids was historically wrong, because this was with the Victorian First Infantry. And Victoria was using Australian Rules. David and I went and knocked on Peter's door and said, "We're leaving the movie, if you make it a rugby league game! It must be Australian rules!"

[laughs] So, Peter said, "Ok, you're both gonna be in it!" So Dave Williamson and I are in that scene playing football. [pointing to the photograph] That's me there. And that's Robert Grubb, the actor. And that's Robert Stigwood, one of the producers.

Tibbetts: But what a lovely idea. What a lovely moment.
Boyd: Yep. And there I am with John Seale.

Tibbetts: Yeah. The two of you crouching at the base, the tents look like pyramids. [laughs]
Boyd: Yeah, they do. I'm sure that was designed that way. There's the crew shot on top of the pyramids. I don't know if you remember the scene. We went up very early one morning when the sun was rising behind them, and they're sitting down. Mel has a cigarette. He and the other actor, Mark Lee, are talking. And there's Peter. I've often said this to students here in Australia, not only American audiences. Gallipoli, in Australian folklore, represents coming of age to Australia, where a lot of young men went to war thinking it was going to be a great adventure. In fact, a lot of them didn't come home. And to me, that was a great period of our history that needed to be told. I'm just so pleased that Peter told it in such a wonderful rounded way, where the two guys got together, ran against each other in competition then finished up going all the way across to Gallipoli.

Tibbetts: I would guess that even Australian viewers learned a lot.
Boyd: Well, that's what I'm saying. I'm very glad that Peter made that film to present that to the Australian public in such a wonderful way.

Tibbetts: What were some of the different locations for the shoot?
Boyd: Firstly, the film was funded partly by the South Australian Film Corporation. So, it was desirable that we shot a fair proportion of the film in South Australia. So a lot of trouble was put into finding a place that looked similar to Gallipoli. In other words, facing out to sea, facing west, with similar sand hills. The ones in the film were quite misty but it was a very good facsimile of the real Gallipoli. We shot most of the film on the beach and in the hills west of Port Lincoln. And then we went to the pyramids to show a bit of the story of the Australians who camped in Egypt either before going off to France or Gallipoli, during the war, where they had more training. That was a hard, high moment of the film as well. So, the film was shot mostly in South Australia, and partly in

Egypt. In Gallipoli where the battle did take place, the entire area has become a heritage-listed venue for both the Turks and Australians, who now have a very friendly relationship. Every Anzac Day, a lot of Australians, I think twenty-thousand nowadays, go there for Anzac Day, which is April 25, the date in 1915 when the Anzacs arrived on Gallipoli Cove. There's always a big ceremony there. There are still artifacts being dug up, like picks that were used to dig the trenches. I've got one at home that was actually used in Gallipoli, in the First World War anyway.

Gallipoli is a very emotional part of our history. I remember during the scene when the guys were just about to go out of the trenches to face the Turks—Peter had everybody in tears, including the crew. He'd been talking to them very intensely, telling him their characters were facing almost certain death. And he was playing music on his little boom box. I can't remember exactly what he was playing, but he turned the volume right up. Gallipoli was a real coming of age for Australians, you know. Anzac is a derivative of the words "Australian and New Zealand Army Corps." So, that's the word, "Anzac." We celebrate that as a battle we lost. Whereas most military battles are celebrated by whichever country won that battle.

Tibbetts: But is it the kind of thing where the battle was lost but in some ways the war was won, for Australian identity?
Boyd: Well, the Australian identity really came to the fore, and that's one of the key elements in the film. We were a bunch of farmers before then, but after that we were part of the rigors and fatalities of war, which is very sad. Here's fond memories for us on Anzac Day, 2004, which is eight years ago. There's Pat Lovell, one of the producers of *Gallipoli* on Anzac Day. When I say "up," Pat only lives a few miles from here. John and I, a few of us who were part of the film, would go to a great lunch on Anzac Day.

Tibbetts: Now we're looking at the images from *The Year of Living Dangerously*.
Boyd: Shooting in Indonesia was interesting, but, as you may know, we actually had to leave Indonesia before completing filming. There was a political problem. The character of Billy Kwan visited a poverty-stricken young mother, in a very poor area, poverty-stricken area. And so we picked a village to shoot those scenes in. The village was full of Muslims, 'cause they are very downtrodden in Manila, 'cause Manila is basically a Catholic population. So, after we did, Peter and the producers started to

get threats that the production would be harmed in one way or another. The threats got more serious. They'd get phone calls in the middle of the night. We took into that village a whole lot of extras who were actually Catholics. It caused a lot of friction between the Muslims and Catholics, so the Muslims who really wanted to earn the money as paid extras were pushed aside. Unknown to us, we offended them very deeply. So, that's when the threats started coming. So we packed up and came back to Australia and finished, I think, maybe the last three weeks of the film, which was a big job for the art department to recreate that little village.

Tibbetts: A lot of us just remember the scenes with Billy, and we see the *wayang*, we see the shadow-plays. Were you on set shooting those scenes with your operator?
Boyd: We shot that several weeks after we came back. Peter found some authentic *wayang kulit* puppets. I think he even got some Indonesians to do the puppet show, to play the puppet show. So we shot that as the title sequence. I don't think it was anywhere else in the film, it's been a while since I've seen it. It may have been. Balinese culture is really quite extraordinary. And the *wayang kulit* is a way of entertaining the children. Long before television, obviously. It's always associated with kids going out for the early evening, before they go to bed; and this puppet show is performed for them. The lovely gamelan music is very eerie. I've actually seen those shows performed in Bali, which is part of Indonesia.

Tibbetts: Is there a moment as a cinematographer that you recall especially from that film, whether it be a challenge, a moment, an anecdote, shooting that film?
Boyd: You know, Peter is very interested in the play of light. He pointed something out to me that I hadn't thought about, but turned out to be important. He said, "I want you to light the streets in such a way that as we're walking along, going in and out of the little markets, the lights will flicker in intensity. The electricity is not full voltage. I want you to light it like that, if you can." So, I struggled with that for a while. I had to figure out where and when the light would drop off into darkness. That was the sort of lighting suggestion he makes to me that I've never forgotten. Not only that, but there was always a bit of dust in the air, so there was always a slight mistiness to the light, as well. We talk a lot about light. In other instances, he doesn't want anything to look artificially lit. I don't either. I hate seeing something on the screen that looks like somebody's been fussing with the lighting. It just looks phony. In preproduction he'll get

a lot of visual research material together, lots of documentary materials, other films, coffee table books. We'll sit down for quite a long period of time just leafing through them, like you and I are leafing through these photos and papers here.

Tibbetts: Total immersion.

Boyd: Yep, yep. You know, I'll pick up some visual ideas from it that might return to me later.

Master and Commander

Tibbetts: When did you first know you were going to team up again with Weir, after a twenty-year gap?

Boyd: I remember it clearly. One day, purely, by accident, we were sitting on an aircraft going to Los Angeles. We were going for completely different reasons. And we sat, side by side. I think Peter might have arranged that, actually. We were in first class, in those days, and there was nobody else at all in that section. So there was no problem sitting next to each other. He started telling me about this seafaring film he wanted to make, and he was going over to see the people at Fox, because it was starting to gather some momentum. He told me it was called *Master and Commander*, from a series of books by Patrick O'Brian. And it was from the first and tenth novels, I think.[8] Anyway, Peter explained the story almost scene by scene for me. And I thought, Oh, yeah, I'd love to shoot that film! He didn't offer it to me on the flight. But I did get a call from him in Los Angeles that night, and he said, "Let's have dinner tomorrow night. I'm going to drop the script over to you to read, 'cause I'd love you to shoot it." When he said that, I immediately rang my wife: "Guess what Peter's asked me to do, *Master and Commander!*" Peter knew that I loved sailing. So, I read the script and loved it, of course. Eventually, when he got the movie going, in full swing, I went over and we did some scouting for locations, including the Galapagos Islands, once to scout and the other time to shoot. I was so pleased to have been able to work with him again.

Tibbetts: Were you surprised at the time to find out how little of the film would actually be shot on the water?

Boyd: Yes, well, interestingly enough, he originally wanted to shoot it *entirely* on the water, which was a great notion, except that we would have had to have a floating ship trailing along with us. But as soon as we wanted to do a reverse angle, we realized the support vessels would be in the shot, unless we would have to wait half an hour for it to get out of the shot. That and other problems made it not a practical idea at all. It just wasn't going to work. And imagine the catering, getting all the sandwiches brought on board at lunchtime! That's when Peter and I first formulated the idea that maybe we should build a set of the top decks and one in a tank somewhere, which would be the gun deck below it. I think he spoke to Ridley Scott about the tank in Gibraltar, 'cause Ridley had worked on a tank in Gibraltar, although at that stage it had fallen into disrepair. And I think Ridley Scott said, "Peter, I think you'd have to spend a lot of your budget getting it up to scratch again." And a producer came out, Duncan Henderson, and an assistant director came out, and we scoured the north coast of Australia because at that point they thought maybe we'll build a tank in Australia. Ultimately, Peter, after a lot of deliberations, said, "Look, I'm not a civil engineer; I don't want to build a damn tank." So ultimately, we finished up shooting in a tank in Mexico in a tank that James Cameron has purposefully built for *Titanic*.

Tibbetts: I see. The same one?

Boyd: Yep, same one. The tank was fabulous because it had a deep channel where they could put the set on a big gimbal, which moved the big raft fore and aft, left to right. And then it had shallow water all around it so people could actually walk waist deep around the ship, if they needed to. But the stages themselves didn't prove very practical to us. Remember in *Titanic*, when the ship sinks nose first—that set was built on a gimbal, on a stage, that would only do that. And that was no good to us. So, we flattened it out, left it flat in the floor and built one of the cabins on top of that. The captain's cabin was on top of that. Since we couldn't use that gimbal, they put it on rubber tires, inflatable rubber tubes, which you can use for rocking. So, there are a lot of things we weren't able to use that were part of that Mexican tank. In addition to the tank itself, they had a big construction crane on a series of rails. It could trundle anywhere. The reach of the arm of the crane made it useful for construction as well. So, there was a basket constructed by grips that we could hang cameras from. They could be operated remotely from down below.

Tibbetts: Did you go into the box yourself?

Boyd: We did a few times, yeah. I did a few times with the camera operator. I must say, I'm not great with heights, and neither was my camera operator. So we would look at each other and grimace. But that construction crane in the middle of the tank was invaluable, really, for getting shots with the cast from up above. So we would go up in the basket, suspended from that crane. It was a challenge. Well, all films are a challenge, no question of that.

Tibbetts: Near the beginning is that amazing shot where we see through the fog bank a flash of cannon fire from the French warship. That sense of a sinister intrusion reminded me of the opening of *Picnic*.
Boyd: That was mostly a visual effect. We shot the background "plate," knowing that the visual effects team would later add the telescope vignette, more fog, and the cannon flash. It's definitely something Peter likes to do, hint that something is brewing underneath the veil of normalcy. It's an ambience that can be shattered at any moment.

Tibbetts: How about another memorable moment. We're in the Galapagos. Maturin is examining something, and suddenly there's a rack focus revealing a French warship off the coast.
Boyd: Peter wanted Dr. Maturin to be looking closely at an insect in his hand in that scene, because he was a naturalist and he had never seen it before. And Peter wanted the shot where we had the camera tight on him and the water in the distance. He just wanted a slow rack focus from the tight shot of the insect to the *Acheron*, the French ship.

Tibbetts: An electrifying moment.
Boyd: An electrifying moment, it was one of the key moments in the film. But, you know, in fact, there was no ship there at all! I mean, it was a visual effect. The visual effects department had put that ship in there, because we couldn't build a whole ship and get it to the Galapagos from Los Angeles. That would have been next to impossible. So, actually we just photographed an inky sea! The *Acheron* was put in there later.

Tibbetts: It works for me.
Boyd: The first time I ever saw it, it looked to me like a little paper model of a ship floating around at sea. I don't think an audience would have picked that up. I always know when that shot's coming up and I always know that I'm gonna get a giggle out of it.

Tibbetts: Have you ever seen anything before or since like the Galapagos locations?
Boyd: Ahhh, I loved those locations! I think they're one of the great wonders of the world. You could walk amongst the birdlife. So many

different birds, so many colors, with so many different calls. They're very protected. You're not allowed to get off a certain track. You always have a guide and the guide will say, "You can't walk there because there might be turtle eggs buried there waiting to hatch." The whole experience was so different from anything else I'd ever experienced. I'd love to go back there.

Tibbetts: I understand that the actors were not permitted to touch the animals.
Boyd: Absolutely. In fact, sadly, recently, the giant tortoise that was there called "Lonesome George" died just recently. He was from a particular island in the Galapagos, and they were trying to breed from him, to find a mate exactly the same genetically. The different islands had different turtles slightly different in genetics. He was well over a hundred years old. There's a scene with the doctor feeding one of the other giant tortoises. He was able to feed it but he wasn't able to touch it. The tortoises actually reacted very well because we shot them at a special feeding time, and under the watchful eyes of the rangers on the Galapagos. You're not allowed to touch any of the animals, for any reason whatsoever.

Tibbetts: So there you are in this seemingly isolated environment and yet all around you are guides and people to make sure you behave yourself.
Boyd: Absolutely. In fact, I think permission was very, very hard to get. Because, only a few documentary makers have been allowed to shoot film on the island, let alone a big Hollywood dramatic production. So it took a long time, a couple of years of negotiation.

Tibbetts: Were there restrictions on how much camera equipment you could bring?
Boyd: Not so much, but we could only be there during daylight hours. We'd be ferried off the islands just as the sun was setting. We stayed on a tourist ship. That's where we spent our nights and ate our meals. You can't take any foodstuffs onto the islands themselves because it might be bad for the native fauna. But despite all the restrictions, it was completely wonderful to be there. And I loved the experience because I love sailing. It kindled my interest in that historical period of sailing. And it was great to work with my regular crew again in Hollywood. And the chance to explore something different, like shooting below decks on ships with very limited headroom. Peter was very, very careful to make

sure that everything was correct historically in the set, including the height of the deck beams. Just the challenge to light those spaces appealed to me enormously.

Tibbetts: And, of course, the film brought you an Oscar.
Boyd: The Oscar was the icing on the cake for us. Unfortunately for Peter, although the film was nominated for quite a few Academy Awards, Peter Jackson's *Lord of the Rings* trilogy took most of the awards. Apart from mine, one other was for Sound Editing.

The Way Back

Tibbetts: Now who would have thought after such exotic locations, that you would move to totally different set of circumstances and climates for *The Way Back*!
Boyd: Yep, *The Way Back* had its own exotic locations, but unfortunately, some of them were snowy and freezing! Anybody who's seen the film understands that it was a very physical project. Even in some of the forest scenes, which we constructed on one of the huge soundstages in Sophia, in Bulgaria, it was quite cold. We had to wear our parkas and our ski pants to work because it was just as cold onstage as it was working outside.

Tibbetts: Did the cold cause any problems with the cameras and the film?
Boyd: No, there's no physical problems with the cameras or the film being too brittle or anything like that. It's just the comfort level of everybody involved. It's rugged and you can barely talk to each other—really, there's icicles hanging from your nose!

Tibbetts: And then hot environments. You went to Morocco.
Boyd: Yep, then we went "on the road to Morocco"! [laughs] I quite enjoyed Morocco, my first time. I must say, I prefer warm weather, and the minute we hit Morocco, I was in shorts and t-shirt and sandals for the remaining three or four weeks.

Tibbetts: Everybody from the beginning knew what they were in for, I guess, or could you have foreseen that?
Boyd: I don't we could have foreseen it, though I generally get, particularly with Peter's films, a fairly long preproduction period, where we go

through all the locations and go through every scene in the script; and I plan with my crew how to light for scenes. So we're there far ahead of the main crew. Department heads were well and fully aware of what we were in for. Because all that preproduction period was in snow and pretty cold weather, as well.

Tibbetts: You guys just don't sit back and take it easy. But are there times when it's like, "Peter, let's go home"? [both laugh]
Boyd: Yeah. Well, there might have been a few times, but I never said that. You know, filmmaking as a craft wasn't meant to be easy. Great films have to be difficult to make. But you must always maintain a sense of humor. Peter's great with that and it lightens the tension. And we all become a family, a great big family for the short time we're thrown together.

Tibbetts: Are you someone who regards your work as a cinematographer as more of a privilege as a job?
Boyd: It's a total privilege. It's not a matter of being a romantic. It's a job, for sure. It's a hard job, but I feel much more privileged to be able to do that than going to work in a bank every day. Now, *that* would be a job! I count all of us very fortunate to be able to work in this business.

Tibbetts: You can't be in a bank and tomorrow somebody says, "Tomorrow, we're going to Morocco." It won't happen.
Boyd: No, I don't think so. [laughs]

Tibbetts: But really, you could look back on all of these years, this was what you were meant to do on this earth.
Boyd: You know, if I'm shooting tomorrow, I would jump out of bed itching to get to work. Even on feature films, when day after day after day, week after week after week, and you get very tired both emotionally and physically, you're out of bed at 5:30, and your feet hit the ground, and you're into the shower and have some breakfast and go off to work. That day's a whole different experience from the previous day. I still love my work, even if's only a television commercial. There's always a challenge and there's always camaraderie.

Tibbetts: Maybe we could call it, "CAMERA-raderie."
Boyd: Oh, there you go.

The Oscar

Tibbetts: Here's a picture with you holding up your Oscar. Check the smile on your face!

Boyd: The photos we're looking at right now are from the Academy Award night, where I was lucky enough to receive the Oscar for *Master and Commander*. 2002. Just a month before, when the nominations were first announced, all the nominees who have been awarded the nomination for the Academy Awards got together and had their photograph taken and went out for lunch. I went with my agent that day, and she knew quite a few people; so, it was just a very nice, relaxed wonderful lunch where we could get together.

Tibbetts: And colleagues there? John Seale?

Boyd: John Seale was there because he was nominated that same year for *Cold Mountain*. In fact, when I won, I heard this, "Whoopee!" from the other side of the auditorium, and it was John. He was quite happy I won, even though he was nominated that year, too. John had already won an Oscar.

Tibbetts: Everything that you say about him speaks to me of an ongoing friendship, professionally as well as personally.

Boyd: We don't see an awful lot, John and me socially, our lives do part ways, and we both have grandchildren. But we certainly enjoy it when we get together, probably only two or three times a year. Talking shop and things. Once I had been nominated for the Academy Award, for *Master and Commander*, I thought, "Definitely, I hope I can win one." But before that, my career had never been fashioned or designed around consciously going around trying to win an Academy Award. I don't know that any cinematographer's career goes that way. But, to be honest, I was extremely pleased; it was a great night. My wife Sandy, who you've just seen a picture of, had a fall just before we got on the flight to go to L.A. She severely twisted her ankle. She tripped over a garden hose, when we came home from dinner one night. She was limping badly so we went into the auditorium very early so she could sit down. We were almost the first people in the auditorium, only about four or five rows back from the front. This gentleman came up and said to Sandy, my wife, "Hi, I'm Mickey Rooney." [laughs] And he sat down next to her, and we thought that a seat hadn't been assigned for him. So he started chatting away to my wife, and the next thing we know, there's a tap on his shoulder.

[laughs] And one of the attendants came up, "We're sorry, Mr. Rooney, but your seat's back there." [laughs]

Tibbetts: The presence of your wife wouldn't have had anything to do with him selecting that seat.
Boyd: Well, knowing his reputation, maybe it did. I don't know, it could have been, you might be right.

Tibbetts: Well, anybody who married Ava Gardner may still have a little something going for him.
Boyd: I was one of the "labor" awards that come first. I think after me were the "serious" awards, Best Film, Best Director, Actors, and all of that. So, I didn't get to go back and sit in the auditorium. What happens is you go around back of the auditorium, back of the stage, where there's 150 photographers with flashes. Uma Thurman escorted me around there. She's really tall! So then, you go around the back and thousands of cameras start flashing and that's where these photographs were taken.

Tibbetts: Rendering you permanently blind?
Boyd: Just about. It was a bit daunting, I must say, to have people yelling out, "Mr. Boyd, blah, blah, blah; how do you feel?" At one stage, I held the Oscar up and gave it a kiss and they said, "Do it again, do it again, do it again!" So, I must have done it a hundred times.

Tibbetts: [laughs] That's Hollywood. Did a lot of these people know your work, across the board?
Boyd: I'm not sure about the still photographers who were there from newspapers and all sorts of media outlets. But the film had been released, so maybe they knew, maybe they'd seen it.

Tibbetts: But did they know of who you are?
Boyd: To be honest, I doubt it. I'm used to that. When the studio put together a book about the background and shooting of *Master and Commander*, they didn't come to me for a single question. They spoke to every department head about the film and what their jobs were, and all that; but nobody came anywhere near me. The Director of Photography is not even mentioned! I thought that was a bit weird. . . .

Tibbetts: It's not just weird, it's kind of obscene.
Boyd: Anyway, after meeting the press, everybody goes upstairs where

a huge table was set out with a great four-, five-course meal, cooked by a chef called Wolfgang Puck, who is famous. (You've probably heard about him!) A beautiful meal. And after that is the Governor's Ball. And from there people leave for the parties. By that time, my wife and I had been in L.A. for a week, and out nearly every night for various functions. So we didn't go to any of the parties. We just went back to the hotel. My wife went straight to bed, and I just sat there. I opened a bottle of wine, red wine, relaxed, and every time I looked at the Oscar, I started giggling. The next day or so I had quite a few interviews with various press agencies, mostly Australian ones. We came home the next night. Going through customs at L.A. airport aroused a commotion. When my Oscar statuette stopped on the x-ray, the person behind the x-ray and everybody else came rushing to have a look at it. It was a fun few nights, actually. A totally unexpected experience. It won't happen again. As I've said to people, you don't need more than one Oscar, anyway, ha, ha, ha.

Tibbetts: And then you come back home and took out the trash. . . .
Boyd: Yep.

Tibbetts: Life goes on.
Boyd: Exactly. Back in the garden, pulling weeds.

Notes

1. For overviews of four of these outstanding young Australian cinematographers emerging in the early 1970s—Mike Malloy (*Mad Dog*), Geoffrey Burton (*Sunday Too Far Away, Harness Fever*), Peter James (*Caddie*), and Russell Boyd—see "New Vintage Cinematographers of Australia Speak Out," *American Cinematographer*, no. 9 (September 1976): 998–99, 1038–39. For a general historical overview, see Martha Ansara, *The Shadowcatchers: A History of Cinematography in Australia* (Sydney: Austcine Publishing, 2012).

2. For an account of Russell Boyd's work on Norman Jewison's *A Soldier's Story* (1984), see Donald Chase, "Russell Boyd," *American Cinematographer*, December 1984, 81–87.

3. Raymond Longford (1878–1959) was a prolific Australian film director, writer, producer, and actor during the silent era, who directed *The Sentimental Bloke* (1919) and *The Blue Mountains Mystery* (1921). His career faltered in the sound era and he directed only one film, *The Man They Could Not Hang* (1935). The AFI Raymond Longford Award was established in 1968. Peter Weir (1990) and Russell Boyd (1988) are among the recipients.

4. Michael Thornhill directed Russell Boyd's first feature as a cinematographer, *Between Wars* (1974). He has had an extensive career in the Australian film industry. In the late 1970s

and early 1980s he was a director of the New South Wales Film Corporation. He has also worked as a producer for Australian television.

5. See the interview with Peter Watkin in John C. Tibbetts and James M. Welsh, *The Cinema of Tony Richardson: Essays and Interviews* (Albany: State University of New York, 1999), 38–45.

6. See also "Russell Boyd: *Picnic at Hanging Rock*," *American Cinematographer*, no. 9 (September 1976): 1038–39.

7. After working as a camera operator with Russell Boyd, John Seale, ASC, ACS, has gone on to an Oscar-winning career in Australia and Hollywood as a Director of Photography. He has photographed several Peter Weir films, including *Witness* and *Mosquito Coast*. He won an Oscar for his work in *The English Patient* (1996).

8. Patrick O'Brian (1914–2000) wrote twenty novels about the seafaring adventures of Jack Aubrey, captain of HMS *Surprise*, and Stephen Maturin, the ship's surgeon. The first, *Master and Commander*, was published in 1969 and the last, *Blue at the Mizzen*, in 1999.

Appendix: Notes on *Gallipoli*

Peter Weir and Executive Producer Francis O'Brien discuss the research and subsequent release of *Gallipoli*.

Interview with Executive Producer Francis O'Brien

We begin with O'Brien's account of the film's release in America and the role it played in the growing popularity of Australian film with American audiences. O'Brien's interview, which transpired in Kansas City, Missouri, on September 30, 1981, is a snapshot in time of the days and weeks of the film's first American release. It has never been published.

John C. Tibbetts: This is an unusual opportunity to talk to a producer that has followed a film from its inception on down to the screenings that are going on right now. Tell me how a nice kid from Ohio gets involved in the production of an Australian film!
Francis O'Brien: Well, it's a long road to Australia! I had been with Paramount for a number of years before this. I started out in the marketing division and eventually I worked up to the production division. In 1979, I decided to go off on my own and produce films. After a lot of conversations with various people, I decided that some of the most interesting films in the world today were being made in Australia. We were not yet all that familiar with Australian films, but we had seen early Peter Weir films, *Picnic at Hanging Rock*, *Last Wave*; and *My Brilliant Career* by Gillian Armstrong. They were catching our interest in Hollywood. But we didn't know why or what was going on there. Again, Australia is fifteen thousand miles away, and I didn't know anybody who had been there.

Tibbetts: Of course, there's an important Australian connection with Paramount Pictures in the person of Robert Stigwood.
O'Brien: Yes, Robert Stigwood was producing films with Paramount. He's Australian and had produced *Grease* and *Saturday Night Fever*. We met and became friends. He said to me, "Why don't you go down to

240

Australia, and see what kind of film industry is there?" He hadn't been there in fifteen to twenty years. So that's in 1979, in the fall; and I went down and spent two months there meeting everybody, producers, writers, technicians—just everyone in the industry. It doesn't seem as complicated as it might be, because first of all, Australia only has fourteen million people in it so we're not talking about a very large industry. Anyway, I came home, and I recommended that we should set a company up in Australia and make movies down there that could be commercial around the world.

Tibbetts: Why suddenly do we see now this burgeoning of Australian filmmaking?

O'Brien: Again, I think only in America do we find things so suddenly! All of a sudden, Australian films are the flavor of the week in Hollywood. I'm afraid to say not too many people know that the Australian film industry goes way back, almost as long as ours. It almost parallels our history. They had a very vital and alive industry up until World War II. After the war, American cinema moved in and then something worse happened, television came along, in terms of the film industry. And then the Australian film industry went into total decline. Not until 1970, when the government stepped in and revitalized it. Up until this year, almost all Australian films were financed by the government, and there just wasn't any private money coming into the market. The economics weren't favorable for private investment. We're about the first company to step in with private money. Now the government has passed new tax laws and hopefully, other private investors will come in. You're a doctor, you're a lawyer, invest some money in the film industry and you get a substantial tax break. So the hope is commercial directors like Peter Weir, like Bruce Beresford, like Fred Schepisi, won't have to go back to the government anymore and can look to the private sector for financing.

Tibbetts: We have scarcely heard about the story of Gallipoli before.

O'Brien: Gallipoli is a peninsula in southern Turkey. It's a name and a story that is very familiar to Europeans and obviously to Australians. Our advertising poster says, "From a place you've never heard of." We realize American audiences are not aware of the name. The fact is, *Gallipoli* is the most expensive movie ever made in the history of Australia. It cost $3 million, which by American standards is very low today since the average cost is $10 million. I myself first became aware of *Gallipoli* when I was down in Australia and I had met Peter Weir. He told me about the story in Hollywood parlance—he "pitched" it, you would say. I thought it was a terrific idea. So, I committed to it. We set up the financing for it and got the writer, David Williamson.

Tibbetts: And you got the cameraman, Russell Boyd.
O'Brien: I think that Russell Boyd is one of the most talented cinematographers in the world today. You look at both *Picnic* and you look at *Gallipoli*, he composes scenes so beautifully. They're photographs or paintings the way he does it.

Tibbetts: And for the character of "Archy" you got Mark Lee, who had never appeared in a major film.
O'Brien: You're right. We had long discussions about that. Could he hold up against Mel Gibson? Well, I think clearly he did. A lot of that credit obviously has to go to the actor, Mark Lee, but it has to go to the director, who can draw so much out of an actor. Mark and Mel won two different awards, Mark for Best Newcomer to Film, and Mel Gibson for the Best Actor Award, the Australian equivalent of our Academy Awards.

Tibbetts: I suppose there was never any question that the locations would have to be authentic.
O'Brien: To the degree possible. Again, you always have to remember making a movie, you set a budget and you try to live within or get very close to that budget. So, we tried to be authentic as possible, within reason. And I think we were able to get most every location authentic with the exception of the Gallipoli beach. We used a beach in Australia instead simply for economic reasons, and selected it through photographs and from people who were actually at Gallipoli. For the Cairo locations, you have to give Russell Boyd credit here. Cairo is not the way it used to be. There's a lot of smog, pollution, etc., in the air. And somehow the cinematographer seemed to eliminate all that and just made them spectacularly beautiful. We picked locations into the interior of Australia where it took two days to reach by land rover. They were very desolate areas. It's not quite what I had imagined producing a movie! I mean, where's our limousine??? Although we were shooting during the winter, the temperatures in the desert would still get up to 100, 115. And then at night, it would plunge to the low 30s. Since we were shooting on this man's property, a sheep ranch, we slept in the sheds, with of course no heat! (There was no one but us in the sheds!) We shook with the cold all night. Everyone lived the same. The actors, the director, the producer, and it gave a real sense of family.

Tibbetts: Any conflicts with Weir during the shoot?

O'Brien: Not really. Peter and I grew to trust each other. It was give and take. Take the big ball scene. That was never in the script at all. And only after we were watching dailies, the footage we were shooting every day, did we realize we were missing something in this movie. Well, if I was sitting back in Hollywood and I got a Telex from this director, way out in Australia, that said, "It's essential to have ball scene!" I'd think, "uh-oh, here we go, it's *Heaven's Gate* time!" Like here was a director just wanting an extravagant ballroom scene for no reason! But we all talked about it and came to the same conclusion, that it was essential. So we shot it and increased the budget. You know, Peter is becoming much more of a storyteller as a director than in his earlier films. I think for me, it's wonderful to watch somebody like that in transition. He deals with emotion for the first time, as he's never done in his films before.

Tibbetts: When do you begin to sense what the total film will look like?

O'Brien: Well, you assemble the film. You put it in very rough assemblage, put scenes together to see if you have anything. And then if you do, you go into the editing room for the next three or four months, as we did, and you edit and you mix and add the dialogue. After getting the final cut—what in the business we call the release print—we now have to find someone who's going to distribute the movie for us. In this case in the United States, I brought the film back and showed it to all of the major distributors, Paramount, Columbia, Warner Brothers, Universal, United Artists, etc. And you hope one of them is interested. In this case we were very fortunate, three studios were interested, Warners, Columbia, and Paramount. We chose Paramount for two reasons: One, they paid us the most money; but more importantly for this film, they fell in love with it, and they showed a great deal of enthusiasm in their marketing department. They were going to take this film and make it their "cause."

Tibbetts: Now, here in Kansas City, it soon will be playing as an exclusive engagement at just one theater. How many other cities right now is it playing?

O'Brien: Right now, it's playing in fifteen other cities. When we open in Kansas City, we'll open in another thirty cities at the same time. Again, we're opening quicker than we originally thought, simply because, in the fifteen cities we're in, we're breaking house records in every city we're playing in. We opened it originally in New York City, the Baronet Theatre. That first week we broke every house record. We had to move the film next door to the Coronet because it holds more people. The ex-hibitor ran the film twenty-four hours a day over the Labor Day week-end, again an unusual experience. And now, we've broken every record at that theatre.

Tibbetts: On reflection, just what kind of film is *Gallipoli*?
O'Brien: You're talking about the sort of film that I think we used to make in this country. It's film that has a beginning, it has a middle, it has an end. It's a story about relationships. It's a story we can identify with; and it doesn't matter if it's made in Australia or wherever. But it's under-standable. It's a movie that *entertains* above all. I think the lack of that factor elsewhere explains we see a fall-off in general movie attendance.

Peter Weir's Anzac Lecture

Given April 26, 2001, at the Center for Australian and New Zealand Stud-ies, ICC Auditorium, Georgetown University, Washington, D.C. Never before published. Printed by permission of Peter Weir.

> With [the West Australian 10th Regiment] went the flower of the youth of Western Australia . . . they rushed straight to their deaths; Gresley Harper and Wilfred, his younger brother, the latter of whom was last seen running forward like a schoolboy in a foot race. . . .
> —C. E. W. Bean, *Official History of Australia in the War of 1914-1918*

Growing up in Australia in the 1950s, Anzac Day was a very significant day in the school calendar—because it was a holiday. Well, practically. There was the church service, but you got most of the day off. Remem-brance Day was more important at our school, a separate day when we remembered the Old Boys who "fell." We had a service in the school cha-pel, a turgid, never-ending affair, the school chaplain intoning away . . . "Yea, verily, I say unto you, SACRIFICE. They did sacrifice themselves . . . that *you* might be here today." You felt vaguely guilty, and you couldn't wait for it to be over. And as far as the Anzac story went, well, it was a defeat. Not likely to appeal to a ten-year-old, and it was so long ago, and there'd already been another war or two. So you couldn't wait to get out, get away from that stuffy atmosphere and go to the beach or whatever we did.

Not to say I wasn't fascinated by war, because I had all the comics— *Blackhawk* I particularly loved. And neighbor's garages: they often con-tained war souvenirs. They'd be puzzled when I asked to see their garage on some pretext. That's where you'd be liable to find a German helmet or a captured Japanese Samurai sword.

My own father, rejected on medical grounds, had been an air-raid warden. Not much heroism in that, but at least he'd been on duty the night two Japanese subs got into Sydney Harbour. He remembered the sound of a shell bursting, and I got him to tell me the story over and over. And I had his gas mask. . . . Uncle Jack, who was a bachelor and a veteran, visited us sometimes. Me: "Did you ever personally kill anyone?" Mother: "Don't ask Uncle Jack questions like that!"

By the time I was twenty, we were involved in Vietnam, and later I found myself in the anti-war movement, and anything to do with our martial history was derided by most of the Arts community, an attitude reflected in books and plays of the time. Yet, little more than ten years later, I decided to make a movie about Gallipoli. My friends, and many in the growing film community, were mystified. It was 1976, I'd made two films, and the choice of Gallipoli as a subject seemed to make about much sense commercially as filming the phone book, apart from seeming politically incorrect.

Prior to settling on Gallipoli as a subject, I thought I'd set the story in France. I probably wanted to make a war-movie for all the wrong reasons—I'd been working with original material, and a genre film seemed to offer the chance to coast for a while to be buoyed up by the genre itself, to "hitch a ride," as it were. . . . I'd loved the classics of the genre, *Paths of Glory, All Quiet on the Western Front,* and so on, and as a boy I used to pore over my grandfather's copies of the great war history by Bean, studying the photographs of soldiers and mud and death.

A friend said, "Why not Gallipoli?" But the very mention of the word brought back those mornings in chapel, the voice declaiming away about sacrifice and "Yea, though I walk through the Valley of the Shadow. . . ." But, something stuck there, and I was going to London for the opening of a film of mine. So why not detour to Turkey? Anyway, it was a chance to visit Troy, which seemed a more interesting battlefield.

A word about battlefields: I slept in one on my first trip to Europe in 1965. I was hitchhiking around Greece, and found myself in a remote town in the Peloponnese as night was falling. I'd spotted a park, a timbered peninsula jutting out into the ocean, just out of town, an ideal place to spend the night. I unrolled my sleeping bag in a depression under the pines, the fallen needles making an ideal mattress, and dropped off to sleep. The world was more innocent then; you could sleep anywhere without fear of being disturbed, particularly in Greece, so I was puzzled when something woke me up about 1:00 A.M. I was instantly awake, instantly afraid. That kind of animal fear, the cold sweat, the special alertness you can feel in a moment of profound danger. But why? There was no one about. I hadn't been dreaming and yet I knew instinctively I had to get out of there. Just move slowly, don't run, don't show any fear, just go.

Back in town, I spent an uncomfortable night sleeping behind a bus station. Next morning I found a Greek man beside me on the bus who spoke good English, and I told him of my strange experience. "Didn't you know?" he said, "It's a famous battlefield." He mentioned some date back in the B.C.s . . . a terrible battle, much loss of life, the dead are buried there. "It's been a memorial ever since," he said.

I'm particularly susceptible to the ambience of place, battlefields in particular. I think of the preserved trench system at the Newfoundland's memorial at the Somme, and Truk Lagoon in the Pacific, you can feel it there even underwater. . . . The wrecks of the Japanese ships, their guns still pointing skyward at the American planes that sank them. Gettysburg is very powerful, and, of course, Gallipoli. It's always been a military zone, and apart from the war graves, it's as it was in 1915.

From my diary:

Saturday, October 2nd, 1976: Leave hotel at dawn for drive to Troy . . . in early light I stopped at an old Turkish battery and memorial facing the narrows. This was one of the key batteries of the great sea battle of 18 March 1915, the day the British/French fleet was defeated. The graves of the battery commander and those of his men killed lay in a grove of pine trees. Over a ploughed field I walked to see the narrows and imagine the battle. The guns are still in place! Scarred and rusted, but still pointing toward the expected renewal of the attack. Beautiful, still morning . . . Drive back to Cannakle and take ferry to Eceabat, anxious to get to Anzac. By 10:30, I am driving along the upper road to the memorials at Johnson's Jolly. I walk/scramble over Plateau 400—souvenirs everywhere. I pick up a button with "Commonwealth of Australia" on it; a belt buckle with webbing still on it; a bullet; a tin, ripped open by a bayonet. Down into the trenches, choked now with pine trees. Drive to Lone Pine and again into trenches. Then drive along coast to northernmost extent of Anzac positions. I'm in a kind of dreamy state. Very hot and thirsty. Peel off and dive into the Aegean, just north of Ari Burnu. Rusted ribs of two boats on edge of the water: landing craft? The water is divine. I drive around closer to Anzac cove, then walk to the beach itself. So small! And very shallow. I now understand when authors write of the conges-

tion on the beach. Again I swim. What water—the temperature . . . perfect
. . . under water the most beautiful, blue-green/turquoise colours . . . sand-
covered bottom in deeper waters, closer in weed-covered rocks, river stones as
big as a man's head formed quite a soft if unsteady carpet. Water lapped onto
river stones, which covered half the beach, then sand and soft layers of dried
seaweed I could have swum for hours. Out to dry off in the sun and faint
breeze, then, hiding my coat, book, etc., under some bushes I set out, feeling
great, to walk up Shrapnel Gully. I'll never forget the two-hour walk. The
eerie stillness; felt ghosts all about me. Found water bottles, shells, French tin
hors de Concourse 1900. Eno's Fruit Salts bottle, thousands of shards of broken
stoneware "made in Tamworth," and piles of tins. Ridges towered above me.
"Yea, though I walk through the Valley of the Shadow of Death" occurred to
me. Back to the beach, exhausted, flop into the sea. Drive to Quinns Post and
the N.Z. memorial at Chunuk Bair. Felt very emotional then, and later that
night at the hotel.

After that visit, I knew there was no question but that I *must* make the
film about Gallipoli, and make it for them, for the men who died there.
I had no story. That would take four more years.
It's curious how you can know a thing happened. I mean, know it intellectually . . . but how much different that other "knowing" is. To see
and to touch—to *feel* it as a truth.
I confess to taking the Eno's Fruit Salts bottle—a stomach-settler, di-
gestive aid, a familiar Australian brand name to be found in the medicine
chest of most homes even today. That bottle lying unbroken amongst
the shrapnel and shell casings became a sort of talisman over the next
years. I even put it in the film—Mel Gibson is seen receiving it in a care
package in one scene.
On most films I have a prop that holds something of the spirit of
the film in the early stages; I have it on my desk while working on the
script—not for good luck or anything like that; I've never been one for
good-luck charms—it's more than that.
I once found a Roman head in North Africa under curious circumstances: a marble sculpture no bigger than the head of a child's doll. I
kept it and later wrote a movie inspired by it. Perhaps it came from my
early work in sketch comedy, way back before I started in films. I used to
write sketches with a friend and to provoke ideas we'd often turn up with
an object, something curious or evocative, turn on the tape and start
talking about it: you know, he'd say, "Is that your father's?" I'd say, "No,
if he knew I had one he'd kill me," or something like that. I love props

and used to collect them; I have a garage full of odd objects I thought contained a story.

I made *Gallipoli* in 1980, four years after that initial visit to the battle-field. In the meantime, I made two other movies, one for television and one for the cinema, all the while working with Australian playwright David Williamson on the script. During that period I went to Egypt to visit the key areas mentioned in the war histories, as the Australians and New Zealanders trained in Egypt prior to embarking for Gallipoli. One account mentioned Australians carving their names on the pyramids. I'd read of French soldiers doing the same when there with Napoleon.

I used a guide who told me he knew *exactly* what I was talking about: "Australian soldiers? First War? Yes, carved names. I can show you." We haggled over a price, he went off and came back with two horses. We rode away from the pyramids, which made me suspicious, but he seemed to know all about it. We stopped after some miles and he led me down to a small tomb. There were no other tourists about, and I thought, "Ei-ther I am about to be killed or I am about to find what I'm looking for." He pointed to some hieroglyphs above the tomb. "Australians," he said proudly.

So I let him go, and later, back at the Cheops pyramid, having given up the search, I thought I'd just play the tourist. I climbed up to see the Pharaoh's tomb and, on the way down, took a look at the Queen's burial chamber. I'd been told not to bother with it; those of you who have done this tour will know it is an awkward thing to do, doubled up as you make your way along the corridor to the empty chamber. Not for the claustrophobic.

The room is covered in graffiti, some as recent as last week. I was about to leave when something made me turn around, something on the wall behind me. A set of initials—*CH . . . LT . . . DH . . . TMH . . . 1915 . . . NSW . . . AIF. . . .*

I'll read this entry from my diary made on that visit:

Wednesday, 8 March 1978. PM:
Met an old man in a photographic shop. He speaks excellent English, asks me what I'm doing in Cairo. He tells me he remembers the Australians! As a small boy he stole a hat-badge off one of their hats. . . . "They were magnifi-cent big men, but oh! They could get very angry if they thought they had been robbed! Such a sight to see three or four abreast coming down the street. . . ." He went on to say that his parents had told him they were "the sons of bad Englishmen, criminals of the worst type, exported to Australia!"

There were a number of veterans still alive in the late seventies, and many of their recollections were folded into the story. They were all of a similar type, gentlemen in a way, generally married, and the interviews followed a similar pattern. The wife would discreetly leave after the tea had been poured, and they would then begin to talk. All appeared to have photographic memories of those years, years lived so intensely. Precise details, recalled across sixty years with such clarity. They mostly wanted to relate humorous moments, but with gentle nudging they took me into the trenches, and the terrible sights and sounds were recounted as though they had happened the week before. In nearly all cases they had never told anyone what they were telling me, or the researcher. After the war they either didn't want to recall their experiences or they were not asked.

With the script, David and I went through many drafts. Initially, we tried too large a canvas. We had two friends, one who went to the war, one with an Irish background who refused to go. This character got involved in politics on the left, and at the end of the war the two met, the veteran and his would-be champion, the politician. They didn't recognize each other. The draft had the conscription referendums in it. As many of you would know, Australians voted twice as to whether we would support conscription, and in both cases it was a "no" vote. So we had all of that in it—by the way, I think that was "the birth of the nation," as much as the valour of the men in the field. Anyway, we were attempting too much; it perhaps would have made a mini-series for television, but we were getting nowhere.

Then came the breakthrough. Reading through the voluminous, brilliant, *Official History* of C. E. W. Bean, I came on a description of a battle at a place called "The Nek," at Gallipoli. The Nek was a small, open patch of ground on the heights above the beach, no bigger than two tennis courts. The Australians were to attack there as part of a feint, while the main British force was to attempt to break through at Suvia Bay. It was a disaster.

They were to attack at 4:40 A.M., after a furious land and naval bombardment, which was intended to blast the Turks out of their opposing trenches. Reading from Bean's *History*:

For some reason, which will probably never be explained, the bombardment ended . . . seven minutes before 4:40 A.M. . . . . There seems little question that there had been a mistake in the timing of the watches. Whatever the cause, the shelling of the enemy's forward lines ceased. For three minutes hardly a shot was fired, but during that time the Turks gradually raised their head, and, realizing that there was no fire upon them, manned their trenches two-deep in anticipation of the assault which they knew must be imminent. One line seated on the parapet and the other standing behind it, they nestled their rifles to their shoulders, took aim, and waited. Their machine guns here and there rattled off a dozen shots as they made ready for the action.

Behind the Australian parapet, a few of the officers, looking at their watches, were perplexed at the sudden cessation of shell fire. "What do you make of it?" asked Lieutenant Robinson; "there's still seven minutes to go." "They may give them a heavy burst to finish," was the reply. But none came. "Three minutes to go," said Colonel White. Then, simply, "Go!" In an instant the first line, all eagerness, leapt over the parapet. Facing them, not a stone's throw away, were hundreds of the enemy, lining two deep in their front trench. The instant the Australians appeared, there burst upon them a fusillade that rose within a few seconds from a fierce crackle into a continuous roar. . . . Watchers on Poe's Hill saw the Australian line start forward across the skyline and then on a sudden grow limp and sink to the earth "as though," said one eyewitness, "the men's limbs had become string."

. . . The first line, which had started so confidently, had been annihilated in half a minute; and the others, having seen its own down, realized fully that when they attempted to follow, they would be instantly destroyed. Yet, as soon as the first line had cleared the parapet, the second took its place . . . and exactly two minutes after the first had gone, without hesitation every man in the second line leapt forward into the tempest.

As the third and fourth lines made ready to follow, men of the West Australian 10th, efforts were made by the Regimental leaders to discover whether further sacrifice was necessary. . . . About this time a staff officer from Brigade headquarters asked why the third line had not gone forward. But Brazier, their officer, doubting that annihilation of further troops could serve any interest except that of the enemy, determined to raise the question, as he had the full right to do, before allowing that line to start. He consequently went to Brigade Headquarters, but here Colonel Anthill told him Australian marker flags had been seen in the enemy trench and that the "the 10th Regiment *must* push on at once!" Among the West Australians every man assumed that death was certain, and each in the secret places of his mind debated how he should go to it. Many seemed to have determined that they would run as swiftly as possible, since that course was the simplest and most honorable. . . . Mate having said goodbye to mate, the third line took up its position. . . . It was about 4:45 A.M. The roar of the small arms, which had been called forth by the lines of the 8th subsided to almost complete silence, but as the men rose above the parapet, it instantly swelled until its volume was tremendous. With that regiment went the flower of the youth of Western Australia, sons of the old pioneering families, youngsters—in some cases two and three from the same home—who had flocked to Perth at the outbreak of war with their own horses and saddler—men known and popular, the best-loved leaders in sport and work in the West, then rushed straight to their deaths. Gresley Harper and Wilfred, his younger brother, the latter of whom was last seen running forward like a schoolboy in a foot race. . . .

David and I abandoned all our previous drafts, dropped our convoluted plots and our attempts to make a "significant" film, and went instead for a very simple storyline. The story of a friendship, of two mates, athletes, track stars, who would end up at The Nek. One would survive, and one would have to make his final run toward the Turkish guns.

I remember a quote of Ingmar Bergman's, in which he said, "You can do anything on screen but kill someone!" The audience will not suspend their disbelief at this moment. He may be right, and I concentrated therefore on the idea of *preparing* to die. There is little overt death or violence in the film. Some criticized the film at the time on this point—as if I'd avoided the showing of the "the reality" of war, and somehow softened the film for audiences, avoiding the horror. And they were right, at least in one sense, because I wanted to make this final sacrifice all the more powerful. The power lay in watching this young man make his final preparations for death. Prepare to give up his life. An athlete, barely seventeen years old, in the fullness of life, who must find his courage and "go to his death."

The film centered around the friendship of these two young men— and they were mates. Much has been written about the concept of mateship in the Anzac legend and indeed in the story of these two young countries, Australia and New Zealand. Did it originate, in the case of Australia, with the male convicts? On the goldfields, in the outback? Was it the many wars both countries took part in? Probably all these things. Veterans talked of it; they said, "Everyone had a mate, often odd combinations, the tall with the short, the educated with the uneducated—perhaps you "palled up" with someone who had a talent you didn't have." One old soldier put it well: "Your mate would watch your back and you would watch his." He went on to say that this applied particularly to the battlefield. The fear was that if you were hit you might be left but if you had a mate, he would make sure you were looked after.

Will Dyson wrote in 1917, in his book *The Mate*: "Most of the boys are of that age at which friendship is not the tepid give and take of years of discretion. Remember our friendship at twenty? At that age, friendship is a thing intense and unquestioning—it is a blasphemy to think of it as anything less than eternal. . . . Normally, these wither painlessly in their season, but this generation, or what maimed fragment of it lives through it all, will live with the memory of heroic friendships cut off at the height of their boyish splendor, and which can never suffer the slow deterioration of disillusionment."

Thank you.

Additional Sources

Research Sources

National Film and Sound Archive, Headquarters Canberra. McCoy Circuit, Acton ACT 2601. Offices are also located in Sydney and Melbourne, with Access Centres available in State Libraries in Hobart, Brisbane, Adelaide, and Perth. www.nfsa .gov.au.

The Australian Centre for the Moving Image is located at Federation Square, Melbourne. Inside is the Australian Mediatheque with permanent displays of film, television, and digital culture. www.acmi.net.au.

Australian producer Anthony Buckley's www.buckleyfilms.com is a rich resource of Australian film history.

The Hanging Rock Research Centre is located at South Rock Road, in Woodend, Victoria, Australia 3442. Visit macedonranges.com/natural-attractions/hanging rock.

Selected Interviews and Websites

http://www.peterweircave.com (collection of articles on Peter Weir)
Anon. "Dialogue on Film: Peter Weir." *American Film* 11, no. 5 (1986): 13–15.
Brennan, Richard. "Peter Weir." *Cinema Papers*, no. 1 (1974): 116–17.
Campbell, Virginia. "Love, Fear and Peter Weir." *Movieline*, September 1993, http://www.eterweircave.com/articles/articleb.html.
Caputo, Raffaele and Geoff Burton (eds.). *Second Take: Australian Film-makers Talk*. St. Leonards, NSW: Allen & Unwin, 1999.
Champlin, Charles. "Peter Weir: In a Class by Himself." *Los Angeles Times*, June 4, 1989.
Dempsey, Michael. "Inexplicable Feelings: An Interview with Peter Weir." *Film Quarterly* 33, no. 4 (1980).

Farber, Stephen. "Natural Dangers: A Conversation with Peter Weir." *New West,* 1979, 99–106.

Magill, Marcia. "Peter Weir." *Films in Review* 32, no. 8 (October 1981): 474–75, 478–79.

Murray, Scott and Gordon Glenn. "Production Report: *The Cars That Ate Paris*: Informal Discussion with Jim and Hal McElroy and Peter Weir." *Cinema Papers,* no. 1 (1974): 20–21.

Prouty, Howard. "Peter Weir: Director." *American Film Institute,* 1985.

Rayner, Jonathan. *The Films of Peter Weir.* New York and London: Continuum, 2003.

Tibbetts, John C. "Peter Weir: A View from the Apocalypse." *The World and I,* April 1994, 122–27.

Spines, Christine. "Peter Weir, the Director of the *Truman Show* Discusses the Very Real Manipulations of Moviemaking." *Premiere,* July 1998, 39–41.

Thomas, Kevin, "Peter Weir Climbs Hollywood Beanstalk." *Los Angeles Times,* September 21, 1979.

Ventura, Michael. "Witnessing *Witness*: The Nuts and Bolts of Peter Weir." *Los Angeles Times,* February 8–14, 1985.

Weir, Peter. "*Gallipoli*: Shooting History." In *Amongst Friends: Australian and New Zealand Voices from America,* edited by Patty O'Brien and Bruce Vaughn. Dunedin: University of Otago Press, 2005.

Weir, Peter. "The Director's Voice 2," in *Third Take, Australian Filmmakers Talk,* edited by Raffaele Caputo and Geoff Burton. Australia: Allen & Unwin, 2002.

Index

Academy Awards, ix–x, xv, xvii, xxii, 19, 108, 179, 189, 192, 200, 204, 234, 236–38

Ace Ventura films, xviii, 185–86

Adventures of Barry McKenzie, The (film), 46n2, 81

Alfred Hitchcock Presents (television series), 105, 153

Alien (film), 114–15, 130, 132

All Quiet on the Western Front (film), 245

Alvin Purple films, 81

Amagula, Nandjiwarra, 23, 90–92, 106–7, 140, 142, 226

Amish community and culture, xi, xxiv, 109, 189

Anzac Day, 37, 228, 244–52

Armstrong, Gillian, xvi, 38n6, 47, 158, 205, 213, 240

Artaud, Antonin, 115

ATN7 Television, xiv, 48, 51, 54, 56, 59, 65

Aunty Jack Show, The (television series), 67–68, 69n5

Australia, origins of, 3, 5n1

Australian Broadcasting Corporation, 38n7, 50, 53, 55–56, 58

Australian Film Development Corporation (AFDC), xvi, 75, 79–81

Australian Film Institute (AFI), xv, 62, 118, 205

Australian National Film and

Television School (NFTS), xvi, 49, 158

Australian New Wave (1970–1980), xvi–xvii, 19–20, 38n6, 172, 179

Awakenings (film), 7, 23

Ballard, J. G., 126

Bean, C. E. W., 249–51

Bear, Greg, 26, 39n11

Beatles, The, 182, 186

Beethoven, Ludwig van, 30, 161, 173

Bell, Greg, 146

Beresford, Bruce, xvi, 20–21, 38n6, 46n2, 58, 115, 158, 205, 241

Bergman, Ingmar, 123–24, 150, 158, 251

Between Wars (film), 204, 206

Bizet, George, 26

Biziou, Peter, 191–99

Blake, William, xviii, xxv, 24

Boccherini, Luigi, 27

Bond, Grahame, 62, 67–68, 116, 131–32

Bosch, Hieronymus, 17, 37n4, 114, 168–69

Botticelli, Sandro, 134, 168, 174n1

Boyd, Russell, xxi, 101–2, 147n2, 204–38, 242; on Australian light, 4, 206; early years, 204–6; photographing Gallipoli, 102, 204, 224, 226–28; photographing Master and Commander, 204, 208–9, 230–34; photographing

Picnic at Hanging Rock, 102, 204, 206–8, 213–24, 232; photographing *The Last Wave*, 204, 207–8, 223–26; photographing *The Way Back*, 204, 234–35; photographing *The Year of Living Dangerously*, 204, 208, 228–30; receiving Oscar, 204, 234, 236–38; working methods with Peter Weir, 209, 234–35

Bramston Show (television series). See *Mavis Bramston Show, The*

Bridges, Jeff, 17–18, 22–23, 168, 171

Brown, Helen, 146

Buñuel, Luis, 32

Bush Christmas (film), 43

Caddie (film), 83

Cameron, James, 231

Campion, Jane, 20, 38n6, 158–59

Cannes Film Festival, 19–20

Carpenter, John, 114

Carrey, Jim, xii, xviii, 25, 185–88

Carrière, Jean-Claude, 31–32, 35

Cézanne, Paul, 17

Chamberlain, Richard, 91, 120, 132n4, 134, 179, 224–25

Chandler, Raymond, 154

Chaplin, Charlie, 64, 118

Chariots of Fire (film), 144

Chauvel, Charles, 43, 46n1

Chesterton, G. K., xxiii–xxiv, 15

Cleese, John, 132, 135, 139

Close Encounters of the Third Kind (film), 132

Cold Mountain (film), 236

Coleridge, Samuel Taylor, xxv

Comic books, 41–42, 244

Commonwealth Film Unit (CFU), xvi, 11, 38n7, 55–65, 67, 72

Cook, Captain James, 3–4, 6

Copping, David, 76

Coppola, Francis Ford, 84

Corman, Roger, 71

Crocodile Dundee (film), 205

Dali, Salvador, 88, 116

Davies, Piers, 72

Dawn, Norman O., 47

De Niro, Robert, 23

De Palma, Brian, 25

Depardieu, Gerard, xv, xviii, 28–29, 148, 169

Dickens, Charles, 113, 187

Don't Look Now (film), 140–41

Dyson, Will, 251–52

Ealing comedies, 158

Ebert, Roger, 24

Eisenstein, Sergei, 22, 64, 119, 162, 209

Elstree Studios, 66

Etaix, Pierre, 31

Experimental Film and Television Fund (EFTF), xvi, 10, 66–67, 81

Farrell, Colin, 202

Fauré, Gabriel, 28

Fawlty Towers (television series), 131

Film Australia, 72

Fitzgerald, F. Scott, 33, 114

Flash Gordon (serial), 113

For the Term of His Natural Life (film), 47

Ford, Harrison, xi, 4–5, 151–52, 161, 163–65, 176, 179, 189

Freud, Sigmund, 136

Friedrich, Caspar David, xxv

Galapagos Islands, xxii, 208, 230, 232–33

Gallipoli, history of, xvii, 20, 37, 38n9, 94–96, 146, 150, 227–28, 244–52

Gance, Abel, ix

Gassner, Dennis, 193

Gattaca (film), 192

Getting of Wisdom, The (film), 84n1

Gibson, Mel, xi, xv, 103, 108, 212, 227, 242, 247

Górecki, Henryk, 18, 37n5, 173

Gothic tradition, xxv

Gow, Keith, 13, 37n2, 72

Green, Cliff, 137

Greer, Germaine, 115

Grieg, Edvard, 173

Griffith, D. W., 64, 193

Guard, Dominic, 82

Gulpilil, David, 90–92, 142, 146n1

Hall, Ken G., 33, 39n14

Hammer Films, 5, 105, 158

Hanging Rock Reserve, 84n2, 215

Harbutt, Sandy, 16

Harris, Ed, xii, 186, 188, 201–3

Hawke, Ethan, 180

Hawks, Howard, 114, 118

Heaven's Gate (film), 243

Hellman, Jerome (Jerry), 161–62, 164–65

Hesse, Hermann, 39n12

Hillcoat, John, 38n6

Hiller, Arthur, 130

Hitchcock, Alfred, xii, 63–64, 66, 76–77, 108, 112, 114, 117–19, 121, 132, 134, 153, 158

Hopper, Dennis, 186

Humphries, Barry, 45, 46n2, 52

Hunt, Linda, xvii, 27, 97–98, 108

Huxley, Aldous, 114

Indiana Jones films, 36

Invasion of the Body Snatchers (1956 film), xii

It Happened One Night (film), 148

James, Henry, xxvi

Jedda (film), 43, 46n1

Jewison, Norman, 238n2

Jung, Carl, 117–18, 122, 132n2, 136

Jurassic Park (film), 156

Kafka, Franz, 183

Katzenberg, Jeffrey, 29, 176, 181, 189

Keats, John, xxv

Khan, Nusrat Fateh Ali, 109

King, Richard, 19

Koch, Christopher, 128

Kotcheff, Ted, 33

Kubrick, Stanley, xii, 84, 114, 117, 120, 131–32

Kurosawa, Akira, ix, 63, 118, 152

Lambert, Anne, 82, 218–19, 222–23

Lang, Fritz, ix

Lawrence of Arabia (film), x

Lee, Mark, 227, 242

Leonard, Robert Sean, 177, 180–81

Lewis, Jerry, 70–71

Lindsay, Lady Joan, xiii–xiv, 82, 84n2, 85, 214

Linney, Laura, 187

Lloyd, Norman, 153

Longford, Raymond, 205, 238n3

Lord of the Rings films, 234

Lovell, Pat, 51, 68n1, 129, 221, 228

Lucas, George, 41, 132

Luhrmann, Baz, 33, 159

Luke's Kingdom (television series), 135

MacDowell, Andie, 28

Mad Max films, 16

Magus, The (film), III

M*A*S*H (film), 81

"Mateship," 38n9, 95–96, 103n2, 251

Matisse, Henri, 16–17

Mavis Bramston Show, The (television series), 45, 51–52, 54–56, 61

McElroy, Hal and James, 68n1, 76, 78n1, 87, 130, 143, 206, 221

Miller, George, 16, 38n6, 86

Monty Python's Flying Circus (television series), 10–11, 68, 135

Morris, Judy, 60, 141

Morse, Helen, 82, 218–19, 222

Mozart, Wolfgang Amadeus, 145

Murdoch, Rupert, 87

Murray, Les, 21

My Brilliant Career (film), 240

National Film and Sound Archives (NFSA), xxvii, 47

Ned Kelly (film), 76, 78n1

New World Company, 71

Niccol, Andrew, xi, 25, 184, 192

Nicholson, Jack, 151

Noble, Thom, 164

Novalis, xxv

Noyce, Phil, xvi, 213

O'Brien, Francis, 240–44

O'Brien, Patrick, xv, 230, 239n8

"Ocker Comedies," 84n1

Orpheus Myth, xxvi. *See also* "Threshold Effect"

Papadopolous, John, 213

Parker, Alan, 192

Paths of Glory (film), 245

Penderecki, Krzysztof, 173

Perez, Rosie, 170–71

Poe, Edgar Allan, xxv

Polanski, Roman, 84, III

Pop Art, 116

Portrait of the Artist as a Young Man, A (novel), 44

Prisoner, The (television series), 192

Pudovkin, Vsevolod, 64

Rafferty, "Chips," 4, 43

Rawicz, Slowomir, 201

Renoir, Jean, 63, 118

Richards, Keith, 27

Roberts, Rachel, 82, 218

Roberts, Tom, 88, 103n1

Rockwell, Norman, 193

Roeg, Nicholas, 33, 79, 83, 98, 140

Ronan, Saorise, 202

Rooney, Mickey, 236–37

Rosenberg, Mark, 170

Rudin, Scott, 25, 185–86

Russell, Ken, 66

Sacks, Oliver, 7, 23

Sarris, Andrew, 23–25

Schepisi, Fred, xvi, 20–21, 38n6, 47, 58, 158, 241

Schrader, Paul, xi

Schubert, Franz, xxv

Schumann, Robert, xxv, 30

Scorsese, Martin, 149

Scott, Ridley, 115, 132, 231

Seale, John, 101–3, 164, 179–80, 182, 208, 216, 218, 227, 236, 239n7

Seaside, Florida, xii, 194

Selznick, David O., 153

Seven Samurai (film), 63

Shakespeare, William, 42, 151, 162, 175, 177, 181, 187

Shelley, Percy Bysshe, xxv, 177

Shelton, Ron, 205, 212

Sheridan, Jim, 192

Sherlock Holmes, 154

Shiga, xxii, 14, 37n3

Shirley, Graham, 213

Smeaton, Bruce, 30

Soldier's Story, A (film), 238n2

South Australian Film Corporation, xvi, 79–80, 227

Spielberg, Steven, 25, 41, 132

Star Wars (film), 114

Stevenson, Robert Louis, 5

Stigwood, Robert, 227, 240–41

Stites, Wendy (wife), 10, 18, 55, 87–88, 101, 178, 180, 190

Stone (film), 16

Straub, Peter, 35

Strauss, Richard, 27, 39n12

Sturgess, Jim, 200–202

Sundowners, The (film), 33

Surrealism, 115–16, 119, 127

Sydney, Australia, xiv, xvi, 19, 38n7, 63, 136, 190; Film Festival, 54–55, 105–6

Sydney University, xiv, xviii, 5, 24, 44, 115, 139

Tati, Jacques, 31

Tenant, The (film), 111

Tennyson, Alfred, 176

Theatre of the Absurd, 115–16

Theroux, Paul, xi, 161, 164

Thing, The (film), 114

Thoreau, Henry David, 177

Thorn Birds, The (television series), 129–30, 132n4, 138–39, 143, 159–60

Thornhill, Michael, 62, 69n4, 206, 213–14, 238n4

"Threshold Effect," xxiv, xxixn7

Titanic (film), x, 231

Truffaut, François, 158

Turner, Ann, 38n6

Twilight Zone, The (television series), 105, 111

2001: A Space Odyssey (film), 113, 120

Ullmann, Liv, 83

Van Gogh, Vincent, 16–17

Vangelis, 144

Venice Film Festival, 169

Vertigo (film), xii

Vian, Boris, 115

Vincent Report, The, 58, 68n2

von Stroheim, Erich, ix

Von Sydow, Max, 83

Wages of Fear, The (film), 5

Wagner, Richard, 162

Wake in Fright (film), 33

Walkabout (film), x, 33, 140

Walt Disney Studios, 176, 181

Warhol, Andy, 116

Watkin, David, 211

wayang kulit, 229

Wayne, John, 151

Weaver, Jacki, 82

Weaver, Sigourney, xi, xv, 99

Weir, Peter: on adaptation, 6, 33–34; on angels, 21–23; on apocalypse, xxiii, 21, 25–27, 38n10, 170; on Australian aborigines, xxiv, 23, 83, 90–92, 106–7, 109, 140; on Australian identity, 43, 63; on auteurism, xx, 86, 135, 151; collaboration with Russell Boyd, 101–2, 204–10; on documentary, 14, 56, 113, 123, 162, 184; early years, xiv, 3–5, 40–46, 105, 131, 154, 178, 244; on editing, 109–10, 121, 125, 162; on

Hollywood, xviii, 8, 17, 80–81, 108, 157, 169–71, 176; as humanist, xii; on institutionalized education, xiv, xxvi, 23–25, 43–44, 154, 178; on "Jack and the Beanstalk," 171; on music, xx–xxi, 7–8, 26–30, 35, 109–10, 127, 145–46, 157, 162–65, 173, 180–82; as Peter Pan, xxiii, 9; on politics, 15, 17, 179; as Romantic artist, xxv; on screenplay writing, xx, 6–7, 15, 35, 72, 92, 162, 189, 249, 251; on sense of wonder, 36; on sexuality, 98, 136–37, 140; as storyteller, 123, 154; television years, xiv–xvi, 9–13, 46, 50–55, 106; on unrealized projects, 6–7, 61, 200; on Vietnam War, xxiv, 50, 80–81, 86, 106, 116, 172, 245; on water motif, 94; on World War I, 94, 129, 150, 244–52; on World War II, 4, 11, 14, 245

Films: *The Cars That Ate Paris*, x, xv, xvii, xx, 11, 16, 53–54, 58, 65, 68, 70–78, 79, 81, 85, 111, 120, 126, 128, 133, 135–36, 143, 179, 201, 206, 208, 213–14; *Count Vim's Last Exercise*, xv, xix, 8–11, 36, 48, 52, 54, 56, 106; *Dead Poets Society*, xiv–xv, xviii, xxiii–xxv, 12, 23–25, 28, 108, 153, 157, 169, 175–82, 187; *Fearless*, ix–xi, xv, xxiii, 3, 8, 17–18, 21–23, 30, 109, 167–74, 185, 202; *Fifth Façade*, 13; *Gallipoli*, x–xi, xv, xvii, xxiii, xxv, 6, 18–20, 26–27, 38n9, 85–88, 94–95, 97–98, 100–102, 129, 134, 139, 144–46, 150–52, 171, 176, 179, 201, 204, 224, 226–28,

240–52; *Green Card*, xv, xviii–xxiv, 28–29, 148–49, 154–56, 159, 169–70; *Green Valley*, 11–13; *Heart, Head and Hand*, xxii, 14; *Homesdale*, xv, 53–54, 65–67, 72, 76, 81, 85, 96, 111, 127, 143, 213; *The Last Wave*, x, xv, xvii, xxii–xxv, 21, 23, 26, 50, 64, 83, 85–86, 89–92, 102, 106, 111, 115, 117–18, 120, 128, 132, 133–34, 136, 139–42, 149, 152, 155, 173, 179, 201, 204, 207–8, 223–26, 240; *The Life and Flight of the Rev. Buck Shotte*, xv, xxiii, 8–10, 54–56, 59; *The Man on the Green Bike*, 53; *Master and Commander*, x, xix, xxi–xxii, xxv, 6–8, 18–19, 22, 27, 200–202, 204, 208–9, 230–34, 236–37; *Michael* (episode in *Three to Go*), xv, xxiv, 12, 61–62, 69n3, 81, 86; *The Mosquito Coast*, ix, xi, xv, xviii–xx, xxiii, 16–17, 21, 23, 148, 151–52, 161–66, 177, 179–80; *Picnic at Hanging Rock*, x, xv, xvii–xviii, xxi–xxv, 4, 13, 21, 24, 29–30, 38n10, 68n1, 78n1, 85–89, 98, 100, 102, 111, 120, 122, 126, 128, 133–34, 137–38, 145, 152, 154–56, 159, 168, 173, 179, 201, 204, 206–8, 213–24, 232, 240, 242; *The Plumber*, xv, xvii, 28, 87, 93–96, 111, 125, 127–28, 130, 138, 141–43, 149; *Stirring the Pool*, 60; *The Truman Show*, ix, xi–xii, xv, xviii–xix, xxii, xxv, 8, 11–12, 21, 25, 183–90, 191–99, 202; *The Way Back*, ix, xi, xiii, xv, xix–xxii, xxvi, 7–8, 21, 26, 39n10, 200–203, 204, 234–35;

Witness, xi, xv, xviii–xxiv, 4–5,
    8, 17–18, 21, 109, 153–54, 163–64,
    172, 176, 179, 189; *The Year of
    Living Dangerously*, xi, xv, xvii,
    xix, xxi, xxiii–xxiv, xxvi, 21, 27,
    86–87, 94, 96–101, 103n3, 107,
    122, 128–30, 139, 151–52, 176,
    179, 201, 204, 208, 228–29
Welles, Orson, ix, 153
Wenders, Wim, 158
White Men Can't Jump (film), 205, 217
Whitman, Walt, 28, 177
Williams, Robin, xv, 23, 157, 175–78,
    180–82, 187
Williamson, David, 144, 226, 242,
    248–49, 251
Wilson, August, 35

Yglesias, Rafael, 170

Zaentz, Saul, 165
Zallian, Steve, 7
Zamfir, Georg, xxi, 29–30
Zapruder film, 209
Zinnemann, Fred, 33

Printed in the United States
By Bookmasters